measuring
underemployment

demographic indicators for
the United States

STUDIES IN POPULATION

Under the Editorship of: H. H. WINSBOROUGH

Department of Sociology
University of Wisconsin
Madison, Wisconsin

measuring underemployment

demographic indicators for the United States

Clifford C. Clogg

Department of Sociology and
Population Issues Research Center
Pennsylvania State University
University Park, Pennsylvania

ACADEMIC PRESS

A Subsidiary of Harcourt Brace Jovanovich, Publishers

New York   London   Toronto   Sydney   San Francisco

ACADEMIC PRESS, INC.
111 Fifth Avenue, New York, New York 10003

United Kingdom Edition published by
ACADEMIC PRESS, INC. (LONDON) LTD.
24/28 Oval Road, London NW1 7DX

Library of Congress Cataloging in Publication Data

Clogg, Clifford C
    Measuring underemployment.

    (Studies in population)
    Includes index.
    1. Underemployment––United States––Statistical
methods. I. Title. II. Series.
HD5716.2.U5C58   331.1'3   79–22916
ISBN 0–12–176560–1

PRINTED IN THE UNITED STATES OF AMERICA

79 80 81 82   9 8 7 6 5 4 3 2 1

contents

9 some new directions for mathematical demography

10 conclusion

preface

The research reported in this volume was begun in 1974, during the worst recession since the 1930s. It was my belief then that the usual unemployment statistic, the chief quantitative measure derived from the "labor force" approach, did not adequately portray the labor force dynamic in a market society. After 5 years of more-or-less continuous work on this project, I am even more convinced that this conclusion is correct. The unemployment rate is, by itself, an inadequate labor force indicator—it cannot describe the across-time dynamic or the cross-sectional differentials in the labor force with the clarity demanded by modern social science. It should be replaced as soon as possible by a more complete framework for measurement: One purpose of this work is to present an approach by which this might be accomplished.

That I undertake this study was suggested by Teresa Sullivan and Philip Hauser, who had proposed a measurement scheme referred to as the Labor Utilization Framework. The Labor Utilization Framework posits the existence of three dimensions, or forms, of underemployment, each one of which requires a conceptual and operational apparatus for its measurement. These three forms may be simply delineated as the time, income, and skill-utilization forms. Implicit to this conception of underemployment is the recognition that there are only three principal rewards distributed to workers directly through the labor market: work time, wage or other work-related income, and the utilization of worker skills or human capital. An individual-level measure of underemployment corresponding to each of these rewards was devised, and a certain combination of these measures was used to construct the multi-state variable that is the main product of the Hauser–Sullivan approach.

At the outset of this research I had very modest intellectual objectives. It was my task at first merely to apply the Labor Utilization Framework to time-series data from the United States, in the hope that this would either demonstrate the efficacy of the framework in a compelling way or suggest ways it could be improved. During the course of the analysis, however, it became apparent that a study of somewhat broader significance would be possible, a study that could help reorient sociological and demographic thinking about the labor force aggregate in an advanced industrial society. It is this broader objective that has really motivated the "substantive" part of the work. The frequent "methodological" excursions are related, if only indirectly, to this broader theme.

The main issue of this work is the Labor Utilization Framework of Hauser and Sullivan: its conceptual groundwork, its operational measurement, and, especially, its implications for the way the labor force aggregate is described and interpreted. The present volume is based on the analysis of repeated cross-sectional surveys, and demographic–statistical methods suited for this type of data have been adopted. The basic variable in question is discrete and qualitative: one aspect of the study was the systematic use of recently developed statistical methods for log-linear models. The methods for latent structure analysis (Chapter 5) and for cohort analysis (Chapter 6) deserve special mention in this regard. I have tried to address the essential elements of the sociodemographic theory of the labor force with the logical unity provided by both the Labor Utilization Framework and the specific methodologies adopted for its analysis. Topics such as the theory of frictional underemployment; the "class structure" governing the distribution of labor market rewards; the tempo of social change in the labor force; the "productive value" of a population; the "true" dependency on productive labor; and other topics have been given some attention. The substantive merits of this book consist of its integration of a set of apparently different labor force topics into a single set of empirical contingencies that can be plausibly studied from the viewpoint of the Hauser–Sullivan framework. I believe that the book, taken as a whole, is on the right track in unifying our thinking about many vital issues in the labor force area.

ACKNOWLEDGMENTS

My indebtness to several individuals will be clear to even the casual reader of this book. Leo A. Goodman, Philip M. Hauser, and Evelyn M.

Kitagawa, all of the Department of Sociology and the Population Research Center, University of Chicago, deserve my most sincere thanks. This book is an application of their work and has been made possible largely through their encouragement. My greatest debt is to Leo Goodman, a gentleman, scholar, and good friend. Any rigor achieved in my work is the result of my desire to duplicate the painstaking rigor so forcefully exhibited in the 70-or-more scientific papers of his that I have studied. A better teacher than he would be very difficult to find.

Teresa Sullivan, also of the University of Chicago, has provided much stimulus for this work. Her important labor force study, *Marginal Workers, Marginal Jobs* (University of Texas Press, 1978), was often in my mind. The valuable comments made by Alfred Adewuyi, Patricia Anderson, and Darwin Sawyer are also gratefully acknowledged. Steven A. Tuch, graduate sociology student at Pennsylvania State University, read the entire manuscript and located several errors and inconsistencies in logic. None of these persons are responsible, however, for any faults that remain in the book.

My institutional affiliations over the past 5 years have been most conducive to research, and it is not an exaggeration to state that this work would have suffered greatly without them. The Center for Health Administration Studies (Odin W. Anderson, director) and the Population Research Center, University of Chicago, enabled me to earnestly begin the study. The Population Issues Research Center, Pennsylvania State University, provided a hospitable and stimulating climate where I could finalize it. My colleagues Warren Robinson and Gordon DeJong have been particularly helpful in making my transition from graduate student to university professor a smooth one. A lectureship in the Department of Sociology, University of Chicago, as well as support from Population Council Grant D74043C, the National Center for Health Services Research PHS Grant HS00080, and a Research Initiation Grant from Pennsylvania State University provided many of the financial resources which I drew upon in the course of this work.

measuring underemployment

demographic indicators for
the United States

introduction

Since the Depression era, the industrialized nations of the West have relied upon unemployment statistics in order to determine both the economic condition of the labor market and the social condition of the labor force. The conceptual approach adopted in the 1930s separated the population of working age at any point in time into two structural groups, each group being distinct from the other according to its proximity to the labor market. The first group was composed of persons who, of their own accord, did not work for pay or profit and hence did not directly contribute to the formal economic product. These persons were only indirectly attached to the labor market, and they were accordingly designated as the *economically inactive* population. The second structural group was composed of persons who did work for pay or profit as well as those who were involuntarily out of work but were actively seeking a job. Both the loss of employment and the inability to find employment were presumed to indicate a failure in the socioeconomic mechanisms that allocate employment opportunity. Persons in this second group were all thought to be exposed to the "risk" of employment and disemployment, and so this segment of the population was referred to as the *economically active* population or, simply, the *labor force*. In this fashion, the population of working age was dichotomized into the structural groups through which virtually all subsequent work force statistics have been collected and interpreted (compare Hauser, 1949).

The main labor force indicator developed within this approach was the crude *unemployment rate*, which was merely defined as the number of economically active persons without employment expressed as a percentage of the total labor force. In spite of its apparent simplicity, this so-called unemployment rate has been a master socioeconomic indicator since its inception in the mid-1930s. The changing economic condition of the labor market was thought to be evidenced by time-period change in the unemployment rate. The social condition of the labor force was thought to be adequately described by cross-sectional comparisons of unemployment rates for the various sociodemographic categories of the labor force. As Gordon (1972) has observed, "At both the macro- and micro-levels, [labor market and labor force] problems were defined and measured by the unemployment rate" [p. 5]. It is difficult indeed to conceive of another socioeconomic statistic that has been more influential in public policy debate, more critical in the shaping of modern political cleavage, or more central to social scientific theory about the socioeconomic order.

The underlying premise of this book is that the unemployment statistic is no longer an adequate indicator of the economic condition of the labor market, or of the social condition of the labor force, and therefore does not represent the best possible work force information for public policy or social science consumption. In the past decade, it has been concluded that statistics of *under*employment, in addition to statistics of *un*employment, are required in order to describe adequately the quantity and quality of work provided by society to its economically active population. This need to measure underemployment has required a new conceptualization of the structure of the labor force in the modern economic setting. It has also required techniques to operationalize the various concepts of underemployment. Finally, it has demanded different methodological tools in order to summarize in a meaningful way the complexity of structure that emerges from the consideration of several different forms of underemployment.

This book is a demographic treatise on the measurement of underemployment, including unemployment, and attempts to meet the need to measure the different forms of underemployment in the modern labor force. The empirical base for this endeavor consists of sample data on the civilian population of working ages in the United States from 1969 to 1973. This time span contains 1 year often regarded as one of "full employment" (1969) and 2 years of recession (1971–1972), and it therefore contains sufficient labor market variability for a meaningful application of the new methods. The conceptual basis laying the groundwork for the study is contained in a resolution concerning the measurement of underemployment adopted by the Eleventh International Conference of Labor Statisticians in 1966. That resolution (see International Labour Office, 1976) reads in part as follows:

> Underemployment exists when a person's employment is inadequate, in relation to specified norms or alternative employment, account being taken of his occupational skill (training and working experience). Two principal forms of underemployment may be distinguished: visible and invisible.
>
> (1) Visible underemployment is primarily a statistical concept directly measurable by labour force and other surveys, reflecting an insufficiency in the volume of employment. It occurs when a person is in employment of less than normal duration and is seeking, or would accept, additional work.
>
> (2) Invisible underemployment is primarily an analytical concept reflecting a misallocation of labour resources or a fundamental imbalance as between labour and the other factors of production. Characteristic symptoms might be low income, underutilization of skill, low productivity. Analytical studies of invisible underemployment should be directed to the examination and analysis of a wide variety of data, including income and skill levels (disguised underemployment) and productivity measures (potential underemployment) [pp. 33–34]. . . .

This conference suggested that different forms of underemployment should be considered in the attempt to measure both the imbalance of supply and demand in the labor market as regards volume of work and the general quality of work provided to economically active or marginally economically active workers. The dimensions of *time* spent in employment, *income* derived from work, the *productivity* of work, and the *skill utilization* of workers were singled out as being necessary components to the measurement of work force "underutilization," or underemployment. Reports published in the *Monthly Labor Review* show that much effort has already been expended to measure these labor force characteristics. The time dimension of underemployment has received central consideration for the 40 years of modern work force statistics. It is visible because it is readily observed and recorded on labor force surveys routinely conducted around the world; indeed, most labor force surveys are conducted with the primary objective of measuring the time dimension of underemployment. The income, productivity, and skill utilization dimensions are "invisible" characteristics of the quality of work—invisible because they are not customarily considered by labor force indicators now in existence, invisible because of the extreme difficulty in measurement, and invisible because up until the present time very little was known about their characteristic features.

Following a proposal for the measurement of underemployment recently suggested by Philip Hauser, three forms of visible underemployment and two forms of invisible underemployment are presented here as composite socioeconomic indicators of labor force structure. It will be evident through the course of this work that the above concepts of underemployment have been captured at least in part by the approach to be set forth. It will also be apparent that the methods developed to summarize the structure of underemployment have produced very parsimonious descriptions of the modern United States' labor force.

1.1 THE LABOR UTILIZATION FRAMEWORK

The labor utilization framework (LUF) was first proposed by Hauser (1974, 1977) to deal with deficiencies in the unemployment measure as applied to the work forces of the developing nations. Studies by Myrdal (1968), Turnham (1971), and many others summarized in poignant detail the failure of the Western definition of unemployment for developing societies and concluded that the volume of unemployment actually measured with the labor force approach was only a small fraction of the "subproductive" or "underutilized" labor force. The labor force concept brought into existence in the West during the Depression was simply not exportable to the developing regions of the world, a proposition that had been advanced much earlier (Moore, 1953) but had been relatively neglected throughout the post–World War II experience. Although many studies documented the failure of the unemployment statistic to indicate the structural imbalances of the work force in developing areas that could account for their slow growth in economic productivity, there were few frameworks proposed through which a superior measurement scheme could be devised.

The labor utilization framework, however, was proposed and implemented on a massive scale and was conceived with the explicit objective of remedying the deficiencies in the labor force approach noted by Myrdal and Turnham and summarized in the recommendations by the International Labour Office (ILO). At the time of this writing, the LUF has been successfully applied in several developing nations, including Thailand, Indonesia, Singapore, Malaysia, the Philippines, Taiwan, Hong Kong, and South Korea. The LUF now appears likely to replace the labor force approach in several developing countries, although various modifications of it will necessarily occur. It is beyond the scope of this book to describe the manner in which the LUF was implemented in the developing nations, and it is not expedient here to summarize the detailed analyses that have already been conducted with the LUF. It should suffice to note, however, that the framework has been seriously entertained for use in the developing nations, and the natural question to ask is whether the LUF, or some close relative to it, can be used with equal justification in developed societies like the United States.

That the unemployment statistic was not comprehensive enough in its scope, and hence did not measure the true incidence of worker underutilization, was recognized very soon after the labor force approach was adopted. One of the many critiques was presented as early as 1936— almost before the modern labor force standard was adopted—when Robinson (1936) described the existence of a substantial amount of "disguised" unemployment that could not be uncovered by the now conventional approach. Some years later, after nearly 2 decades of experimentation through the Current Population Survey, the National Bureau of Economic Research (1957) sponsored a conference on the meaning and measurement of unemployment. It was evident to the participants in this conference that the meaning of unemployment statistics was still unclear even after extensive experimentation and comparative analysis. Several of the participants in this conference (e.g., Gertrude Bancroft and Albert Rees) suggested slightly different measurement schemes, although general proposals for the measurement of *under*employment were conspicuously lacking. In the early 1960s, President John F. Kennedy commissioned a special committee assigned to appraise unemployment statistics, perhaps the first indication since the Depression of governmental dissatisfaction with labor force measurement procedures. The Gordon Committee, as it came to be called, did much to foster a public awareness of the deficiencies in the labor force approach. Recommendations for moderate revisions in definitions were made, but few incentives were given in this policy directive whereby measures of underemployment could be devised (see U.S. President's Committee to Appraise Employment and Unemployment Statistics, 1962). Proposals stemming from the Gordon Committee were largely aimed at obtaining sharper measures of unemployment itself, sharper measures of part-time unemployment, and minor redefinitions of the population universe to which these measures would apply. In recent times, the controversy over unemployment measures has expressed itself most vividly in the cycle of events that led to the passage of the Comprehensive Employment and Training Act of 1973 (CETA). The CETA legislation contained a mandate for governmental statistical agencies to develop measures of *under*employment and constituted a dramatic change of direction in the general activity of labor force measurement. Various proposals for measuring underemployment have indeed been suggested (see Appendix A), but up until the present, no conclusive results have been obtained. No single proposal of the many that have been considered has thus far evoked a sufficient degree of consensus among the labor force statisticians of the United States. In 1977, President James Carter commissioned another committee of experts headed by Sar Levitan, partly with the purpose to appraise the various proposals for the measurement of

underemployment. The LUF is now one of the frameworks being evaluated by this important committee (Sullivan and Hauser, 1978).

At the risk of some oversimplification, it seems fair to conclude that
past controversy has essentially hinged upon two different issues. The first
is the need to further refine the measures of unemployment, perhaps
including in the process a refinement of the labor force definition itself.
Certainly this has been the dominant theme in the controversy about the
unemployment statistic from the Depression through the 1960s. The second issue is one that is logically distinct from the first: the recognition of a
need to develop supplemental labor force indicators, including measures
of underemployment or underutilization. The labor utilization framework
used throughout this study is directed to the second objective almost
entirely. But it could be easily modified to accommodate itself to antici-
pated changes in basic labor force and unemployment definitions. One
immediately obvious advantage of Hauser's framework is that it does not
abandon the labor force approach of the past but could, at the same time,
be made consistent with changes in basic labor force definitions that will
almost surely arise in the future. A description of the forms of underemployment considered in the LUF can now be outlined.

The five forms of underemployment of this study pertain, with one
exception, to persons who are members of the economically active work
force. A person is a member of the active work force if and only if he or
she is working for pay or profit or is actively seeking such work. (Unpaid
family workers are an exception to this definition; they are included in the
active work force even though their compensation is not easily expressed
in a money wage.) One long-standing criticism of the labor force approach, and of its unemployment statistic, revolves about the statistical
treatment of *marginally* economically active workers who are out of work
but who refuse to actively seek work, presumably because of their past
discouragement in job-seeking activity. These "discouraged workers"
fluctuate in number with economic growth and recession. The charge
against the labor force approach has therefore been that they should be
included in the measurement of the underemployed, since their numbers
so obviously depend upon the transitory economic exigencies (see Flaim,
1973). Nevertheless, the standard approach has been to exclude them
from the universe of the economically active, and hence from the definition of the unemployment rate. Periodic publications do, however, keep
track of the discouraged worker phenomenon, so that for practical purposes, "discouraged workers" are now considered in present attempts to
measure underemployment. We have not been able to isolate discouraged
workers exactly in accordance with official definitions with the data that
are at our disposal. However, a proxy to them has been obtained instead.

We refer to persons obtained by our proxy method as the *sub-unemployed* to reflect the apparently greater severity of underemployment for these persons relative to unemployed persons. Because discouraged workers are very much like the unemployed, this proxy sub-unemployment category is properly understood as a form of visible underemployment.

The standard visible underemployment measures associated with the labor force approach are also included in this study, and the official definitions of them have been in no way altered by our approach. *Unemployment* is one such visible underemployment form. Another form is closely related to unemployment, inasmuch as time spent in employment is also the criterion used. This other form is *involuntary part-time employment* and characterizes a worker who, although at work, is working less than a full-time workweek because of economic reasons. The visible underemployment forms considered here have been routine components of labor force reporting for several quinquennia.

The obvious common denominator of these three visible underemployment forms is the concept of work time lost. The implicit assumption is that hours of work provided by the economy are homogeneous units of uniform quality and that therefore the measures of work time lost will indicate total underemployment. If an assumption of homogeneous time units of work were true, then clearly there could exist only one kind of underemployment; statistics summarizing the amount of work time lost would provide a gauge of income adequacy, of productivity of the work force, of the utilization of workers' skills, as well as of the imbalance in supply and demand as regards the volume of work. Gilroy (1975) has recently refined the visible underemployment measures by taking into account finer detail on the reporting of hours worked. The tacit assumption of Gilroy and those seeking to modify the measurement of the time dimension of underemployment is still that, for practical purposes, the time units of employment are homogeneous. That social science study is essentially preoccupied with the dimension of work time lost is illustrated well by Bowen and Finegan's (1969) impressive study of labor force participation. In their study, the fullness of participation in the work force is indicated only by the hours worked in a week or by the weeks worked in a year; the implicit conception of adequate employment (or of underemployment) is centrally linked to the amount of time worked. Most social scientific work concerning underemployment has heretofore focused almost entirely upon the time dimension of underemployment, to the exclusion of the other dimensions or forms.

The obvious criticism of approaches with an exclusive focus on the time dimension of underemployment is that the time-divisible work units in the modern setting are *not* homogeneous in character. In modern economics characterized by an extreme division of labor, the work units are much more heterogeneous than they were in the Depression era when the original measurement scheme was proposed. In a modern economy a strategy is required that will take account of what the ILO has referred to as invisible underemployment, measures of which reflect the qualitative diversity of time-divisible work units. Clearly, time spent in employment can be further classified along dimensions of income derived from work, of productivity of work, and of skill utilization of workers. Further classification of the labor force would then permit an appraisal of how the other labor market rewards were being distributed and how productive the full-time workers actually were.

In addition to indicating the quality of time spent in employment, the invisible underemployment measures should also be designed to measure the changes that occur over time in the imbalance of supply and demand in the labor market, since in the modern regulated economy the usual measures of visible underemployment are now thought to be insufficient even in this task. In heavily regulated labor markets of the mixed economy, time lost by the labor force may not reflect changes in supply–demand schedules but may be inordinately influenced by, say, governmental controls and trade union pressure. The economic exigencies that presumably would have forced employers in a free labor market to decrease the hours of employment extended to workers may now instead force a lowered effective wage rate, a stifling of per-worker productivity, or a shifting of skilled labor to unskilled positions, all the while maintaining the same number of time units of work. In order to measure the strength of economic forces that were originally measured by the visible underemployment measures, supplemental indicators are now needed.

Some workers in this new labor force may be working full time and hence be counted as adequately employed workers by the standard methods, but their work wages may not be sufficient to provide them with adequate income. These workers are referred to in this study as *underemployed by low income*. Levitan and Taggart (1974), among others, provide several techniques whereby the work force is ranked according to "income adequacy," partly satisfying the need for measuring an income form of underemployment. However, their procedures represent a major departure from the labor force approach, as can be seen most clearly in their treatment of unemployed workers. The focus of their Earnings Inadequacy Index is to assess the need for income, which is a very different thing from measuring need for employment. Their index actually ignores some unemployed workers who nevertheless have adequate income (in the form of compensation, for example). We consider a measure of the income form that is compatible with the standard labor force approach and does not abandon the more usual visible underemployment measures at all.

The ILO concept of job productivity, a most difficult characteristic to measure with labor force survey data, is not directly measured in the labor utilization framework. However, an indirect measure of work productivity is afforded by the measure of the low-income form just discussed. Since under conditions of perfect competition, the wage income obtained by a worker exactly corresponds to value of the product produced, the worker who is underemployed by income may also be considered subproductive. Thus the invisible underemployment measure that we refer to as the low-income form does attempt to satisfy indirectly the need for a *productivity* measure, in the same sense in which income derived from work will indicate the true productivity of work. There is, of course, no exact correspondence between wage income and productivity in a modern economy, and so the low-income underemployed may not represent the subproductive except in an approximate way.

Another kind of invisible underemployment occurs when workers are fully employed as regards time spent in work but are inadequately employed because their skill attainments—their accumulated fund of human capital—are considerably greater than the skill requirements of their jobs. These persons are denoted as the *mismatched* in this study. To our knowledge, in the burgeoning literature on labor force indicators, there has been no other attempt to measure systematically the extent of skill underutilization or mismatch in the labor force as a whole. Hauser's innovation in the "labor utilization framework" is the method for measuring invisible underemployment in general, and the mismatch form in particular.

As Appendix A makes evident, these underemployment forms may occur singly or jointly; a given worker may be underemployed by two or more of the above criteria. A worker who is mismatched as regards his or her current occupation may be temporarily unemployed and so on. Following Hauser's conventions, we shall for most purposes define these forms in a way that makes them mutually exclusive. (More comment will be made about these conventions in Chapter 5.) With these conventions, persons of working ages may be classified into seven different statuses, including the statuses that denote the five underemployment forms of this study:

1. Not in the labor force (or economic inactivity)
2. Sub-unemployment (a proxy to the "discouraged worker" status)
3. Unemployment
4. Part-time employment (or part-time unemployment)
5. Underemployment by low income

6. Mismatch
7. Adequate employment or utilization

The conventional labor force is composed of persons classified in any of statuses 3 through 7, and statuses 1 and 2 taken together denote the usual not-in-labor-force category of official reports. Since status 2, a proxy to discouraged workers, is composed of persons thought to be at least marginally economically active, we occasionally redefine a *modified labor force,* a more inclusive subpopulation conceived to be a risk to underemployment, as comprising persons in the statuses 2 through 7. The distinction between the two definitions of the labor force makes a difference in the calculation of the rates of underemployment and will be repeated when the reader is likely to be confused over the ambiguity of nomenclature. These seven labor force statuses produce a classification that is much richer than conventional classifications, and presents, in a single array, the categories that denote various types of inability to secure the main rewards of the labor market.

In summary, Hauser's approach enables us to consider jointly the different forms of underemployment, forms that have at their root different concepts of underemployment. There are three main concepts of underemployment: work time lost, income deficiency, and the mismatch of workers' skill attainment with required job skills, and they all relate directly to three logically related types of labor market rewards. In order to satisfy more fully the need to measure productivity of work, the assumption can be made that income derived from work be regarded as a proxy for work productivity, although a rigorous measure of productivity would be very difficult to construct with the typical labor force survey.

1.2 A CRITIQUE OF THE LABOR UTILIZATION FRAMEWORK

Although satisfying in most respects the practical needs for the measurement of the different underemployment forms, the approach advocated here is certainly not above criticism. Two important areas of potential concern can immediately be raised. The first pertains to the income thresholds used to establish the existence of the low-income form of underemployment. These were taken, as far as possible, from the Social Security Administration's recommendations for the determination of the poverty status of households. Some have charged that the usage of the poverty thresholds implies that the measure of the low-income form is actually an indicator of poverty or need, not necessarily *underemployment* in the labor market, but this charge is actually not justified. Poverty cutoffs were adjusted so that they could be applied to assess the deficiency of *work-related* income on a *per-worker* basis, an approach that is quite different from one emphasizing actual poverty of households. The labor utilization framework uses the poverty thresholds merely as benchmark criteria for measuring the low-income form, but other criteria could be invoked as well. These other criteria could lead to vastly different absolute numbers designated to be in the low-income form. The important idea in any attempt to measure such a concept, however, is the application of uniform standards, and that uniformity was obtained insofar as possible here. Since different income cutoffs would lead to very different absolute levels of low-income underemployment, it is to be understood at the outset that absolute numbers of workers observed in the low-income category are difficult to interpret by themselves. Relative comparisons over time or across demographic strata should nevertheless be meaningful, because the standards have been uniformly applied.

A second point of possible criticism is the use of completed years of formal education as a proxy for the skill attainment of the worker. Our technique does not take into account the obvious fact that educational inputs themselves are of varied quality and therefore contribute in different ways to the real skill attainment of different workers. The skill levels of two given workers with the same completed years of education can differ considerably solely because of the different quality of their education. The use of educational attainment as a proxy for skill level does not take into account the obvious influence of on-the-job training or skill accumulation through experience, both of which are also important vehicles for raising the stock of human capital. The approach by which skill underutilization is inferred in this study is clearly less than optimal, but we are unable to think of other alternatives that could be applied to existing data sources. Because of the ambiguity in determining cutoffs for the measurement of both the invisible underemployment forms, the absolute levels of invisible underemployment obtained by Hauser's method are indeed somewhat arbitrary figures. However, relative comparisons across time or across demographic strata should fairly indicate the *differentials* in invisible underemployment. It is our contention that an analysis of these differentials is by far the most important objective of labor force measurement.

The above criticisms pertain to the way in which the forms of invisible underemployment are to be measured with existing data. They do not attack the need to measure the prevalence of the several forms but rather the specific techniques used. Presumably, other researchers will wish to modify our conventions, perhaps by acquiring additional information in future labor force sample surveys. Other criticisms are in our view more harmful and will be much more difficult to remedy in future attempts to measure underemployment. Most of these criticisms pertain to the ambiguity of defining and measuring the various forms of underemployment for certain kinds of workers. In the modern labor force of the West, there are at least three categories of workers for whom it is extremely difficult to define, let alone measure, the existence or nonexistence of underemployment.

1. *Unpaid family workers,* generally characteristic of certain kinds of household enterprise, clearly present a problem in the definition of the low-income form of underemployment, since no money income is received by these workers. Unpaid family workers constitute 1–2% of the American labor force, with women and nonwhites being most susceptible to this kind of labor. Any other kind of worker who receives remuneration for his or her labor in a manner that is difficult to assign monetary value to is also subject to the same ambiguity in classification. Many such workers are recorded as having negligible income and so would be counted as being underemployed by income in most labor force surveys. The low-income form of underemployment as used in this study is clearly most appropriate to the case where a definite wage income can be easily measured.

2. *Agricultural workers* constitute a problem in the measurement of most of the underemployment forms. Much agricultural work, on the basis of the firsthand experience of the writer, is not so easily defined in terms of time spent in employment, income received from work, or skill requirements, even in a time when agribusiness threatens to destroy the traditional organization of agricultural work about the household. As is the case with the more usual labor force statistics, the underemployment forms of this study are best suited to the measurement of labor force conditions in the manufacturing and service sectors. Agricultural workers comprise between 2 and 5% of the active work force in the United States, depending upon technical definitions.

3. *Secondary earners* generally pose a serious problem in the definition of all the underemployment forms. At issue is the question of the severity of underemployment, as well as the degree of involuntariness of underemployment, for the secondary worker who is formally dependent upon some primary worker. Primary earners typically have an attachment to the labor force that is of long duration, and their attempts to secure the labor market rewards are more likely to be planned in reference to a long-term career. Secondary earners, on the other hand, have a more transient attachment to the labor force, reflected in their multiple entries to and exits from the labor force through the life cycle. (It is, of course,

the very transience of employment for secondary workers that contributes to the advantage of the primary earner in seeking out the rewards of the labor market.) Presumably, the criteria by which the underemployment status of secondary workers is determined should differ from those criteria used for primary earners. Secondary workers, by most definitions, belong to households, and these households are organized about a primary earner who is conceived to be optimizing his or her capacity to seek out adequate employment. If the several earners in a given household were all optimizing their capacity to seek out adequate employment (in the sense of maximizing individual-level utility), then this would necessarily imply that households as we generally conceive of them could have only a momentary existence. The necessary geographic mobility that accompanies a worker's optimal work-seeking strategy would dissolve households containing several workers in only a short span of time. But we know that some households with several workers apparently persist through time, indicating that employment priorities within the household have been assigned. These different priorities, as between the degree to which the primary earner and the secondary earner are permitted to optimize their employment-seeking behavior, imply that different standards for ascertaining underemployment for each type of worker should be developed. Such standards would be necessary to reflect the apparently different severity of underemployment for these two types of workers. For example, primary workers who are unemployed apparently experience a more severe kind of underemployment than do secondary workers who are unemployed, the reason being that primary workers have "done their best" to find adequate employment, whereas secondary workers could not have "done their best" to find adequate employment because they have remained in the household where their employment priorities are of secondary importance to those of primary earners. Some adjustment of the criteria used in the determination of the income form for secondary workers was undertaken in this study, by virtue of the above considerations. But no similar attempt was made to adjust criteria used for the determination of the other forms. Technical definitions of secondary workers are certain to change in the near future, but there will almost certainly be an increase in the proportion of workers whose attachment to the labor force is transient, secondary, or dependent on the labor market experience of fellow household members. Evidently, this criticism of underemployment measurement applies primarily, although not exclusively, to women in the labor force.

The problem of measuring underemployment by any method thus far suggested in the literature is far from a trivial one when these kinds of workers are encountered. Currently almost one-half the active work force in the United States are unpaid family workers (or workers very similar to unpaid family workers), agricultural workers, or secondary workers. Labor force indicators in general would be greatly improved if a method for dealing with these kinds of workers—which did not abandon the conceptualization of different underemployment forms—could be developed. This subject is currently overburdened with ideological overtones, especially regarding the statistical treatment of secondary workers, so no rational solution would seem to be immediately forthcoming. It is necessary that these considerations be kept in mind in order that the statistical summaries of underemployment, especially of differential underemployment, will be treated cautiously in the remainder of this work.

1.3 THE DATA

The principal source of data for this study is the March Current Population Survey (Annual Demographic File) for the years 1969 to 1973. These data constitute one of the best—if not the best—sources for the analysis of the labor force currently available anywhere in the world. They certainly comprise the primary empirical data with which any study of the U.S. labor force must reckon. Winsborough (1975) has even argued that the Current Population Survey (CPS) could soon serve as a central data base for establishing a comprehensive system of social accounts for the United States, accounts that could supplement the purely economic accounts that have proliferated in government statistics since the World War II. The extensive training of survey enumerators, the 30 years refinement of questionnaire schedules, the unequaled stock of financial resources available to the agencies conducting the survey, the excellent comparability among the cross sections that make up the series, and the highly professional character of the data preparation itself all point to the high degree of confidence that can be placed upon the data that constitute the empirical base of this study (compare Shryock and Siegel, 1973, Vol. I, p. 73; Morton, 1969). The present work, which rests upon this high-quality data source, can be considered as a step toward establishing a particular kind of social account based upon the CPS vis-à-vis the labor force indicators of Hauser.

Since the series is composed of repeated cross-sectional samples and does not in any way constitute a panel, methods for estimating the parameters of time-period change that are different from the methods for panel data suggested by Richard Stone (1966) are clearly appropriate. Duncan

(1969) has convincingly argued that social indicator models, in the near future at least, will be centrally concerned with repeated cross-sectional surveys of the type found in the CPS. The demographic accounting methods of Stone and others will simply have to await the development of a continuous population register or extensive sampling analogues to it. Repeated cross-sectional surveys can, in the interim, provide us with much concrete information of interest to social science, as this book will hopefully demonstrate. The methods of analysis that the data base constrains us to use will hopefully then be of general importance in the social indicator branch of sociology.

Large-scale social indicator models based upon the CPS pose special strategic problems concerning the manipulation of data and the statistical models to be employed in defining parameters for the time-period change in evidence across the successive time points. Each of the CPS data files contains approximately 200,000 records or cases, so that, obviously, the data retrieval problem is immediately burdened by cost considerations. The recent development of efficient computer software that is capable of retrieving data from a hierarchical record structure such as is found in the CPS data files circumvents somewhat the difficulties of data retrieval. Only a few years ago, these cost considerations would have made a study such as this prohibitively expensive, but now cost is simply not a restricting factor. Regarding data analysis itself, it should also be mentioned that the computer programs associated with hierarchical log-linear models are also sufficiently developed so as to make data analysis costs of manageable proportions. In our view, these newer methods of data analysis are to be recommended not only on purely statistical grounds but also in terms of cost efficiency.

Every kind of serious statistical study of data like the CPS requires the use of the computer and cannot be attempted at all without the aid of several different computer programs. Over 30 computer programs were used in this study, most of which were written or modified by the writer for the purposes of this research. But even with the data-retrieval analysis problems associated with a study of such proportions, the overall computing costs were kept at less than $3000, and this amount included the purchasing and initial preparation of much of the data. (The three computer programs described in the appendixes were also developed mainly with the funds allocated for this project.) Social indicators of the type proposed in this study have therefore become feasible for academic consumption and are by no means restricted to the governmental and private research organizations with virtually unlimited resources. The potential now exists for empirical social science to monitor socioeconomic change in ways that have not been previously possible.

1.4 THE ORGANIZATION OF THIS BOOK

The underlying theme of this book is that the more usual methods for the measurement of underemployment require extensive modification. This rounding-out of our measurement procedure should begin with a recognition that work time, wage income, and skill utilization are the principal factors distributed to workers through the labor market and that each of these labor market rewards has a counterpart in an individual-level measure of underemployment. Underemployment itself can be conceived merely as a deficiency in giving workers a sufficient amount of work time, income, or skill utilization, a conception of underemployment that appears general enough to accommodate itself to various theoretical approaches to the labor market. To expand upon this orientation to the analysis of structure in the labor market and labor force, however, three logically distinct intellectual activities are required.

The first requirement is of a purely theoretical character, and this is the reconceptualization of the labor force aggregate in terms of its ability to secure the main labor market rewards. There is no dearth of studies purporting to analyze the factors of work time, wage income, or skill utilization, but most of these studies isolate one particular dimension to the exclusion of the others. A basic tenet of the labor utilization framework is that the three dimensions should all be considered simultaneously and that they should always be analyzed in the first instance as characteristics that are inherently related to the workings of the labor market. A conscious attempt is made to follow this strategy throughout the book, a strategy that affects our interpretation of the models proposed in subtle but nevertheless profound ways. One example of this orientation is found in Chapter 5, in which the relationship *among* the measures of underemployment is considered at length. Such an analysis only makes theoretical sense if we are given the assumption that the three basic labor market rewards should be conceived in a simultaneous manner. We believe that results presented in the body of this work will provide evidence for the necessity to adopt such a theoretical orientation. But the ramifications of this theoretical perspective are by no means completely worked out in this book or in the treatise by Sullivan (1978), which uses an approach similar to the present one. Clearly, much more theoretical work is required before the labor utilization framework can be made maximally relevant to labor force theory.

A second intellectual activity, and one that will surely inspire vociferous debate, pertains to the operational procedures actually adopted for the empirical measurement of the underemployment forms. Our operational criteria are outlined in Appendix A, and they are similar to those used by Sullivan (1978). But other criteria could be used with perhaps equal validity, implying that much experimentation with operational procedures must be carried out. But at this stage in the development of measures of invisible underemployment, such controversy is to be devoutly hoped for. We encourage others to experiment with the cutoffs used in our work to measure the underemployment forms, and we sincerely hope that such endeavor will soon lead to superior measurement schemes. We have actually experimented with several different criteria for operational measurement, but this activity has so far been largely informal and certainly not rigorous. The work reported in this volume, it should be emphasized, is not an experimentation with alternative strategies of operational measurement, and so we must leave the comparative analysis of alternative strategies to future research.

A third activity will consume the bulk of our attention in the following chapters, and this is the determination of proper statistical methodologies for the analysis of work force characteristics as they are conceived and empirically measured with the labor utilization framework. This framework measures different underemployment forms by partitioning the population of working ages into discrete categories, as opposed to an arrangement of the work force along scale points of some quantitative, unidimensional continuum. Since there are several categories of underemployment isolated by this framework, a complexity of structure emerges that is actually ignored by the more conventional measurement schemes but that nevertheless must be squarely faced. Methods for the analysis of a multistate categorical variable are required if the ultimate objective of measurement is to be fully achieved. In this book, new statistical methods for the analysis of qualitative data will be applied throughout, hopefully producing as an end product a reasonably concise summarization of the demographic structure and across-time dynamic of the U.S. labor force. Most of our work, therefore, is directed toward this type of intellectual activity; hopefully the results obtained thereby will be of some enduring importance even if the basic concepts and operational procedures of the labor utilization framework are ultimately modified or even rejected.

Chapter 2 presents the main empirical results obtained by applying the labor utilization framework to the U.S. work force for the years 1969 through 1973. The age, race, and sex differentials in underemployment are brought out, and the reader can thereby ascertain the value of including measures of invisible underemployment into a general labor force measurement scheme. The goal of this presentation is to demonstrate that a radically different conception of the labor force—and labor market— readily emerges from the application of the Hauser-Sullivan approach.

One fundamental issue underlying the various proposals for the measurement of underemployment is the belief that the customary measures "disguise" the "true" levels of underemployment and hence bias any analysis of differentials in labor force structure across various sociodemographic categories of workers. It is often claimed that the conventional measures of the time form of underemployment mask real differentials in labor market experience (say, by age, race, or sex) or that they are insensitive to the measurement of across-time change in the labor market. These considerations imply that new measures, of whatever genre, should provide information about *differentials* in labor market experience that will substantially increase the knowledge about these differentials that would be inferred from the measures of the time form. In Chapter 3, the statistical information in the new measures of invisible underemployment is discussed, using standard results on the collapsing of cross-tables and a statistical information concept. Our findings are that the new measures add substantially to our fund of information about both demographic differentials and time-period change in the labor force, implying that, indeed, much relevant information concerning "true" labor force characteristics is "disguised" or attenuated by the more customary measures.

Different subpopulations have very different intrinsic levels of risk to the different underemployment forms. For example, young workers are at extremely high risk of experiencing all the forms of underemployment, and this empirical regularity is not so much a function of current labor market conditions as it is a function of the age-graded opportunity structure about which the rewards of the labor market are organized. If the relative share of persons in the labor force at high risk of underemployment changes over time, then the crude rates of underemployment will not measure "true" underemployment risks in an unambiguous manner. The highly aggregative rates that are often used to summarize underemployment levels will confound the underemployment risks associated with the current labor market and with the changing (demographic) composition of the labor force. Chapter 4 considers the influence of changing demographic composition upon the underemployment rates, a legitimate research question owing to the dramatic changes in the demographic makeup of the American labor force that are known to have occurred in this time span. We provide estimates of the across-time change in underemployment that are "controlled for" or "purged of" the extraneous influence of demographic composition, and we attempt to draw the connection between these estimates and the theory of frictional underemployment.

In Chapter 5, we exploit the fact that an individual can be simultaneously underemployed with respect to two or more of the underemployment forms. For example, a part-time unemployed worker can also be mismatched, and so forth. By reference to new latent structure methods, we examine the *scalability* of underemployment as measured by the labor utilization framework. New indicators of underemployment are developed that take account of the fact that the extent of multiple underemployment changes appreciably with economic fluctuation. The models of this chapter also have direct bearing on the characterization of labor force classes, such as is attempted by theorists of the dual or segmented labor market. A basic tenet of the segmented labor market theory (theories?) is that the time, income, and skill dimensions of underemployment are inextricably related. For example, a person whose work-related income is very low over the long run can be expected to have a high risk of unemployment. Using this point of view, which implicitly treats the underemployment measures as indicators of labor force marginality, models are developed in Chapter 5 that characterize *latent* labor force classes indirectly observed in aggregative labor force data. This chapter lends quantitative expression to the theory of the "dual" labor force or "dual" labor market.

A fundamental part of demographic method is the examination of the dependence of the phenomenon under study on the age, time-period, and cohort category in which individual-level observations are made. Changes in underemployment over time are usually thought to result, in large measure, from the influence of the economic exigencies. The dependence of underemployment on the age of the individual, when removed from the influence of time-period fluctuation, is regarded as an indicant of the age-graded social structure through which the rewards of the labor market are organized. (Economists conceive of the age-underemployment relationship as being due almost entirely to the role of experience; i.e., experience is taken as the concept actually measured by age.) Chapter 6 introduces the cohort concept (occasionally referred to as a "vintage" concept in economics) into the analysis of underemployment for the age group 20–34. Differentials among cohorts with respect to labor force experience are documented for some race-sex groups. An attempt is also made to purge the observed time-period variation in the prevalence of certain labor force statuses of the distortions resulting from the cohort variable. We also present identified cohort parameters showing the "tempo" of social change viewed through the cohort perspective, and we provide a rationale for cohort analysis of a discrete dependent variable. The "diagonals parameter" model used by Goodman in the social mobility context is shown to be of considerable utility in the demographic analysis of rates.

Chapter 7 contains material somewhat tangential to the rest of the work, inasmuch as explicit measurement devices are not directly considered. One goal of social indicator research generally is the forecasting or prediction of the relative numbers in various social statuses of interest. The subject of this chapter is the time-trending of the relative sizes of the various labor force statuses considered elsewhere in the work. One approach is a log-linear time-trend model, and a second is related to the familiar process of population projection.

Chapter 8 views underemployment within the perspective of the life table or stationary population model of demography. We here draw out the implications of currently observed age-specific underemployment rates upon the expectation of years of life to be lived per person in any of the labor force statuses. A new labor force indicator, which we designate as the "eventual productive life years" or "eventual productive value" of a person, is developed. By considering "jointly stationary" populations, we also show in a mathematically tractable manner how labor market rewards are allocated to the race–sex groups, given constraints on the number of "favorable" labor force statuses that can be provided by society to its population. In the process, we are led to entertain some very different ideas about underemployment differentials and the manner in which they should ultimately be conceived.

In Chapter 9, we suggest a new measure of *dependency,* an important concept in demography, at least since Coale and Hoover's (1958) use of it in a population-economy model. We also examine the age distribution of underemployment risks and show that the age *elasticity* of underemployment, when properly defined, appears to remain unchanged despite economic fluctuation. Empirical regularity summarized in this chapter seems to beg for further analytic appraisal; mathematical demographers will hopefully be encouraged by these results to use their special skills for a more formal demographic analysis of labor force structure.

Several technical appendixes complement the material of several of the chapters and provide additional methodological material that we believe will be relevant to those concerned with the analysis of repeated cross-sectional surveys, including labor force surveys. These appendixes provide the operational criteria actually used to measure the underemployment forms (Appendix A); a modified life-table approach to the analysis of age-graded social statuses (Appendix B); a general computer program for latent structure or latent class analysis (Appendix C); an analysis of the quality of age data in the Annual Demographic File (Appendix D); a rationale for calculating normed measures of interaction in log-linear models (Appendix E); a statistical technique for analyzing the way the cohort variable "translates" across-time change in demographic rates (Appendix F); a computer program for cohort analysis (Appendix G); and a technique to "adjust" rates within the framework of multiplicative models for cross-classified data (Appendix H).

2

underemployment in the
United States, 1969–1973

In this chapter, the main results obtained by applying Hauser's labor utilization framework are presented and briefly discussed. The objective is the description of underemployment in terms of simple two-variable relationships observed over time. The tables presented in this section contain, in certain respects to be discussed later, all the information that is necessary to characterize the time-period change in underemployment for the age–race–sex groups. Some comments concerning the adequacy of Hauser's indicators are made on the basis of these simple comparisons. Although there are many contingency tables that could be of interest, the ones presented in this chapter will hopefully be found provocative. They will also suggest the importance of examining underemployment differentials using Hauser's framework or some close relative to it. The theme of this chapter, elaborated upon throughout the remainder of this book, is that an entirely different description of labor force (and labor market) structure emerges with the inclusion of the measures of invisible underemployment.

Table 2.1, "Time by Labor Force Status," pertains to the total civilian population 14 years old and over, recorded on successive March CPS files.[1] Five underemployment forms are represented in that cross-table: sub-unemployment (a proxy for "discouraged workers"), unemployment,

---

[1] Raw frequencies obtained in the categories of underemployment are presented in Table 2.1 so that other researchers might duplicate our results. Procedures for obtaining this cross-table are made explicit in Appendix A.

TABLE 2.1
Underemployment in the United States, 1969–1973, for the Total Population and the Total Labor Force, 14 Years and Over

Year (1)	Not-in-labor force[a] (2)	Sub-unem-ployed (3)	Unem-ployed (4)	Invol-untary part-time (5)	Low income (6)	Mis-match (7)	Adequate (8)
1969							
Number	45887	779	2233	1476	4483	5640	48017
Percentage of total	42.3	.7	2.1	1.4	4.1	5.2	44.2
Percentage of labor force	–	–	3.6	2.4	7.2	9.1	77.7
Percentage of modified labor force	–	1.2	3.6	2.4	7.2	9.0	76.6
1970							
Number	43705	670	2840	1554	4120	5560	45299
Percentage of total	42.1	.6	2.7	1.5	4.0	5.4	43.7
Percentage of labor force	–	–	4.8	2.6	6.9	9.4	76.3
Percentage of modified labor force	–	1.1	4.7	2.6	6.9	9.3	75.4
1971							
Number	44956	933	3874	1819	3945	6219	44373
Percentage of total	42.4	.9	3.7	1.7	3.7	5.9	41.7
Percentage of labor force	–	–	6.4	3.0	6.5	10.3	73.8
Percentage of modified labor force	–	1.5	6.3	3.0	6.4	10.2	72.5
1972							
Number	42939	1001	3677	1680	4234	6363	42811
Percentage of total	41.8	1.0	3.6	1.6	4.1	6.2	41.7
Percentage of labor force	–	–	6.3	2.9	7.2	10.8	72.9
Percentage of modified labor force	–	1.7	6.2	2.8	7.1	10.6	71.6

(continued)

TABLE 2.1 (continued)

Year (1)	Not-in-labor force[a] (2)	Sub-unem-ployed (3)	Unem-ployed (4)	Invol-untary part-time (5)	Low income (6)	Mis-match (7)	Adequate (8)
1973							
Number	41685	911	3121	1455	4261	6766	42350
Percentage of total	41.5	.9	3.1	1.4	4.2	6.7	42.1
Percentage of labor force	–	–	5.4	2.5	7.4	11.7	73.0
Percentage of modified labor force	–	1.5	5.3	2.5	7.2	11.5	72.0

Source: *March Current Population Survey,* for years 1969 through 1973.
[a]See text for discussion of the definition of labor force and modified labor force.

involuntary part-time unemployment, underemployment by low work-related income, and mismatch. Different summary percentages are presented in that table. These are underemployment "ratios," with the total population as base; "rates" of underemployment, with the usual labor force as the base; and "rates" of underemployment, with the "modified labor force" as the base. The modified labor force is the sum of columns 3 through 8; that is, it includes the sub-unemployed along with the more usual labor force as the universe of persons "exposed" to the risk of underemployment. All of these underemployment categories, except for the mismatch form, are directly comparable over time. Owing to changes in occupational classifications beginning in 1971, there is a possible distortion in the mismatch change 1970–1971, but this distortion is apparently minimal in view of the regular trend over time in the percentage mismatched. We see from Table 2.1 that mismatch apparently increased from 9.4% in 1970 to 10.3% in 1971, and this increase of .9% could be partly due to the incomparability of occupational classifications essential to determining mismatch between these two periods. This magnitude of change does not appear unreasonable, however, since the change 1972–1973 was also .9%, and the occupational classification for those 2 years was entirely comparable.

Restricting our attention to the rates of underemployment with the usual labor force as the base (the sum of columns 4 through 8), the following characterization of underemployment emerges. Unemployment increased from a low of 3.6% in 1969 to a high of 6.4% in 1971. The low-hours form of underemployment showed similar changes, although the absolute magnitude of those changes was not nearly so great as with unemployment. The income form gives us surprising information in addition to the unemployment and hours forms, themselves routine indicators for several decades. We see that 1969–1970, where unemployment had *risen* from 3.6% to 4.8%, the income form decreased from 7.2% to 6.9%. By looking at unemployment (or low hours) alone, then, we would have been misled in characterizing labor market change, since the two forms tended to progress in opposite directions. In terms of providing adequate income to full-time workers, the year 1970 was somewhat better than unemployment statistics alone would have led us to believe.[2] But from 1971 to 1973 the converse was true. Unemployment and low hours declined substantially, the former by two full percentage points, but the income form *increased* from 6.5% to 7.4%. This documented variability of the income form apart from variability in the "visible" forms of underemployment is evidence for the need to include an income measure in underemployment statistics. Similar conclusions were also reached by Levitan and Taggart (1974), although their income measures were considerably different from our own.

The trend in mismatch seems to be a fairly regular one, increasing from a low of 9.1% in 1969 to 11.7% in 1973. A disturbing feature of the mismatch trend is that it seems to increase steadily, despite the rise and fall in the visible underemployment forms. As an indicator sensitive to the transitory economic exigencies that are clearly reflected in the visible underemployment indicators, mismatch does not, at first glimpse, seem very appropriate. That mismatch seems to rise steadily in spite of countervailing trends in the other underemployment forms could, however, be indicative of socioeconomic forces impervious to those that cause fluctuation in visible underemployment. That the relative number of persons working in jobs not fully commensurate with their educational (i.e., skill) attainment is rising at the rate of over .6% per year is a fact of far-reaching importance for labor force policymakers and social scientists alike. The trend in mismatch, then, cannot be explained by the trends in any of the other underemployment forms, and so we conclude that this form is an indicator of forces largely independent of the factors producing visible underemployment.

[2] This statement needs some qualification, since the income measure is based upon the *past* year's experience, and we have assumed that past year's experience as a proxy for the current incidence of the income form. If the series are adjusted to a more current basis, by applying the income form of year $t + 1$ to year t, the series appears much more regular with respect to the income form, and this adjusted series is more in line with the trend in unemployment during this period.

The trend in sub-unemployment, by reference to column 3 of Table 2.1, exhibits a pattern not unlike that of unemployment rates. Since our measurement of these marginally active persons is admittedly crude, we should be cautious in concluding that either the relative changes in or the absolute numbers of the sub-unemployed are valid measures of the discouraged worker phenomenon. But they are certainly suggestive, and they correspond to official figures concerning the trend in the numbers of discouraged workers in this time span.

A few comments concerning the comparability of our figures with other results are in order. The figures here pertain to the population (or the work force) 14 years old and over, whereas the usual labor force tabulations since the 1960 census are based upon ages 16 and over. Minor departures from published figures are therefore expected.[3] The unemployed and the low-hours forms in our study, exactly comparable to standard definitions of these forms, produced results virtually identical to published data. There is no way we can corroborate our low-income measurement procedure, even though it is based upon the federal poverty thresholds that have become ubiquitous in national statistics. The income figures reported here refer only to members of the labor force, and only to those members of the labor force who were not classified as unemployed or part-time unemployed. In addition, published figures on the incidence of poverty pertain to households, not necessarily to individuals or to individual workers. Finally, our income measures provide an adjustment for weeks worked in the past year and only pertain to work-related income. (With these qualifications in mind, it should be quite clear that the low-income measure is *not identical* to a poverty or need measure, as some critics have charged.) One standard for comparison is Sullivan's (1978) similar usage of the income criteria, and our results are virtually identical to her's. On the basis of internal consistency and certain external comparisons, our results appear reasonably error free. We do not therefore address this problem further in this work, but researchers could check our results in more detail by applying the methods outlined in Appendix A.

Since the measures represented in Table 2.1 are in part novel, it is appropriate to examine them for their contribution to gauging across-time variation in underemployment. Time-trend in these measures should re-

---

[3] Some official publications that are based upon the March CPS for the years of this study and that allow the corroboration of results are U.S. Department of Commerce (1975) and Bureau of Labor Statistics (1975). Of course, literally hundreds of other sources could have been used to corroborate the results for almost as much detail as we needed. We did not do so, but we noted that the overall table (Table 2.1) was almost identical to official results. Other sources using similar data are Sullivan and Hauser (1975), Sullivan and Hauser (1978), and Sullivan (1978).

veal characteristics of the changing labor market that are not described by unemployment rates alone. Ideally, we should compare these results with other socioeconomic indicators of demonstrated validity pertaining to labor force characteristics over this time span. Unfortunately, such a comparison would be limited by the availability here of only a small number of data points (five time-period observations in all). Crude measures of the variability evidenced in the measures of the five underemployment forms will be discussed instead, the justification for which being that variability in these indicators through a period of economic fluctuation is a necessary condition for validity of the measurement scheme.

In Table 2.2, coefficients of time-period variation for each of the five underemployment forms are presented. With regard to the three measures of *visible* underemployment (i.e., sub-unemployment, unemployment, and part-time unemployment), the *absolute* numbers obtained by our method are meaningful, if only because they rely upon the customary procedures used to measure the time dimension of underemployment. For the two measures of *invisible* underemployment (the income and mismatch forms), the absolute figures obtained are perhaps less meaningful because of the arbitrariness in definition of these forms. But *relative* changes over time

TABLE 2.2
Coefficients of Time-period Variation in Underemployment Rates
(Modified Labor Force as Base)

	Underemployment form				
Coefficient	Sub-unemploy-ment	Unemploy-ment	Low hours	Income	Mismatch
1. Arithmetic mean	1.4	5.2	2.7	7.0	10.1
2. Standard deviation	.2	1.0	.2	.3	.9
3. Coefficient of relative variation	.2	.2	.2	.0	.1
4. Mean absolute deviation from the mean	.1	.4	.1	.1	.4
5. r^2, the squared correlation coefficient	.60	.48	.07	.00	.83
6. $1 - r^2$	.40	.52	.93	1.00	.17

Source: Table 2.1, this volume.

should be meaningful for purposes of assessing these measures, because the standards by which these forms are determined have been uniformly applied to each of the time-periods.

Measures that assess the across-time variability are the simple standard deviation, the ratio of the standard deviation to the mean (i.e., the coefficient of relative variation), and the mean absolute deviation from the mean. These were calculated from the underemployment rates of Table 2.1, where the modified labor force was the base in those rates. Since labor force indicators should necessarily show across-time variability in a time span where we know a priori that considerable economic fluctuation occurred, measures that show large variability are probably to be preferred. For the visible underemployment forms, we see that the unemployment rate, a master socioeconomic indicator for several decades, by far performs the best, with, for example, a standard deviation of 1.0%. The standard deviation of the mismatch rate, owing to the steady increase over time in the incidence of mismatch, also shows considerable time-period variability. The coefficient of relative variation shows the usual unemployment statistic to be superior to the other measures of visible underemployment.

Another way to view the time-period variation of this admittedly short series is to consider variation about a linear time-trend. A substantial linear time-trend may by itself point to socioeconomic changes of long duration, and variation about this time-trend will indicate the "shocks" of the transitory economic exigencies. By examining the correlation coefficient of the underemployment rate with time, the evidence of linear time-trend in some of those rates is clearly brought out. The proportion of unexplained variance, $1 - r^2$, is similarly showing transitory shocks in other of those rates. Strong correlations were obtained for sub-unemployment, unemployment, and mismatch, indicating the existence of linearity in these rates. More important, in our view, is the variability about the time-trend line. The income form, with moderate overall variation ($s = .3$), has no time-trend component whatsoever but would apparently add considerably to our understanding of transitory underemployment changes. The same is true of the low-hours form.

On the face of it, then, it can be said that in terms of absolute and relative variability, unemployment and mismatch seem to be the best indicators. Mismatch by itself has a very heavy linear time-trend component, and the income form could contribute to our understanding of transitory changes, although there is no apparent trend at all in the incidence of the income form. The questions of this study pertain in part to the validity of Hauser's measurement of the invisible forms of underemployment. These measures appear to show the necessary degree of variability, in one

TABLE 2.3
Underemployment during 1969–1973, "Condensed" Table (Modified Labor Force as Base)[a]

Year (1)	"Economic" underemployment[b] (percent) (2)	Mismatch (percent) (3)	Adequate (4)	N^c (5)
1969	14.4	9.0	76.6	62628
1970	15.3	9.3	75.4	60043
1971	17.2	10.2	72.5	62363
1972	17.8	10.6	71.6	59811
1973	16.5	11.5	72.0	58864

Source: Table 2.2, this volume.

[a]The "modified labor force" includes the sub-unemployed plus the usual labor force.

[b]"Economic" underemployment is the sum of sub-unemployment, unemployment, hours, and the income forms of underemployment.

[c]Denotes the number in the modified labor force upon which the percentages are based; that is, sample size.

sense or another, for their measurement to be valid. In a labor force as dynamic as the one represented in this study, variability in underemployment measures is a necessary, although certainly not a sufficient, condition for assessing the adequacy of our measures.

For reasons that will be more apparent later, we choose to summarize the rather unwieldy results of Table 2.1 in a condensed version, Table 2.3. We there combine sub-unemployment, unemployment, part-time unemployment, and the low-income forms into one class and maintain the mismatch category as another distinct class. Briefly, the reasons for collapsing our results are that the first four forms of underemployment are very similar in character (e.g., in their *economic* character), whereas the mismatch form is distinct conceptually and statistically from these other forms.[4] Table 2.3 therefore represents an overall view of underemployment in this 5-year time span, where unnecessary detail is eliminated. Unemployment rates themselves, a master socioeconomic indicator for the last 4 decades, account for most of the time variation in the collapsed category. We refer to the collapsed category as "economic underemployment" in Table 2.3 and throughout the rest of this book.

As a second step in describing underemployment across time, the above results are broken down further by sex and race. The results are shown in Table 2.4. Across-time variation in all the underemployment forms is not

---

[4] See related results in Chapter 5.

TABLE 2.4
Underemployment by Race and Sex, 1969–1973 (Modified Labor Force as Base)
(in Percentages)

	1969	1970	1971	1972	1973
White male					
Sub-unemployed	.7	.7	.9	1.1	.9
Unemployed	2.8	4.0	5.6	5.5	4.5
Hours	1.8	2.0	2.2	2.3	2.0
Income	3.4	3.4	3.5	4.0	4.0
Mismatch	10.3	10.5	11.5	12.3	13.2
Adequate	81.0	79.4	76.3	74.8	75.4
Nonwhite male					
Sub-unemployed	2.0	2.0	2.4	2.5	1.9
Unemployed	5.6	7.0	9.2	9.3	8.1
Hours	3.9	4.6	4.5	4.4	3.3
Income	4.4	4.7	5.0	4.8	4.6
Mismatch	6.9	7.0	8.5	9.1	9.6
Adequate	77.2	74.7	70.5	69.9	72.5
White female					
Sub-unemployed	1.8	1.4	1.9	2.1	2.1
Unemployed	3.9	5.0	6.4	5.9	5.4
Hours	2.6	2.7	3.3	3.1	2.9
Income	13.1	12.1	11.0	12.0	12.2
Mismatch	7.4	7.7	8.6	8.5	9.3
Adequate	71.2	71.2	68.9	68.4	68.1
Nonwhite female					
Sub-unemployed	3.4	3.0	4.3	4.1	4.0
Unemployed	7.7	8.4	10.6	11.1	10.3
Hours	5.5	6.2	6.8	4.8	4.1
Income	12.6	12.2	10.0	10.5	10.9
Mismatch	8.2	8.6	8.4	8.6	9.9
Adequate	62.6	61.6	59.9	60.9	60.8

unlike that given previously for the total modified labor force. Unemployment rates increased about 3% from 1969 to 1972 for each of the groups; the low-hours form again exhibited less variation than unemployment. Mismatch increased steadily for all groups, and the time-trend in the low-income form is not peculiar for any group given the overall results. (One anomaly to this description is the sharp *fall* in the income form 1969–1971 for women in general.) More interesting are the race–sex comparisons for any given cross section of time. We see that females had rates of the low-income form approximately four times that of white males and over double that of nonwhite males. For mismatch, we see that white males exhibited the highest rates, with the other groups being approximately equal to each other for each time-period.

For purposes of providing a more condensed view of the sex–race–time variation in underemployment, Table 2.5 is presented. This table corresponds to Table 2.3 presented earlier for the total modified labor force, where again the first four underemployment forms are collapsed into one "economic underemployment" category. With the table collapsed in this fashion, we see race and sex differentials in underemployment that are more marked than consideration of visible underemployment statistics alone would have shown. The new measures contribute much to our understanding of the social organization of the labor force, since new race and sex differentials in labor force experience are now evident.

Age is another master demographic variable with which the underemployment forms also vary. Because of the relationship of age to the socioeconomic mechanisms that allocate employment opportunity, age variability in underemployment is expected. We consider this problem in detail in Chapter 4, but for now the broad outline will be discussed. Table 2.6 shows the age variability in underemployment over time; the time variation is again not unlike that detailed above, except that for the age group

TABLE 2.5
Underemployment by Race and Sex, 1969-1973, "Condensed" Table
(Modified Labor Force as Base) (in Percentages)

	1969	1970	1971	1972	1973
White male					
"Economic" underemployment	8.7	10.1	12.2	12.9	11.4
Mismatch	10.3	10.5	11.5	12.3	13.2
Adequate employment	81.0	79.4	76.4	74.8	75.4
Nonwhite male					
"Economic" underemployment	15.9	18.3	21.1	21.0	17.9
Mismatch	6.9	7.0	8.5	9.1	9.6
Adequate employment	77.2	74.7	70.5	69.9	72.5
White female					
"Economic" underemployment	21.4	21.2	22.6	23.1	22.6
Mismatch	7.4	7.7	8.6	8.5	9.3
Adequate employment	71.2	71.2	68.9	68.4	68.1
Nonwhite female					
"Economic underemployment	29.2	29.8	31.7	30.5	29.3
Mismatch	8.2	8.6	8.4	8.6	9.9
Adequate employment	62.6	61.6	59.9	60.9	60.8

Source: Table 2.4, this volume.

TABLE 2.6
Underemployment by Age, 1969-1973 (Modified Labor Force as Base) (in Percentages)

	1969	1970	1971	1972	1973
14-19 years					
"Economic" underemployment[a]	29.2	30.1	32.9	35.9	35.6
Mismatch	2.3	2.4	2.5	2.8	2.8
Adequate employment	68.5	67.5	64.6	61.6	63.8
20-34 years					
"Economic" underemployment	17.1	18.1	21.0	21.0	19.3
Mismatch	11.1	11.5	13.0	13.9	15.5
Adequate employment	71.8	70.4	66.0	65.1	65.2
35-49 years					
"Economic" underemployment	10.3	11.5	12.6	12.7	11.7
Mismatch	10.0	10.0	11.0	11.2	11.6
Adequate employment	79.7	78.5	76.4	76.1	76.7
50-64 years					
"Economic" underemployment	10.1	10.8	11.9	11.6	10.8
Mismatch	7.8	8.2	8.8	9.2	9.8
Adequate employment	82.1	81.0	79.3	79.2	79.4
65 and over					
"Economic" underemployment	13.8	12.3	15.2	14.6	13.4
Mismatch	7.7	8.7	8.1	8.3	8.0
Adequate employment	78.5	79.0	76.7	77.1	78.6

[a]Economic underemployment is sub-unemployment, unemployment, low hours, and the income form in one aggregate figure.

20-34, economic underemployment increases absolutely with economic recession more than in the other groups. The mismatch trend in ages 20-34 is also striking, since we see that mismatch for that age group increased dramatically (a full 4.4% in 5 years), and it is not difficult to show that most of the overall variation in mismatch owes to fundamental changes in mismatch rates for this critical age group. These observations are certainly in line with Freeman's (1976) assessment of "overeducation" relative to demand for educated labor for this broad age group, even though our measure of educated underemployment is different from that used in Freeman's work. The age trends in economic underemployment are precisely those that are expected: extremely high risk of underemployment in youth, low risk in the middle ages, rising risk in the older labor force ages, with moderately high risk over age 65. The dependence of mismatch upon age is, of course, confounded by both the fact that the very young ages have not yet completed their education (accounting for their very low mismatch) and the fact that the older ages completed schooling in an era where educational attainment in general was vastly different than in recent times. Regarding the mismatch rate for ages 20–34, it might be argued that these figures will be *conservative* estimates of the real excess of educated labor supply over demand for that labor. The reason for this assertion is simply that a part of the age group 20–34 is still acquiring the type of education (i.e., higher education) that puts them at especially high risk of mismatch.[5] Presumably, the observed rate of mismatch would be much higher if labor force entry were not being postponed by those persons at especially high risk of mismatch.

Other tables broken down with greater age detail show much the same pattern as does Table 2.6, so we will not go into more detail than that which has been presented. Of special importance to the demography of the labor force in this era is the changing *age composition* of the labor force. Since risk to underemployment varies regularly with age, and since this regularity may be assumed to persist through time, relative changes over time in the size of particular age categories will affect overall rates in ways unrelated to the changing age-specific risk to underemployment. These age "distortions" are the subject of further analysis in Chapter 4.

These, in broad outline form, are the results obtained by analysis of underemployment over time as conceived by Hauser's labor force indicators. These tables were chosen for presentation because, in certain respects to be mentioned later, they contain information that is sufficient to characterize across-time changes in underemployment for the age–sex–race groups. Although these tables are sufficient to characterize that change, it is not clear how that information should be summarized in the form of unambiguous statistical indicators.[6] Finding suitable methodological tools that summarize this information in meaningful ways is a subject taken up at length in the remainder of this book. The above tables can be taken now as an approximation to the underemployment history of the U.S. labor force 1969–1973. Further statistical manipulations to be conducted in this book will, for the most part, attempt to isolate the

---

[5] See Appendix A for further comments. According to our operational definitions, only workers who have completed at least one additional year of schooling beyond high school are subject to mismatch. Since many persons completing 1 or more years of school beyond high school will still be out of the labor force during at least part of the age span 20–34, the apparent mismatch is probably less than the mismatch that would obtain if those persons were participating in the labor force.

[6] We will find in Chapter 4 that acceptable log-linear models for the age × race × sex × time × underemployment table will include the marginal tables presented above as *sufficient statistics*. That is, these marginal tables contain statistical information that is sufficient to describe the relationships observed in the full cross-table, and this finding led to our inclusion of these marginal tables here. On the concept of sufficiency, see Rao (1973).

structure underlying these basic demographic contingencies. Results similar to these, or indicators comparable in substance to them, are largely absent from the abundant literature on the measurement of underemployment or labor force underutilization. The description of labor force structure embodied in these tables is considerably at variance with other descriptions that ignore the incidence of invisible underemployment.

3

information in the measures of invisible underemployment

This chapter considers the following problem: Since it is not directly possible to infer the actual measurement validity of the various underemployment indicators, criteria that are *necessary* for their validity must be suggested. This is the case principally because the *absolute magnitudes* observed in the various categories of underemployment are ambiguous. Unemployment measures, for example, could be affected by as much as 2% by altering one or two of the standards used in determining whether a person out of work has expended a sufficient degree of effort in looking for work. Likewise, the low-hours category could be artificially inflated (or deflated) by using a standard of less (or more) than 35 hr per week as the "full-time" workweek and/or by adjusting the criteria used to establish "economic reasons" for part-time work. Sub-unemployment, our proxy to the "discouraged worker" phenomenon, could also be a contrived figure, given differing conceptions of what that type of marginal labor force participation really is. Since our measures of these three forms have been accepted for some time and have been shown to be necessary measures of underemployment, the need to analyze these traditional measures critically is here ignored. The problem with the newly proposed "invisible underemployment" measures is an acute one, however, if only because of the novel character of their conceptualization and measurement. Those categories could also be adjusted to almost any *absolute* level one wanted to obtain, merely by changing the income thresholds or by changing the years of education used as cutoff points. The new measures cannot be evaluated, that is, merely by inspecting the absolute frequencies observed in categories purportedly signifying the low-income or mismatch forms of underemployment. But *variability* as evidenced by underemployment differentials over time or across demographic strata should exist if our approach to measurement is valid. It is this contention on which the present chapter rests.

In the absence of a means to assess the validity of the absolute magnitudes contained in our invisible underemployment categories, we will propose the following necessary condition: Any new indicator of invisible underemployment must provide additional information regarding across-time and/or across-demographic-strata differentials than would be obtained from the more usual labor force indicators. We know that invisible underemployment is of a different character than visible underemployment, so that whenever differentials exist with respect to visible underemployment—the measurement of which is relatively valid—different kinds of differentials must exist with respect to invisible underemployment. If our technique of measurement does not show this to be true, then it cannot be a valid one. A finding that invisible underemployment exhibits the same kind of variability that visible underemployment exhibits would surely contradict the theoretical literature that dictated the need to consider invisible underemployment. Throughout this chapter, we will make reference to time variation in the labor market and to underemployment differentials that are known to exist with respect to age, sex, race, and other structural variables. Our measurement of invisible underemployment, to be appropriate at all, must provide information regarding those master differentials that are known to exist and that cannot be inferred from the more usual labor force indicators. We first describe a statistical measure of information appropriate for the problem at hand and then apply these methods to infer the information in the new measures of underemployment.

3.1 THE INFORMATION IN FULL VERSUS COLLAPSED CROSS-TABLES

Suppose that we did not have access to our invisible underemployment measures but only to the more usual indicators of visible underemployment. For purposes of exposition, suppose further that these visible underemployment measures were collapsed into a simple dichotomy. (No loss of generality occurs if we maintain the detail of sub-unemployment, unemployment, and low hours in the following.) Now suppose that we wish to examine the information in the usual visible underemployment measures concerning some criterion variable C, which for now we also assume to be a simple dichotomy. Denote the dichotomous variable indicating the presence or absence of visible underemployment as $U(2)$. Class 1 of $U(2)$ corresponds to "visible underemployment," and class 2 of $U(2)$ corresponds to "not visible underemployment." Denote the observed cell proportions as $p_{ij}^*, i, j = 1, 2$. Now suppose that we compute expected cell proportions π_{ij}^* according to an independence hypothesis, that is, $\pi_{ij}^* = p_{i.}^* p_{.j}^*$. The independence hypothesis states that $U(2)$ is homogeneously distributed across the categories of C; it is the demographic hypothesis of no differential underemployment. "Information" in the observed table which modifies our belief about the independence hypothesis is defined as:

$$I_2(p^* : \pi^*) = 2 \sum_{\substack{i=1,2 \\ j=1,2}} p_{ij}^* \log(p_{ij}^*/\pi_{ij}^*) \tag{3.1}$$

(see, e.g., Theil, 1971, pp. 636ff). Associated with Equation 3.1 is 1 degree of freedom (df), as in the usual independence hypothesis for the 2×2 contingency table. We see that statistical information in the sample is proportional to the likelihood-ratio χ^2 statistic L^2, or $I = nL^2$, where n is the sample size. A large value of $I_2(p^* : \pi^*)$ denotes a large amount of information in the $U(2)$ variable that allows us to discriminate between the classes of the C variable. In purely statistical terms, a large value of $I_2(p^* : \pi^*)$ tells us that C and $U(2)$ are not independent of each other or, equivalently, that the $U(2)$ variable is not homogeneously distributed across the categories of C. In more substantive terms, the data (the p_{ij}^*) provide a large amount of statistical information about an underemployment differential.

Now suppose that the income form is included with our underemployment variable, and denote the new trichotomous variable so created as $U(3)$. The first class of $U(3)$ is identical with the first class of $U(2)$, but the second class of $U(3)$ denotes underemployment by low income, unlike the case for $U(2)$. Corresponding to the $C \times U(3)$ cross-table we also have an information measure

$$I_3(p : \pi) = 2 \sum_{\substack{i=1,2 \\ j=1,2,3}} p_{ij} \log(p_{ij}/\pi_{ij}) \tag{3.2}$$

and a large value of that measure corresponds to the case where underemployment, including the visible forms and/or the income form, are not homogeneous with respect to the classes of C. In Equation 3.2, the p_{ij} are the observed proportions in the $C \times U(3)$ contingency table, and the π_{ij} are the expected proportions under the independence hypothesis, that is, $\pi_{ij} = p_{i.}p_{.j}$. (It can be verified that $p_{11} = p_{11}^*, p_{21} = p_{21}^*, \pi_{11} = \pi_{11}^*,$ and $\pi_{21} = \pi_{21}^*$, and these facts are partly responsible for the results that follow.)

Corresponding to Equation 3.2 are 2 *df,* as is the case for the usual independence hypothesis for the 2 × 3 contingency table. A high value of the information measure $I_3(p : \pi)$ corresponds to the situation where $U(3)$ is not homogeneous with respect to the classes of C; there are visible underemployment and/or income differentials with respect to the criterion variable C. The main result is that $I_3 - I_2$, by a standard result in the partitioning of χ^2 in full versus collapsed tables, is a measure of the *additional information* in the income form, *apart from the information in the visible underemployment form*. It is possible to show using methods presented by Goodman (1968, 1971b) that I_3 is equal to the sum of I_2 and another quantity that is identical to the information measure that would be obtained from the 2 × 2 table derived by *deleting* the first category of $U(3)$ in the $C \times U(3)$ cross-table. The information in the full table thus consists of two distinct components, the first denoting information in visible underemployment alone and the second denoting information in the income form alone. The result generalizes to any table where C and/or U may be polytomous and holds in the case where we examine either a simple independence hypothesis or a conditional independence hypothesis controlling for one or several variables. Statistical independence in this context, to repeat once again, is equivalent to the demographic hypothesis of no differential underemployment, and information about demographic differentials (i.e., the magnitude of the departure from statistical independence) is precisely that which should be used to assess the gain we have achieved in measuring invisible underemployment. All that is required is a specification of the types of criterion variables that should be brought into the analysis.

3.2 THE INFORMATION IN INVISIBLE UNDEREMPLOYMENT RELATIVE TO AGE, RACE, SEX, AND TIME-PERIOD DIFFERENTIALS

In Table 3.1, we have presented indexes of the relative increase in information provided by Hauser's new measures, derived by partitioning the information in the age × race × sex × time × underemployment contingency table. First we obtained the information in the table when a fourfold classification of underemployment was used, defined in relation to the three categories of visible underemployment. Next we obtained the information in the table with a fivefold classification of underemployment (including low-income detail), and finally we obtained the information in the table with a sixfold classification of underemployment (including both low-income and mismatch detail). By denoting I_4, I_5, and I_6 as these re-

TABLE 3.1
Information in the Income and Mismatch Forms of Underemployment in the Age by Race by Sex by Time by Underemployment Cross-table

Criterion variable (1)	Control (2)	Income relative to visible under-employment (3)	Mismatch relative to income and visible under-employment (4)	Income and mismatch relative to visible under-employment (5)
A	RST	.721	.270	1.185
R	AST	.083	.096	.187
S	ART	5.918	.042	6.211
T	ARS	.134	.354	.535
ST	AR	3.709	.072	4.047
RT	AS	.089	.191	.298
AT	RS	.506	.278	.925
RS	AT	2.568	.040	2.712
AS	RT	1.546	.175	1.993
AR	ST	.593	.246	.984
ARST	None	1.183	.171	1.555

Variable key: A = age in five categories; R = race in two categories; S = sex; T = time.

spective information measures, we see that $(I_5 - I_4)/I_4$ measures the information in low-income relative to the information in visible underemployment alone, that $(I_6 - I_5)/I_5$ measures the information in mismatch relative to the information in both low-income and visible underemployment, and that $(I_6 - I_4)/I_4$ measures the information in both the low-income and mismatch forms relative to the information in visible underemployment alone. These three indexes are presented as columns 3, 4, and 5 of Table 3.1, respectively. The additional information in Hauser's new measures is considerable; both of the new measures provide information about differentials in the labor force (or labor market) that is evidently disguised by the usual measures.

The income variable produces the most dramatic results, as inspection of column 3 in Table 3.1 shows. That column contains quantities $(I_5 - I_4)/I_4$, which show the information in the income variable relative to that contained in visible underemployment. When the criterion variable is age (variable A), we find that this index is 72.1%, or that there is 72.1% as much information in Hauser's *single* measure of low income as was contained in the *three* visible underemployment measures. The income variable thus adds considerably to our knowledge about age differentials in labor force experience. This figure gains additional significance when account is taken of the tremendous age variability in the risks to the time form of underemployment; the income measure by itself has 72.1% of the information in the measures of the time form, and there is, of course, much information in the three measures of the time form. For race and time-period, the information in the income measure is 8.3% and 13.4%, respectively, showing that the income variable does not provide us with much information about these kinds of differentials, above that already contained in the visible underemployment measures. Information about sex differentials in labor force experience is 591.8% of that contained in the visible underemployment measures, or there is the dramatic figure of 491.8% more information in the *single* income measure than in the other three measures of visible underemployment. The social organization of the labor force about the sexes is thus very dramatically portrayed by the income measure; conversely, the visible underemployment measures disguise the labor market opportunity for females. Inspection of tables presented in Chapter 2 shows that visible underemployment differentials between the sexes are indeed not very pronounced at all but income differentials are very extreme, and both these facts account for this dramatic increase in information.

Once we have considered the income form, Hauser's mismatch measure adds only moderately to our understanding of age differentials or to our understanding of time-period changes in the labor market. By inspection of column 4 of Table 3.1, we see that mismatch contains 27.0% of the information contained in all the other measures about age differentials and 35.4% of the information contained in all the other measures about time-period change. But such increases in statistical information in the mismatch form could be important in their own right, chiefly because the age and time-period variability in the other measures is very dramatic. It is only by comparison with the income form that the results for mismatch seem somewhat disappointing.

The reader can gain further understanding of the magnitude of these information statistics by studying in detail the several tables presented in Chapter 2. It can be fairly concluded from the results of this section that the *overall* gain to be achieved by considering the new measures is considerable. With the new measures, we are now able to see new differentials in the demographic strata of the labor force—showing the dimensions of social organization in the labor force—and to obtain a more sensitive portrayal of time-trend in the labor market. The overall gain in the new measures, obtained from the last row of Table 3.1, is judged by our method to be 55.5%, since $(I_6 - I_4)/I_4$ was 155.5% for both new measures combined. These measures, then, or ones very similar to them, have a great potential for inferring demographic differentials in the labor force or time-period change in the labor market.

TABLE 3.2

Information in the Income and Mismatch Measures: Region, Family Type, and Place of Residence

	Income relative to visible under-employment	Mismatch relative to income and visible under-employment	Income and mismatch relative to visible under-employment
Region	.221	.886	1.302
Family type	9.513	.107	10.641
Place of residence	.298	1.070	1.686

3.3 THE INFORMATION IN INVISIBLE UNDEREMPLOYMENT RELATIVE TO REGION, FAMILY TYPE, AND PLACE OF RESIDENCE

The preceding section contained results pertaining to the gain in statistical information that can be obtained from the Hauser-Sullivan measures of invisible underemployment. But this analysis was restricted to only three structural variables—age, race, and sex—and to the variable time-period that ostensibly indicates labor market change. The new measures added considerable information to the characterization of these structural differentials and of the labor market change. In this section, we present another appraisal of the information in the new measures, focusing on other structural characteristics. Three structural variables of special importance are region of residence, place of residence, and family type.[1] We now consider the additional information in the new measures for inferring underemployment differentials with respect to these structural variables, again demonstrating that the gain in information is considerable. On the basis of these results, it will again be apparent that an altogether different conception of labor force structure emerges when considering these new measures, adding to the validity of the labor utilization framework.

Table 3.2 presents relative information indexes corresponding to those considered earlier in Table 3.1. One difference between the two sets of results, however, is important to note. In Table 3.2 the information was partitioned in three *different* three-way cross-tables, whereas in Table 3.1 the information was partitioned in a single multiway cross-table. The first

[1] Region was a fourfold variable (northeast, central, south, and west); place of residence was a threefold variable (Central City of a Standard Metropolitan Statistical Area [SMSA]; in SMSA but not Central City; and not SMSA); and family type was a threefold variable (primary families, secondary families and subfamilies, primary and secondary individuals).

row of Table 3.2 pertains to the information in the region by underemployment by time table. We see that the income measure has 22.1% of the information contained in the *three* visible underemployment measures and that the mismatch measure has 88.6% of the information contained in the four underemployment measures (including the income measure). The regional differentials in labor force structure are thus more clearly portrayed by inclusion of the Hauser-Sullivan indicators than would be the case if these new indicators were ignored. The income measure contributes tremendously to an analysis of differentials according to family type of the worker, with a relative information index of 951.3%. The mismatch measure can also be seen to add substantially to the understanding of differences in labor force structure by place of residence, since the relative information index is 107.0% for this comparison. In sum, the new measures seem to be adding substantially to the statistical information describing differentials in labor force experience with respect to these master structural variables.

Using the same principles applied elsewhere in this chapter, it is possible to partition the variability in underemployment into parts due to various sources, including sources resulting from the variability in the new measures of invisible underemployment. As in regression analysis, however, this partitioning need not be unique, owing to the various conceivable orderings of the components considered. But a partitioning can at least be suggestive of the role that the new measures play in describing overall variability in the labor force structure. Table 3.3 is an example of such a procedure, where the sources of *regional* variability are isolated. Rather than converting measures of variability to information measures, as was done previously, we instead rely on the χ^2 statistic obtained from various models.

Model H_0 in Table 3.3 is the hypothesis fitting the marginals (TR) and (U_6), where U_6 refers to the sixfold underemployment measure discussed previously. (That is, U_6 contains *all* the underemployment categories, including both the usual measures and the low-income and mismatch measures.) The χ^2 of this model, as noted in Table 3.3, is a measure of variability resulting from heterogeneity in underemployment over time $(U_6 - T)$, from heterogeneity in underemployment across regions $(U_6 - R)$, and from heterogeneity in $U_6 - R$, which differs across time $(U_6 - T - R)$. With an $L^2(H_0)$ of 3621.82, there is a large amount of variability, and we now attempt to analyze the various sources of it.

Model H_1 fits the margins $(TR)(TU_6)$, fitting $T - U_6$ interactions that were excluded in H_0. A marked reduction in χ^2 is obtained $[L^2(H_1) = 2390.56]$, showing that a proportion $1231.26/3621.82 = .340$ of the variability unexplained by H_0 is due to time-period heterogeneity in the sixfold

TABLE 3.3
Sources of the Regional Variability in Underemployment

Model	Margins fit	Source of χ^2	L^2
H_0	$(TR)(U_6)$	Heterogeneity in U_6-T, U_6-R, U_6-T-R	3621.82
H_1	$(TR)(TU_6)$	Heterogeneity in U_6-R, U_6-T-R	2390.56
H_0/H_1		Heterogeneity in U_6-T	1231.26
H_2	$(TR)(TU_5)$	Heterogeneity in U_5-R, U_5-T-R	1267.66
H_1/H_2		Heterogeneity in mismatch	1122.90
H_3	$(TR)(TU_4)$	Heterogeneity in U_4-R, U_4-T-R	1038.55
H_2/H_3		Heterogeneity in income	229.11

underemployment variable. This component, signified by the absolute difference $L^2(H_0) - L^2(H_1)$, might be thought of as the part of variability that can be attributed to labor market change. It is interesting to see that a full 66% of the unexplained variability of H_0 is not explained by the $T - U_6$ interaction, signifying that other sources of variability exert a strong influence.

Model H_2 is identical to H_1, except for the fact that the underemployment measure used is a *five*fold classification, collapsing the mismatch category. It fits the margins (TR) and (TU_5) in what is by now an obvious notation. The difference $L^2(H_2) - L^2(H_1) = 1122.90$ can be attributed only to the regional variability in mismatch; in relative terms, this says that 47.0% of the variability unexplained by H_1 can be thought of as being due to regional variability in mismatch. Thus, a large part of the overall variability—indicated by $L_2(H_0)$—can be attributed to the regional differences in mismatch levels, a result that squares very well with our earlier analysis in Table 3.2. Model H_3 is considered to isolate a component part resulting from regional heterogeneity in low-income underemployment, and we see a moderate, but not negligible, component of χ^2 resulting from this source as well.

An approach like that of Table 3.3 could also be applied to analyze the sources of variability in underemployment differentials by place of residence or by family type of worker, but such an analysis will not be carried out here. Indeed, by virtue of results presented in Table 3.2, it can be expected that even larger components of variability would be traced to the low-income and/or mismatch differentials. Rather than summarize such an analysis, it should suffice at this point to reiterate the fundamental result of this chapter: Marked differentials in labor force structure exist that can only be fully accounted for by introducing the underemployment detail recognized in the labor utilization framework. We believe that new kinds of differentials in labor force structure are manifestly evidenced by the new measures, and in this sense, the new measures have been efficacious in measuring that which they can reasonably be expected to measure. In the remainder of this work, we will accordingly assume that the labor utilization framework is reasonably valid, at least as far as can be determined on the basis of post hoc statistical analysis.

3.4 CONCLUSION

This chapter has been concerned with the analysis of the additional information that can be obtained from the Hauser-Sullivan measures of invisible underemployment. A standard statistical formulation of information was adopted for this appraisal, and standard results on the collapsing of cross-tables and the partitioning of χ^2 were used to summarize the gain that has been achieved. The gain in information in the new measures was moderate to substantial, implying that the more customary measures of visible underemployment do indeed "disguise" the "true" differentials in labor market experience. The income measure adds dramatically to our understanding of sex differentials. The mismatch measure adds somewhat to our understanding of age differentials in labor market experience and can also be very important for an analysis of time-period change in the labor market. The new measures also add substantially to information concerning differentials in underemployment across region, place of residence, and family type. The approach outlined in the chapter could, of course, be used with only slight modifications in the appraisal of other measures of invisible underemployment (e.g., Levitan and Taggart, 1974). This approach could be used to compare the relative efficacy of the alternative measurement schemes now being proposed.

4

the effect of changing demographic composition on the crude indicators of underemployment

A paradox in the measurement of unemployment is demonstrated in the general recognition that full employment is not the same thing as a zero rate of unemployment, as unemployment is conventionally measured within the labor force approach. Even without appealing to basic tenets of labor economics, it is possible to see why such a paradox exists. At no time in the history of a market society has a zero rate of unemployment been attained, and seldom has unemployment reached as low a figure as 1%. During the economic mobilization for World War II, for example, American unemployment averaged around 2%. It is difficult to envision how a free labor market in the United States could ever produce more effective demand for labor than in these wartime circumstances, so surely a "floor" of 2% represents an extreme lower bound on the unemployment rate for this society. The year 1969, often used in this work as a period of "full employment" to which comparisons can be made, actually had unemployment levels that averaged over 3% for the year. A massive array of evidence could be compiled to show that in the United States, unemployment seldom falls below the 3% figure, even in times of very strong aggregate demand for labor, and that in other market societies, unemployment seldom falls below the 1–2% range. Surely some or many of the empirical situations that we could survey had "full employment" in the sense of ensuring sufficiently high demand for labor, and a natural question to ask is why, then, has unemployment not been redefined to record zero unemployment when in fact full employment conditions exist. Up until the present time, however, no consensus has been reached through which such a redefinition can be proposed.

The paradox just discussed illustrates a fundamental ambiguity in the meaning of the unemployment statistic. Full employment cannot be defined as it might be by the uninformed observer, who would surely understand full employment and zero unemployment as tautologically equivalent, and this implies that the unemployment measure itself requires deeper analysis of its intended meaning. At the risk of some oversimplification, it can be said that measured unemployment is composed of two logically distinct parts, only one of which provides information about the extent of full employment. A first part may be called *frictional* and is defined as the unemployment that is intrinsic to a labor force irrespective of the purely economic forces that change demand. It may be described as the unemployment that is *functionally necessary* for the labor market to work as it is designed to work. Frictional unemployment is the normal job turnover that characterizes a dynamic work force; it is the temporary and "frictional" interruption in employment that results from simple job mobility, progression through the different statuses of occupational careers, and the like. The more dynamic and mobile the labor force, the higher the frictional unemployment will be. It is exceedingly difficult to measure frictional unemployment (compare Rees, 1957), and the standard definition of unemployment (see Appendix A) can surely be seen to include many other types of unemployment besides the frictional kind. There is unemployment that is of long duration, there is unemployment that is persistently high for some groups owing to discriminatory hiring and firing practices, and there is unemployment that exists solely because of a real deficiency in demand in certain industrial–occupational sectors. This type of unemployment is the complement to frictional unemployment and may be simply referred to as *structural*. The conventional unemployment statistic is composed of a mixture of both structural and frictional unemployment, and sociological and economic thinking about this mixture is properly understood as the theory of frictional unemployment. Since full employment is the elimination of all nonfrictional unemployment, which can only be determined after the intrinsic level of frictional unemployment has been pinpointed, theoretical conceptions of full employment are as richly variegated as the theories of frictional employment themselves.

By applying nearly the same logic that leads to a recognition of different types of unemployment, which may be reduced to the frictional and the nonfrictional, or structural, it is clear that the other forms of underemployment can also be said to have frictional and nonfrictional components. That is, there is a level of sub-unemployment that cannot be eliminated, if only because of the close similarity between this form and unemployment itself. There is a level of part-time unemployment that is necessary to a given labor force, if only because part-time work can be viewed, in some cases at least, as a necessary job status for workers to pass through in their search for full-time employment. There is also a level of low-income underemployment that is functionally necessary, because some low-wage jobs exist as established links to adequate wage jobs. Finally, a certain level of mismatch must also be tolerated in a market economy. A status of mismatched employment might, for example, be necessary in the long-term career strategy for many skilled persons; temporary mismatch can, in some cases at least, be regarded as normal and desirable. A certain length of tenure in a low-skill status might be necessary for acquired skills to be proven and for on-the-job skills to develop, which in turn might subsequently open up the proper channels through which a worker's skills can be fully utilized. Each of the forms of underemployment must therefore be interpreted with the utmost scholarly reserve, since the total rates of underemployment that can be more or less easily defined and measured have component parts that have different meaning in the assessment of the degree of employment opportunity.

Now if frictional *un*employment (or frictional *under*employment) could somehow be taken as a constant property of the labor force, then the effort expended to characterize it would be entirely superfluous. If frictional unemployment were always and everywhere, say, at a level of 2%, then we could merely say that full employment would be attained wherever the 2% level of observed unemployment was reached. Of course, cross-national and across-time comparison of unemployment statistics, if they show anything at all, convince one that the frictional component of these measures is a variable property of the labor force. But no kind of simpleminded analysis can adequately describe the changing mix in the component parts, and this fact is largely the reason that some of the most eminent labor economists have gone to such pain to estimate it.

A variety of factors are responsible for the changing mixture of frictional and nonfrictional underemployment in a modern society. These are in part economic in character, but in our view, they are mainly the result of social–structural causes that sociologists would do well to examine. A society that fosters a high job-turnover rate, such as one with an extremely complex division of labor and normal career lines that push workers through many job statuses in a lifetime, is one that will have a high frictional component to all the underemployment forms. A society that inefficiently manages labor turnover owing to social–structural impediments to mobility or to social–structural barriers to the diffusion of job-related information is also one that will necessarily exhibit a high level of frictional underemployment. Recognizing the extreme difficulty in measuring these societal attributes, as well as changes in them over time, and then inferring their relationship to frictional underemployment means that approximate devices must be invoked. The approximation that is suggested in many accounts is to examine the *composition* of the labor force by demographic grouping, thereby inferring by indirect means the strength of changes in the underlying forces that cause change in frictional underemployment.

Rees (1957, p. 51) long ago singled out demographic composition as a proxy variable through which frictional components to underemployment could be monitored. Each demographic group in the labor force, such as a particular age–race–sex group, has a characteristic level of frictional underemployment that is assumed to change rather slowly over time. Young workers, for example, have an exceedingly high risk of frictional underemployment, as can only be the case in view of their rapid turnover in jobs, their transient attachments to currently held jobs, their preparation for participation in full-fledged careers, and the like. Similarly, old workers have a high risk of frictional underemployment, owing principally to the transience of their work activity in the face of retirement. Each demographic grouping has an intrinsic level of risk to each form of underemployment, and over the short run, this is viewed as a persistent feature of the labor force. Given these assumptions, it is claimed, the trend in frictional underemployment can be at least partly monitored by keeping a watchful eye on the changing demographic composition of the labor force. It is this conception that underlies not only Rees's (1957) early work but also that of Perry (1970), Smith *et al.* (1977), and Toikka *et al.* (1977). The work of Easterlin (1968, 1978) and Easterlin *et al.* (1978) also pinpoints the demographic compositional factor as a proxy apparatus through which changes in underemployment should be assessed.

In this chapter the effect of changing demographic composition on the indicators of underemployment is examined in some detail. The purpose of such an appraisal is to document through indirect means the changing mix between frictional and nonfrictional components to underemployment; the results to be presented will convince one that frictional underemployment probably increased substantially from 1969 to 1973. In Section 4.1, certain hierarchical log-linear models are used to examine the role of demographic-compositional changes in the context of overall time-period change in the labor force. In Section 4.2 the across-time change in the labor force is adjusted to remove the effect of changing demographic makeup, showing a time-trend that is quite different from that observed. In Sections 4.3 and 4.4 the analysis is restricted to the age variable alone, a tentative rationale for which is advanced, and it is shown how great the age "distortion" in underemployment rates actually is. It will be demonstrated that demographic composition of the labor force is of the utmost importance in the interpretation of across-time trend in the labor market and that the measurement of true employment opportunity cannot possibly be carried out without acknowledging the demographic factors that are so closely related to a labor force's intrinsic risk to underemployment.

4.1 THE TIME-PERIOD HETEROGENEITY OF THE LABOR FORCE

In the time span 1969–1973, the labor force of the United States was changing its demographic composition to a considerable extent. In general, a civilian labor force can change its demographic-compositional makeup over time through a variety of mechanisms, including (a) changing labor force participation patterns; (b) in- or out-migration (which is highly selective regarding its demographic composition); (c) changing age distribution of the population of working ages occasioned by past fertility conditions; and (d) changing patterns of military recruitment. In the short run, changing mortality patterns, a fifth factor logically distinct from these, could not affect composition as much as the above four factors, at least for this time span in the United States. Factors (a) and (c) seem to represent the most important focus for a "causal" analysis of changing labor force composition in the contemporary United States. In this section, we provide statistical documentation of the time-period heterogeneity in demographic composition, when this heterogeneity is taken in conjunction with other kinds of time-induced heterogeneity in the labor force. Since the various demographic strata of the labor force have different levels of risk to the several underemployment forms, changes in demographic composition over time by themselves can increase (or decrease) the apparent overall risk to underemployment, and it is this simple observation that suggests the importance of considering the magnitude of demographic-compositional changes in the labor force.

To examine time-period heterogeneity in the labor force, we will use a cross-classification composed of the following variables:

Demographic variables:
  Age (variable A) in five categories
  Race (variable R) in two categories (white-nonwhite)
  Sex (variable S)
Time-period (variable T) in five categories
Underemployment (variable U) in six categories

The resulting five-way contingency table has 600 cells, with a total sample size of approximately 300,000. This contingency table contains information that is central to any scheme of indicators proposing to summarize change in the American labor force during this period; it is useless to speak of underemployment change viewed from other perspectives (e.g., economic sector, household type) unless we have first discovered the underlying pattern of underemployment in this basic demographic contingency table.

The *time-period heterogeneity* in the joint variable *ARS* is of central interest in this chapter, since that joint variable is the composite representation of demographic structure. To begin such an appraisal, a set of models suggested by Goodman (1973b) for analyzing the heterogeneity among a set of *T* multidimensional cross-tables will be utilized; in the present context, *T* represents the variable referring to the five time-period observations. The discussion is illustrated when necessary with the notation of "the fitting of marginals." The fitting, for example, of the marginal (*ART*) for a given model would designate that (*a*) parameters reflecting the three-factor interaction *A–R–T* were included in that model; (*b*) parameters reflecting the two-factor interactions *A–R*, *R–T*, and *A–T* were included in that model; and (*c*) parameters reflecting the one-factor "zero-order" interactions *A*, *R*, and *T* were also included in that model. The interpretation of models of any complexity is relatively straightforward, given this kind of shorthand notation.

The possible range of models for the five-way table is tremendous, so a model-fitting strategy that takes into account certain logical orderings among these variables will be followed. It may fairly be presumed that the joint variable *ARS* will affect the level of underemployment (variable *U*) apart from any time-period effects; this is so because of the marked dependence of underemployment on age–race–sex group. The interaction of *ARS* with *U* may be said to denote the "intrinsic" relationship of underemployment to the demographic variables, since *T* does not enter into the configuration of interactions embodied in *ARS–U*. All the models here *control* for the effects of *ARS* on *U* in order to take into account the organization of employment opportunity about the composite structural variable *ARS*. That is, any model will contain the marginal (*ARSU*) as a statistical control. (We will show later that an adequate representation of the data should contain the interactions implied by fitting *ARSU*.) If the joint relationship given in the *ARSU* marginal table were completely *homogeneous* over time, then the model H_0 described by fitting $\{(ARSU)(T)\}$ would be true.[1] In Table 4.1, the fit of this hypothesis is presented, and we

---

[1] Strictly speaking, the (*T*) marginal must be fit in any model applied to these data, to represent the fact that *T* different samples are under consideration.

TABLE 4.1

Hierarchical Log-Linear Models Showing Demographic Composition Changes over Time, and Total Time-period Heterogeneity in the Labor Force for the Civilian "Modified Labor Force" 14 Years and Over, 1969–1973

Model	Margins fit under model	Degrees of freedom, df	Goodness-of-fit χ^2	Likelihood-ratio χ^2, L^2
H_0	$(ARSU)(T)$	476	2285.80	2326.37
H_1	$(ARSU)(TU)$	456	1070.98	1076.17
H_2	$(ARSU)(TU)$			
	$(ARST)$	380	563.47	570.52
H_3	$(ARSU)(ARST)$	400	1692.97	1733.11

Key: A = age in five categories; R = race in two categories; S = sex; T = time; U = under-employment in six categories.

see that with a likelihood-ratio χ^2 of 2326.37, these data clearly contradict this model assuming time-period homogeneity. The likelihood-ratio χ^2 associated with H_0, say $L^2(H_0)$, is a measure of the *total effect* of the time-period variable T upon the joint relationship $(ARSU)$, in the sense that it is a measure of variation *due to T,* controlling for the effects of all other variables.[2] Any model more complicated than H_0 would necessarily introduce time-period *heterogeneity* in one or more of the variables composing the joint variable $ARSU$. The effect of time-period, controlling for the joint relationship implied by fitting $(ARSU)$, is now decomposed by two different routes.

Model H_1 fits the marginals $\{(ARSU)(TU)\}$, or in substantive terms, it provides an allowance for time-period heterogeneity in the level of underemployment [expressed by fitting (TU)]. If the only time-period heterogeneity in the labor force were change in the overall level of underemployment, then H_1 would be true. Model H_1 makes no allowance for time-period heterogeneity in any of the other variables or their relationships to one another (namely, changing age, race, or sex composition, or changing relationships of age, race, or sex to underemployment over time). We see from Table 4.1 that H_1 produces a dramatic reduction in unexplained variation, indicating that, indeed, a large share of the total effect of time-period can be traced to changes in the overall level of underemployment.

---

[2] This concept of a "total effect" is much different from the "total effect" of a variable in econometric or path analytic models. The decomposition of effects in path analysis with linear models (Heise, 1975; Duncan, 1975) has no direct analogue in log-linear models (such as logit models), and so this measure of "total effect" based on the χ^2 statistic is perhaps the easiest way to quantify the "effect" caused by a particular variable.

The $T-U$ interaction in this five-way table can be said to represent "intrinsic" labor market change, since this configuration of interactions does not contain any of the demographic variables.

Model H_2 fits the marginals $\{(ARSU)(TU)(ARST)\}$, or in substantive terms, it allows time-period heterogeneity in both (a) the levels of underemployment [expressed in the fitting of (TU)], and (b) the demographic composition of the labor force [expressed in the fitting of $(ARST)$]. Table 4.2, Part A, examines the parts of the total effect of time-period, or the total variation explained by T, which results from (a) time heterogeneity in

TABLE 4.2
Partitioning the Variation Explained by Time-period

Source of variation	Degrees of freedom, df	Likelihood-ratio χ^2, L^2	$L^2/L^2(H_0)$
A. Time heterogeneity in demographic composition,			
given time heterogeneity in underemployment			
1. Total effect of			
time-period–$L^2(H_0)$	476	2326.37	1.000
Unexplained by			
$(TU)(ARSU)-L^2(H_1)$	456	1076.17	.463
(1) Explained by			
$(ARST) \mid (TU)(ARSU)-$			
$L^2(H_1) - L^2(H_2)$	76	505.65	.217
(2) Unexplained by			
$(ARST)(TU)(ARSU)-$			
$L^2(H_2)$	380	570.52	.245
Explained by			
$(TU) \mid (ARSU)(T)-$			
$L^2(H_0) - L^2(H_1)$	20	1250.20	.538
B. Time heterogeneity in underemployment,			
given time heterogeneity in demographic composition			
2. Total effect of			
time-period–$L^2(H_0)$	476	2326.37	1.000
Unexplained by			
$(ARST)(ARSU)-L^2(H_3)$	400	1733.11	.745
(1) Explained by			
$(TU) \mid (ARST)(ARSU)$			
$L^2(H_2) - L^2(H_3)$	20	1162.59	.500
(2) Unexplained by			
$(TU)(ARST)(ARSU)-$			
$L^2(H_2)$	380	570.52	.245
Explained by			
$(ARST) \mid (T) (ARSU)-$			
$L^2(H_0) - L^2(H_3)$	76	593.26	.255

underemployment alone, (*b*) time heterogeneity in demographic composition alone, and (*c*) time heterogeneity in residual factors unexplained by (*a*) and/or (*b*). The part of the total time-period heterogeneity explained by changing demographic composition, controlling for the effects of (*TU*) and (*ARSU*), is given in line A.1.1 of Table 4.2. We see that time heterogeneity in demographic composition accounted for about 21.7 percent of the total time-period effect in this cross-table, or in other words, nearly one-quarter of the total change in the labor force during this period was due to changes in demographic composition. Another striking feature of these data is the part of total time-period heterogeneity explained by the interaction of (*ARS*) with (*TU*) [i.e., (*ARSTU*) given {(*ARST*)(*TU*)(*ARSU*)}]. This is a full 24.5%, from line A.1.2 of Table 4.2, and represents the influence of time-period heterogeneity upon the *relationship* between the demographic variables and underemployment. Part A of Table 4.2 shows that the total time-period heterogeneity can be considered in three distinct parts, two of which depend centrally upon *demographic composition or changes therein over time*. These are:

1. Main effects of time-period (*TU*) | (*T*)(*ARSU*)   = .538
2. Demographic composition changes: (*ARST*) | (*TU*)(*ARSU*)   = .217
3. Changing relationship of *ARS* to *U*: (*ARSUT*) | (*ARSU*)(*ARST*)(*UT*) = .245

Total effect of time-period   1.000

This partitioning of the time-period variation shows that the demographic composition of the labor force *cannot* be overlooked in a study of underemployment in this time span; about 46% of the total time-period change in the labor force cannot be accounted for without considering time-induced heterogeneity in the demographic composition of the labor force and/or the changing relationships of underemployment to the demographic variables. In the next section, across-time variability in underemployment will be "purged" of the influence of all sources of variability except "intrinsic" labor market change, and the reader can here see reasons why such an analysis can be fruitful.

An alternative partitioning of the total variation resulting from time-period is followed in Part B of Table 4.2. Here the controlling procedure is different from that of Part A, where we examined time heterogeneity in demographic composition only after controlling for the main effects of time-period upon the level of underemployment. The strategy is reversed in Part B by first allowing time-induced heterogeneity in demographic composition to explain the data and then examining the main effects of time-period upon underemployment. The proper sequence is now:

$$H_0: \quad (ARSU)(T)$$
$$H_3: \quad (ARSU)(ARST)$$
$$H_2: \quad (ARSU)(TU)(ARST)$$

The fit of model H_3 is also presented in Table 4.1. Whereas the partitioning method of Part A of Table 4.2 provided somewhat *conservative* estimates of the part of total time-period effect due to changing demographic composition, because it first allowed the effects of (TU) to be taken out, the method of Part B provides a somewhat more *liberal* estimate of this effect, since it does not condition on (TU). By the method of Part B, we see that the part of the total time-period variation resulting from changing demographic composition is estimated as 25.5%. Table 4.3 compares the estimates of the three component parts of the total time-period effect. We see from this table that changing demographic composition accounts for between 21.7 and 25.5% of the total time-period heterogeneity in the American labor force. Between 46.6 and 50.0% of the total time-period heterogeneity in these data involves the interaction of the demographic variables composing *ARS* and time-period. It is thus very important indeed to take into account demographic structure, and changes therein over time, in an analysis of the across-time change in the American labor force.

Since the demographic structure is so important in an analysis of time-period change, we now analyze it further by fitting additional models for these data. Because the partitioning method of Part A of Table 4.2 was more conservative concerning its implications for the magnitude of demographic changes, we will consider a sequence of models built about that first approach.

Table 4.4 presents models logically intermediate between the "baseline

TABLE 4.3
Three-Components to Time-period Heterogeneity, Obtained by Two Different Partitioning Methods

	Partitioning method	
Component	Part A $(H_0 \rightarrow H_1 \rightarrow H_2)$	Part B $(H_0 \rightarrow H_3 \rightarrow H_2)$
Time heterogeneity in underemployment	.538	.500
Time heterogeneity in demographic composition	.217	.255
Time heterogeneity in relationship of demographic variables to underemployment	.245	.245

Source: Table 4.2, this volume.

TABLE 4.4

Models Showing the Time-period Heterogeneity in the Demographic Composition of the Labor Force

Model	Margins fit under model	Degrees of free-dom, df	Goodness-of-fit χ^2	Likelihood ratio χ^2, L^2	L^2/df
H_1	$(ARSU)(TU)$	456	1070.98	1076.17	2.36
H_4	$(ARSU)(TU)$ (AT)	440	676.20	681.47	1.55
$H_4 \vert H_1$	$(AT) \vert (ARSU)$ (TU)	16		394.70	24.67
H_5	$(ARSU)(TU)$ (RT)	452	1045.11	1050.36	2.32
$H_5 \vert H_1$	$(RT) \vert (ARSU)$ (TU)	4		25.81	6.45
H_6	$(ARSU)(TU)$ (ST)	452	1047.77	1052.65	2.33
$H_6 \vert H_1$	$(ST) \vert (ARSU)$ (TU)	4		23.52	5.88
H_7	$(ARSU)(TU)$ $(AT)(RT)$	436	649.86	655.16	1.50
H_8	$(ARSU)(TU)$ $(AT)(ST)$	436	655.41	660.80	1.52
H_9	$(ARSU)(TU)$ $(RT)(ST)$	448	1020.64	1026.23	2.29
H_{10}	$(ARSU)(TU)$ $(AT)(RT)(ST)$	432	627.91	633.66	1.47
H_{11}	$(ARSU)(TU)$ (ART)	420	616.76	623.15	1.48
H_{12}	$(ARSU)(TU)$ $(ART)(ST)$	416	595.93	601.77	1.45
H_{13}	$(ARSU)(TU)$ (AST)	420	635.09	641.31	1.53
H_{14}	$(ARSU)(TU)$ $(AST)(RT)$	416	607.23	613.50	1.47
H_{15}	$(ARSU)(TU)$ (RST)	444	1017.58	1024.21	2.31
H_{16}	$(ARSU)(TU)$ $(RST)(AT)$	428	624.79	631.27	1.47
H_{17}	$(ARSU)(TU)$ $(ART)(AST)$	400	576.47	583.22	1.46
H_{18}	$(ARSU)(TU)$ $(ART)(RST)$	412	592.80	599.74	1.46
H_{19}	$(ARSU)(TU)$ $(AST)(RST)$	412	604.23	610.91	1.48
H_{20}	$(ARSU)(TU)$ $(AST)(RST)$ (ART)	396	573.45	580.10	1.46
H_2	$(ARSU)(TU)$ $(ARST)$	380	563.47	570.52	1.50

models" H_1 and H_2 considered earlier. An index that is useful to gauge the adequacy of the several models of Table 4.4 is the likelihood-ratio χ^2 statistic divided by its degrees of freedom. This index should be approximately unity in an adequate model. (An index *less* than unity would also denote an adequate model but one that possibly contains too many parameters.) Model H_4, which differs from the baseline model H_1 only by considering heterogeneity of age distribution, produces a dramatic reduction in unexplained variation. (Examine the partitioning of H_4, given H_1, showing a decrease of 394.70 in L^2 with the addition of only 16 more parameters.) Changing sex composition and changing race composition also enter substantially into explaining these data, as models H_5 through H_{10} show. But evidently the changing age composition of the labor force by itself dwarfs the other kinds of composition changes. In fact, 78.1% of the additional variation explained by H_2 over H_1 can be explained by the (TA) interaction reflecting time-period changes in age composition, or

$$.781 = [L^2(H_1) - L^2(H_4)]/[L^2(H_1) - L^2(H_2)]$$

This is by itself a demographic change of dramatic proportions and will be the subject of separate analysis later in this chapter.

We noted earlier in connection with Tables 4.1, 4.2, and 4.3 that a large share of the total time-period heterogeneity in these data, some 24.5%, could be thought of as pertaining to the way in which the relationship of underemployment to the demographic variables changed over time. This was indicated by the unexplained variation in H_2 [fitting $(ARSU)$, (TU), and $(ARST)$], which could only be explained by including models more general than H_2. All of these more general models would contain interactions of (UT) with the demographic composition variables. Table 4.5 considers some of these models, all of which are extensions of and include as a special case the baseline model H_2.

Table 4.5 contains models that fit the data remarkably well, considering the extremely large sample size. The index used earlier to assess model adequacy, the likelihood-ratio χ^2 statistic divided by its degrees of freedom, nearly reaches unity for several of the models. In terms of this index, models H_{27}, H_{31}, H_{33}, and H_{36} perform very well, and of these, H_{27} is the most parsimonious. Model H_{27}, with 260 df, is then an adequate summarization of these data; that is, it is an adequate summarization of underemployment and other changes in the American labor force. That model contains over H_2, discussed earlier, (*a*) parameters expressing time-period change in the relationship of age and underemployment, (*b*) parameters expressing time-period change in the relationship of race and underemployment, and (*c*) parameters expressing time-period change in

TABLE 4.5
Models Showing the Time-period Heterogeneity of the Relationships between the Joint Variable Age-Sex-Race and Underemployment: Logit Models

Model	Margins fit under model in addition to (ARSU), (TU), and (ARST)	Degrees of freedom, df	Goodness-of-fit χ^2	Likelihood-ratio χ^2, L^2	L^2/df
Baseline model H_2	—	380	563.47	570.52	1.50
H_{21}	(AUT)	300	394.09	397.92	1.33
$H_{21}\|H_2$		80		172.60	2.16
H_{22}	(RUT)	360	520.80	528.33	1.47
$H_{22}\|H_2$		20		42.19	2.11
H_{23}	(SUT)	360	470.26	475.22	1.32
$H_{23}\|H_2$		20		95.30	4.77
H_{24}	(AUT)(RUT)	280	353.21	358.18	1.28
$H_{24}\|H_2$		100		212.34	2.12
H_{25}	(AUT)(SUT)	280	293.90	296.32	1.06
$H_{25}\|H_2$		100		274.20	2.74
H_{26}	(RUT)(SUT)	340	428.28	433.87	1.28
$H_{26}\|H_2$		40		136.65	3.42
H_{27}	(AUT)(RUT)(SUT)	260	253.59	257.39	.99
$H_{27}\|H_2$		120		313.13	2.61
H_{28}	(ARUT)	200	280.46	286.93	1.43
H_{29}	(ARUT)(SUT)	180	181.82	187.54	1.04
H_{30}	(ASUT)	200	204.56	208.88	1.04
H_{31}	(ASUT)(RUT)	180	165.77	170.58	.95
H_{32}	(RSUT)	320	412.45	417.70	1.31
H_{33}	(RSUT)(AUT)	240	238.12	241.91	1.01
H_{34}	(ARUT)(ASUT)	100	96.08	101.59	1.02
H_{35}	(ARUT)(RSUT)	160	166.35	171.80	1.07
H_{36}	(ASUT)(RSUT)	160	149.14	153.84	.96
H_{37}	(ARUT)(ASUT)(RSUT)	80	79.07	84.40	1.06

the relationship of sex and underemployment. By examining H_{23}, we are led to conclude that the sex–underemployment change over time is the most important, although the other two kinds of change were also important. The American labor force during this time span may therefore be adequately summarized by model H_{27}, which contains the following sets of marginals (or parameters):

1. (*ARSU*):   reflecting structural dependence of underemployment upon the composite demographic variable age–race–sex
2. (*TU*):   reflecting time-period heterogeneity in underemployment or the main effects of the transitory economic exigencies
3. (*ARST*):   reflecting the changing age–race–sex composition of the labor force
4. (*AUT*), (*RUT*), (*SUT*): reflecting the changing relationship of age, race, and sex to underemployment

The above model is parsimonious in that more complicated terms [such as, (*ARUT*)] are not included, indicating that the time-period change in underemployment can be fairly measured by examination of only *three* marginal tables, that is, the *AUT,* the *RUT,* and the *SUT* marginal tables. These marginal tables were all presented earlier in Chapter 2, and these results justify presenting only those tables as a summary set of marginals. Evidently, more complicated marginal tables are not necessary in order to characterize underemployment in this time span. The implication is that time-period indicators of underemployment should be based upon information in these marginal tables and that information in other marginal tables can be ignored.

This model is also fairly simple owing to a large number of degrees of freedom (260), which is a very simple model indeed for a cross-table based upon such a large overall sample size. The model may also be interpreted as a *logit model,* which is a qualitative-data analogue to a multiple regression, where underemployment is viewed as a dependent variable, and age, race, sex, and time are viewed as independent variables (Goodman, 1972b). By proceeding forward from more simple to more complex models, and by taking account of a certain logical ordering among our variables, a good description of the age–race–sex specific trend in underemployment was obtained. By proceeding "backward" from this tentative model, a much more parsimonious model will now be advanced.

Table 4.6 begins with the tentative model H_{27} and considers a series of more *simple* models. Model H_{38} shows us that the inclusion of (*ARSU*) is necessary. We earlier began the model-fitting by assuming that it was necessary to reflect structural constraints in the organization of labor market chances for the demographic groupings and then conditioned on the *ARSU* relationship to obtain H_{27}. The other models of Table 4.6 test the necessity of the demographic-composition–time parameters, and we see from model H_{47} that these are now not necessary at all. Model H_{47} with an L^2 of 318.89 on 312 *df* ($L^2/df = 1.02$) is certainly an adequate model for

TABLE 4.6
Some Other Models

Model	Complete set of margins fit under model	Degrees of freedom, df	Goodness-of-fit χ^2	Likelihood-ratio χ^2, L^2	L^2/df
H_{27}	$(ARSU)(ARST)$ $(AUT)(RUT)$ (SUT)	260	253.59	257.39	.99
H_{38}	$(ARST)(ARU)$ $(AUS)(RSU)$ $(AUT)(RUT)$ (SUT)	280	358.10	360.83	1.29
H_{39}	$(ARSU)(ART)$ $(RST)(AST)$ $(AUT)(RUT)$ (SUT)	276	263.22	267.75	.97
H_{40}	$(ARSU)(ART)$ $(RST)(AUT)$ $(RUT)(SUT)$	292	285.03	289.58	.99
H_{41}	$(ARSU)(ART)$ $(AST)(AUT)$ $(RUT)(SUT)$	280	266.85	271.43	.97
H_{42}	$(ARSU)(RST)$ $(AST)(AUT)$ $(RUT)(SUT)$	292	287.28	291.84	1.00
H_{43}	$(ARS)(ARU)$ $(ASU)(RSU)$ $(ART)(RST)$ $(AST)(AUT)$ $(RUT)(SUT)$	296	396.03	372.70	1.26
H_{44}	$(ARSU)(ART)$ $(AUT)(RUT)$ (SUT)	296	288.91	293.65	.99
H_{45}	$(ARSU)(RST)$ $(AUT)(RUT)$ (SUT)	308	309.92	314.21	1.02
H_{46}	$(ARSU)(AST)$ $(AUT)(RUT)$ (SUT)	296	291.23	295.54	1.00
H_{47}	$(ARSU)(AUT)$ $(RUT)(SUT)$	312	314.14	318.89	1.02
H_{48}	$(ARSU)(AUT)$ $(RUT)(ST)$	332	411.05	415.44	1.25
H_{49}	$(ARSU)(AUT)$ $(SUT)(RT)$	332	356.66	359.62	1.08
H_{50}	$(ARSU)(RUT)$ $(SUT)(AT)$	392	493.49	498.74	1.27

these data and has 52 *df* more than model H_{27} presented earlier. This does not say that demographic composition changes may be ignored, since model H_{47} contains parameters *AT, RT,* and *ST,* which express simple changes in demographic composition over time. Acceptance of model H_{47} does not therefore require rejection of our earlier findings that demographic composition changed significantly over the time span of this study. Instead, model H_{47} says that more complicated kinds of demographic composition changes, expressed in *ART, AST, RST,* and *ARST* parameters, may be ignored, since they are inconsequential. That earlier approach allowed us to make quantitative statements about the *magnitude* of the demographic composition changes in a way that is not directly possible with the models presented in Table 4.6. A possible disadvantage of the models represented in Table 4.6 (including the best-fitting model H_{47}) is that they are not logit models and so may not be directly interpreted as analogues to usual multiple regression models.

The several models applied to the age × race × sex × underemployment × time (5 × 2 × 2 × 6 × 5) table are important because *any* method for measuring underemployment must necessarily begin with information in this basic demographic contingency table. We showed here that the *four*-way table *ARSU* involving *A–U, R–U, S–U, AR–U, RS–U, AS–U,* and *ARS–U* relationships was necessary to describe the organization of underemployment structure about the master demographic variables. We also documented the marked change in demographic composition over time, especially as regards changing *age* composition, and we measured the extent of this change by reference to total time-period heterogeneity in the labor force. Finally, we showed that the time-period change in underemployment generally can be adequately described by considering the time-period change in the relationship of age and underemployment (*AUT*), the time-period change in the relationship of race and underemployment (*RUT*), and the time-period change in the relationship of sex and underemployment (*SUT*). While the *AUT, RUT,* and *SUT* marginal tables, and no others, provide the necessary information upon which indicators of underemployment should be based, it is not yet clear how this information should be summarized. Owing chiefly to changing demographic composition of the labor force, the usual underemployment rates can be misleading.

4.2 THE "INTRINSIC" TIME-PERIOD CHANGE IN THE LABOR MARKET

In the previous section, a "basic" cross-table was analyzed using log-linear models. Certain summary indexes were presented for these models, and a procedure based in part on standard methods of model building and in part on logical considerations peculiar to the data at hand were used to propose candidate models to "explain" the variability in that cross-table. The logical next step would naturally be substantive description of the parameters of some of the most compelling of the models proposed, but such a task can be unwieldy for a variety of reasons. First, even for the more simple models a large number of parameters (200–300) would require substantive interpretation, and this summarization would be complicated even if the most judicious coding of parameters were carried out. Second, the "dependent" variable is a sixfold qualitative variable, so that effects of the explanatory variables on it would once again require most judicious interpretation (Duncan, 1975). And, finally, the parameters of the models are expressed on a logarithmic scale, being defined as certain contrasts of the logarithms of expected frequencies that show how logits are responsive to explanatory variables, whereas in the present case, it seems more natural to examine *rates* of the underemployment variable and the variables that influence their characteristic structure and trend. To circumvent these difficulties, a procedure described in Appendix H and elaborated in Clogg (1978) will be used.

The approach begins by noting that in the basic cross-table there are only three types of variables of direct interest. These are the underemployment polytomy (variable U), the time-period variable (variable T), and the composite variable denoting age–race–sex group, or composite demographic structure. The demographic structure variable is here denoted as variable D. Several possible interactions among these variables were studied previously (compare Tables 4.1–4.6) and were given various substantive meanings. The U–T interactions denoted the "intrinsic" time-period variability in underemployment; we describe these interactions as "intrinsic" because they do not depend on demographic structure in any direct way, nor do they depend on interactions of demographic structure with time-period. It is the set of U–T interactions that we believe should be used to infer the *changes* in the labor market that are related only to the changing risk to underemployment, and it is in this sense that we denote them as interactions ostensibly measuring "pure" or "intrinsic" labor market change. It was found earlier that the U–T interaction was very strong but that it did not exhaustively account for the variability in the data.

A second set of interactions in the U–T–D table is the set of T–D interactions. These denote time-period variability in demographic structure, that is, changing demographic composition of the labor force. The objective of the present analysis is to first note that changing demographic composition has a decided impact on *apparent* trend in labor market characteristics (compare Easterlin, 1978) and that this effect should somehow be purged from the data so that a clear description of "pure" labor market change can be constructed. The results to be presented shortly will effectively purge the data of this confounding set of interactions, and the manner in which this is done is consistent with the model chosen to describe the data.

A third set of interactions is the set U–D, measuring the relationship of underemployment to the demographic structure. Marked dependence of underemployment on demographic structure was documented both in the preceding section and in Chapter 2, and this dependence may be said to reflect in composite form the "intrinsic" relationship of age, race, and sex to underemployment levels. Included in this definition are the obvious factors causing variability (across demographic categories) in the incidence of the unobservable component of *frictional* underemployment, as well as other factors that influence demographic differentials in underemployment. The U–D interactions, since they do not involve the T variable in their configuration, are really nuisance parameters in a study of time-period change, but they will be treated here as a set of interactions to be implicitly included in the analysis. (Actually, it makes no difference whether these interactions are included or excluded in the following.) Finally, in the three-way table cross-classifying U, T, and D, there are three-factor interactions U–T–D, which measure how underemployment changes over time vary by demographic group. For example, we know that young workers generally experience a greater increase in the risk of being underemployed when economic conditions worsen than do middle-aged workers, and this information would be captured in the set of U–T–D interactions. In some cases, it could be of interest to examine time-trend in underemployment allowing the U–T–D interactions to exert their influence, whereas in other cases, it could be of interest to study time-period variability in underemployment where these interactions were ignored. The latter situation would be important, for example, if the U–T–D interactions were themselves judged to reflect the *social* organizational forces influencing labor market opportunity that are different in kind from pure labor market forces; if the objective were to measure labor market trend abstracted from these social factors, then the U–T–D interaction should also be ignored. With these considerations in mind, we now briefly describe the method used to measure time-period variability in underemployment that is in a sense "intrinsic" to the labor market and is not affected by the extraneous distortion of demographic composition.

The three-way cross-table can be completely described by the following saturated multiplicative (or log-linear) model:

$$f_{ijk} = \theta \tau_i^D \tau_j^T \tau_k^U \tau_{ij}^{DT} \tau_{ik}^{DU} \tau_{jk}^{TU} \tau_{ijk}^{DTU}$$ (4.1)

Here f_{ijk} represents the observed frequency in cell (i, j, k), where i indexes categories of the demographic composition variable D, j indexes categories of time-period T, and k indexes the categories of the underemployment variable U. The τ^{DT} parameters refer to the D–T interactions spoken of earlier, that is, they represent the set of interactions between demographic composition and time-period. Loosely speaking, these parameters measure the extent to which demographic composition of the labor force changes over time and, in the present scheme of interpretation, represent a confounding influence that is to be purged from the data. The other interactions of Equation 4.1 can be interpreted in a like manner. The τ^{DU} parameters measure the influence of demographic grouping on the level of underemployment; the τ^{TU} parameters measure the "intrinsic" time-period change in underemployment of primary interest to us here; and the τ^{DTU} parameters measure three-factor interaction, which can, in some cases, be regarded as a set of nuisance parameters to be purged from the data and can, in other cases, be regarded as meaningful parameters that should also serve to define in part the true variability in the labor market across time. The observed *rates* of underemployment depend on the f_{ijk}, which in turn depend on each of the parameters on the right-hand side of Equation 4.1. That is, the rates of underemployment depend on parameters that are not directly related to "intrinsic" change in the labor market measured in the τ^{TU} parameters. In particular, the rates calculated from the f_{ijk} will depend on τ^{DT}, the set of parameters that measures *only* changing demographic composition.

To purge the data of the extraneous influence of D–T interactions, the following simple transformation can be used. Merely take

$$f_{ijk}^* = f_{ijk}/\tau_{ij}^{DT}$$ (4.2)

and note that the "purged frequencies" f_{ijk}^* do not now depend at all on τ^{DT}. Our claim is that *rates* of underemployment calculated from the f_{ijk}^* are free of the influence of changing demographic composition and so can be used to assess "intrinsic" labor market change. Results are presented in Table 4.7.

In order to summarize in a concise way the variability in underemployment across time, we here focus on the *rate of adequate employment*, which is the complement of underemployment. The observed rates of adequate employment are provided in column 1 of Table 4.7. The rate of adequate employment decreased from 1969 to 1970 by 1.26%; it further decreased in the intervals 1970–1971 and 1971–1972. The rate of adequate

TABLE 4.7
Observed and "Purged" Rates of Adequate Employment, 1969–1973

Year	Rate of adequate employment	Purged of D-T	Purged of D-T and D-T-U
	Δ	Δ	Δ
1969	.7674	.7665	.7635
	+.0126	+.0133	+.0112
1970	.7548	.7532	.7523
	+.0293	+.0284	+.0327
1971	.7255	.7248	.7196
	+.0092	+.0067	−.0052
1972	.7163	.7181	.7248
	−.0032	−.0060	−.0034
1973	.7195	.7241	.7282

employment increased from 1972–1973 by .32%, reflecting the modest improvement in labor market conditions in 1973. For purposes of comparison, the successive differences of the rates are presented alongside the rates so that time-period variability can be easily seen.

In column 2 of Table 4.7, the rates based upon the f_{ijk}^* of Equation 4.2 are presented. These quantities are now purged of the interaction between demographic composition and time-period and show a moderately different pattern of time-period variability. We see that adequate employment deteriorated more from 1969 to 1970 than the observed rates showed (1.33 versus 1.26%), and for all other time intervals, the reverse pattern is observed. The decline in adequate employment from 1970 to 1971 was 2.84% (versus 2.93% observed); the decline from 1971 to 1972 was .67% (versus .92% observed—a substantial difference); and the *improvement* from 1972 to 1973 was .60% (versus .32% observed). The trend in the rate of adequate employment is thus somewhat different for the data purged of the influence of demographic compositional changes. Given the model at hand and the specific substantive meaning that attaches to parameters of that model, the quantities in column 2 can serve as "intrinsic" measures of labor market variability. To see how great the effect of changing demographic composition on the observed rate can be, it is worthwhile to note that the difference 1969–1973, representing only *four* time intervals, is 4.79% for the observed rates but is 4.24% for the adjusted rates. Thus we can say that the true deterioration in employment opportunity during the entire interval was nearly .6% *less* than the *apparent* deterioration observed in the data. Further analysis of these rates, broken down by form of underemployment, shows that each form of underemployment increased less than the observed rates show, although the magnitude of the compositional effect on underemployment differed for each form. These results represent the first attempt in this work so far to refine the observed rates with the objective of measuring labor market variability per se.

Yet another conception of "intrinsic" labor market variability in underemployment is that which regards *both D–T* and *D–T–U* interactions as extraneous. In this view, it would be argued that changes in underemployment that are different for the different demographic groupings (measured by the τ^{DTU} parameters) are not pure attributes of the labor market but are confounded by a host of social organizational variables that are only indirectly related to the purely economic forces of the labor market. This conception of the problem directs us to somehow purge the data of both the τ^{DT} and τ^{DTU} parameters, which can be done merely by taking the transformation

$$f_{ijk}^{**} = f_{ijk}/(\tau_{ij}^{DT}\tau_{ijk}^{DTU}) \tag{4.3}$$

Note here that the f_{ijk}^{**} can be expressed as

$$f_{ijk}^{**} = \theta\tau_i^D\tau_j^T\tau_k^U\tau_{ik}^{DU}\tau_{jk}^{TU} \tag{4.4}$$

showing that now *only* the interactions *D–U* and *T–U* are permitted to influence the f_{ijk}^{**}. The f_{ijk}^{**} accordingly reflect the relationship between demographic structure and underemployment (*D–U*), which here may be understood as a structural constraint, and the relationship between time-period and underemployment (*T–U*), which indicates pure labor market variability. Adjusted rates calculated from the f_{ijk}^{**} therefore measure intrinsic labor market variability in a way consistent with the model at hand.

In column 3 of Table 4.7, the rates of adequate employment obtained from the f_{ijk}^{**} are presented. Once again we see a marked difference between the trend evidenced in those adjusted rates as compared to the observed rates. The change over successive intervals is also very different from that exhibited in the rates adjusted only for composition–time-period interaction, and the reader is invited to compare the entries obtained from each method of adjustment. If this conception of pure labor market change were accepted, then the "true" deterioration in labor market opportunity 1969–1973 was only 3.53% (76.35 − 72.82), as contrasted with an observed change of 4.79%. The dramatic difference between these two sets of estimates (nearly 1.3%) provides ample demonstration of the force of demographic structure in defining apparent change in labor market conditions. The estimates presented in Table 4.7 should bring added meaning to the statistical results in Table 4.1 with which we began. True labor market change is very different from observed change in the rates, and an approach similar to that in this and the preceding sections enables us to quantify the importance of factors that cause this difference.

4.3 A RATIONALE FOR CONSIDERING AGE DISTRIBUTION IN THE CONSTRUCTION OF UNDEREMPLOYMENT INDICATORS

The preceding sections presented evidence concerning the extent of time-period change in the demographic composition of the labor force and the effect of this on the across-time variability in underemployment. This section narrows the focus somewhat by considering the effect of changing age composition alone on the *apparent* time-period variation (or labor market change) evidenced in the crude underemployment rates. Sex and race composition can also be important, as previous results can be readily manipulated to show, but for the present, these other demographic-compositional factors will be ignored. Such an omission is made plausible owing to two facts: (*a*) age-composition changes 1969–1973 are by far the most important, dwarfing by comparison the other types of compositional changes; and (*b*) the relationship of age to the hidden level of frictional underemployment—the subject with which this chapter began—is much more clear-cut than are the relationships of sex or race to the level of frictional underemployment, at least for this time span. A more rigorous treatment of the influence of changing demographic structure on the trend in frictional underemployment could indeed be attempted (compare Section 4.2), but in this section, we focus attention only on the role of age, thereby ensuring that results will be *conservative* in their estimation of the rise in frictional underemployment.

The operating assumption is that society allocates the socioeconomic reward of adequate employment in part according to the age of the worker, and the resulting age distribution of employment opportunity is in no way an indication of "structural" underemployment as it should be defined in either economic or sociological terms. Apart from temporary fluctuation in the age pattern of risk to underemployment, the observed age distribution of employment opportunity is the result of the *institutionalization* of role-reward allocation patterns in prior times, the age *structure* of which persists through time. As a result of the persistence of the age-distribution of underemployment, the changing age composition of the labor force can *distort* observed rates of underemployment even if the age pattern of risk to underemployment were to remain unchanged. Underemployment indicators, it is proposed, should unambiguously measure the changing risk to underemployment apart from extraneous age distribution factors. The extent to which this need is not fulfilled is the extent to which the given underemployment indicator is "distorted" by demographic factors of only secondary importance. It will be the argument of this section that the changing age composition of the population of working ages and of the labor force affects *apparent* time-period variation in underemployment (i.e., *apparent* variation in labor market conditions) in ways that cannot be ignored. By straightforward standardization or adjustment of rates (compare Kitagawa, 1964; Fleiss, 1973), we will show that in a span of 5 years, changing age composition alone can account for a *decrease* of approximately 1% in the rate of adequate employment. The material to be presented will forcefully document the claim made by Perry (1970), Easterlin (1978), Easterlin *et al.* (1978), Smith (1977), Toikka *et al.* (1977), and many others that the changing age composition of the labor force demands reevaluation of the true level of "structural," as opposed to "frictional," underemployment in the current economic experience of the United States. Changing age composition alone can distort the degree to which crude or unadjusted underemployment rates are a reflection of the condition of the labor market, since age is a factor with which the hidden level of frictional underemployment is known to vary.

Regarding the concept of age "distortions," both the changing age composition of the population of working ages and the changing age composition of the labor force (reflecting, in addition, changes in labor force participation patterns) are important topics deserving simultaneous treatment. Both need to be considered in tandem, since age distortions can be the result of changes in either the proportion of the total population in a certain age interval or the proportion of the total labor force in a certain age interval. Presumably, the pure age effect and the pure participation effect could cancel each other out, or they could both contribute to an age distortion in the rates of underemployment. (Rates of underemployment are typically expressed with the labor force as the base, or the "at risk" population.) The problem of changing participation rates is considered indirectly here as one of the determinants of the age distribution of the labor force.

As preliminary evidence of the importance of changing *participation* rates in determining the changing age distribution of the labor force, Table 4.8 is presented. In this table, the age-specific labor force participation rates and the ratio of the number adequately employed in an age interval to the total population in an age interval are compared for 2 years.[3] The year 1969 represents very favorable labor market conditions, whereas 1972 was a recession year. Column 6 of Table 4.8 shows that for *every* age,

---

[3] We denote the ratio of adequately employed workers to the total population of working ages as an "adequate employment ratio."

TABLE 4.8
Labor Force Participation Rates and Adequate Employment Ratios, 1969 and 1972, for the Population 14 and Over[a]

Age group	1969		1972		Difference, 1972–1969	
	Participation rate	Adequate employment ratio	Participation rate	Adequate employment ratio	Participation rate	Adequate employment ratio
14–19	.350	.240	.378	.233	.028	–.007
20–24	.684	.438	.706	.391	.022	–.047
25–29	.692	.517	.719	.493	.027	–.024
30–34	.702	.545	.710	.527	.008	–.018
35–39	.713	.562	.732	.545	.019	–.017
40–44	.739	.591	.747	.570	.008	–.021
45–49	.743	.596	.741	.573	–.002	–.023
50–54	.730	.594	.735	.580	.005	–.014
55–59	.692	.570	.678	.540	–.014	–.030
60–64	.560	.465	.546	.431	–.014	–.034
65–69	.300	.239	.268	.201	–.032	–.038
70+	.120	.094	.105	.084	–.015	–.010

[a]The labor force participation rates of this table refer to the "modified labor force" suggested as an alternative to the more usual labor force. That is, both numerator and denominator contain the "sub-unemployment workers," our proxy for discouraged workers. If the more usual labor force definition were used in the calculation of these ratios, the pattern would remain essentially unchanged.

the proportion of the age group adequately employed decreased in 1972 relative to 1969. Column 5 of the table shows that in spite of the worsening of economic opportunity, the labor force *participation* rates in general increased, with substantial increases in the ages typically experiencing high risk of underemployment. This "participation effect" will *distort* the crude rates of underemployment for the labor force in 1972, since the weights that determine crude or overall underemployment rates are the heaviest in precisely those ages where participation increased the most. Couple this pure participation effect with the pure age effect occasioned by past variations in fertility, and the subject of the present section immediately suggests itself.

In order to avoid the cumbersome problems of changing retirement patterns and of early (marginal) labor force participation, both of which are difficult to assess in terms of their implication for "frictional" or "structural" underemployment, the analysis is here restricted to the population aged 20–64. Were it not for the problem of net immigration, which disrupts the unfolding age structure in largely unknown ways, it might have been more appropriate to deal with pure age distortions (i.e., population waves brought about by the peculiar fertility experience of the United States from 1930 to 1960) by the approach set forth recently by Keyfitz (1972). In order to keep the presentation simple, and in order not to ignore the possible immigrant effect upon age structure, the elementary approach of this section will suffice. Before empirical documentation of our claims is presented, some comments concerning the underlying rationale of the concept of age composition effects are appropriate.

When summarizing the strengths of age-specific rates of underemployment from a purely demographic point of view one needs to know the age distribution of the working population (or, alternatively, of the population of persons of working age). Comparisons across demographic strata and/or comparisons over time must "control" for age, since differences in crude rates could be due to dissimilarity in age structure alone. If fertility or mortality were the object of investigation, this problem would be partly resolved by straightforward demographic standardization for age, the rationale for which has generally been the observed *biological* connection of age with these vital processes. However, in the analysis of underemployment the very idea of an age effect is much more subtle, since the *biological* dependence of age and employability is less critical, at least for the ages under consideration here. Some labor force statisticians of radical persuasion might conceivably ignore the age variable altogether, maintaining that within certain broad limits, the age distribution of adequate employment should be nearly uniform, and indications to the contrary are *prima facie* evidence of "discriminatory" employment patterns or even of structural underutilization of labor. We take the contrary point of view here. The rationale for dealing with age distortions is justified in our view by consideration of the central role that age plays in the socioeconomic mechanisms that allocate employment opportunity.

Age is surely a principal criterion by which role positions, including labor force positions, are assigned to individuals. Not only do the roles in which workers find themselves change dramatically with age—the so-called life-cycle effect—but the rewards that a given role secures also change with the age of the individual. Under ideal conditions we can imagine that the individual changes work roles with age approximately in accord with a steady progression from marginal labor force participation in youth to full participation—adequate employment—in a gainful career by middle age. Moreover, within a given work role the *rewards* accruing to a given worker also change with age, perhaps in large measure as a result of the increased experience of older workers relative to younger workers in the same role. It is impossible to disentangle statistically the age–role effect from the age–reward effect with such data as we have at our disposal, but it is nevertheless important that both features be noted in any discussion of age patterns of underemployment. The "human capital" perspective of economics also considers the role of age in a similar fashion, treating the age progression through work roles and through reward patterns within work roles as a natural process whereby human capital is accumulated, the skill of the individual worker is enhanced, and the social rewards—in terms of the provision of adequate employment to the worker—are allocated accordingly. Whether we consider the age pattern of role–reward allocation from the structural view of sociology or as a process of human capital development from an economic point of view, it is nevertheless important that we be cognizant of the *institutionalization* of that age pattern over time. The notion here is that the rigidity of this age pattern persists even though the age structure may shift substantially.

At least three forms of the institutionalization of the age pattern of employment opportunity can be distinguished for consideration. The first is the form whereby a specified *ratio* of all members of a particular age group is allocated adequate employment by society. To examine age distortions given this conception of the problem, the various measures presented in Chapter 2 with the total population (not simply the labor force) as the base for underemployment measures should be considered. A second possible mechanism would be one whereby the *labor force participants* at each age are subject to a rate of underemployment (or adequate employment) that remains unchanged over time, barring economic exigencies. This second possibility calls for data on the rates of underemployment, where the age distribution of the labor force is the central focus. A

third possibility is the case whereby, say, the sex–race groups are subject
to the same sorts of age-allocative mechanisms as in the above two cases
but where the character may be substantially different among the sex–race
specific groups. Each of these possibilities has been considered in turn,
demonstrating that regardless of the form of the institutionalization of
age-distributive mechanisms, nearly the same results emerge. The proper
inference of an "age distortion" in the following depends upon the specific meaning of the age-allocative structure that is presumed to be in
operation.[4]

4.4 AGE EFFECTS FOR THE TOTAL POPULATION AND THE TOTAL LABOR FORCE AGED 20–64

The methods used to infer the age effects on underemployment are
routine standardization methods and so do not need to be rigorously discussed here. Table 4.9 presents the results from these calculations, where
two different types of procedures were employed. The first method involves taking the ratio of adequately employed to the total population, the
result being referred to as the "crude ratio" of adequate employment, and
then adjusting this figure for the changing age composition of the total
population aged 20–64. The adjusted quantities are denoted as "standardized ratios" of adequate employment in column 2. The second method
focuses only on the "modified" labor force and adjusts the rate of adequate employment for changing age composition of the labor force. The
adjusted quantities obtained thereby are denoted as "standardized rates"
in column 4. For each set of calculations, the composition of the 1969
population (or labor force) was taken as the standard set of weights, and
5-year age categories were used throughout this analysis.

Two different conceptions of age distortions are involved in the quantities of Table 4.9. The first is the age distortion in time-period ratios of
adequate employment (with the total population as base in those ratios)
brought about by the changing distribution of the population of persons of

---

[4] In this chapter, for illustrative purposes only, we assume that "pure" cohort-induced
changes in underemployment rates are nil. This assumption is clearly unwarranted, as we
will argue in Chapter 5, but it will allow an analysis of age distortions that will be illuminating, given this basic assumption. By a nil cohort effect, we mean here that *if economic
conditions were to remain constant,* then for any age group the rate of underemployment
would be the same across time. That is, cohorts do not exhibit different rates of underemployment because of some special characteristic of the cohort itself (e.g., the size of the
cohort or the stock of human capital that it possesses relative to other cohorts at prior
times).

TABLE 4.9

Crude and Age-Standardized Rates and Ratios of Adequate Employment, 1969–1973, Total United States Population Aged 20-64 (1969 as Base) (in Percentages)

Year	Crude ratio (1)	Standardized ratio (2)	Crude rate (3)	Standardized rate (4)	Labor force participation rate $(5) = \frac{(1)}{(3)}$	Composition component to ratio $(6) = (2) - (1)$	Composition component to rate[a] $(7) = (4) - (3)$
1969	54.17	54.17	78.20	78.20	69.27	.00	.00
1970	53.50	53.55	76.85	76.93	69.62	.05	.08
1971	51.51	51.71	74.22	74.46	69.40	.20	.24
1972	51.31	51.62	73.57	74.00	69.74	.31	.43
1973	51.50	51.86	73.62	74.28	69.95	.36	.66

[a] Average annual rate of change in composition component to rate in column (7) = .15%.

working age. The second conception is the labor force age distortion in time-period rates brought about by changes in both participation rates and age structure. In column 1 of Table 4.9 we see that the proportion of the total population adequately employed decreased from 54.17% in 1969 to 51.50% in 1973, or a difference of 2.67%. In column 2 the standardized ratios are presented with 1969 as the base year in those ratios. We see that the difference in standardized ratios 1969–1973 of 54.17 − 51.86%, or 2.31%, is less than the difference in crude ratios of 2.67%. We also see that the "composition component" presented in row 5 of column 6 is given as 2.67 − 2.31% = .36%. In relative terms, this figure shows that 13.1% of the difference in crude ratios of adequate employment during the four time intervals from 1969 to 1973 is *due to changing age composition alone.* This is indeed a dramatic figure and by itself casts doubt on the use of unadjusted ratios of adequate employment as indicators of the condition of the labor market. An even more marked age effect is in evidence in the analysis of the crude and standardized rates, which are restricted to the labor force participants. These quantities are presented in columns 3, 4, and 7.

With regard to the rates of adequate employment, where the modified labor force is the base, we see that the rate of adequate employment in 1969 was 78.20% and that this rate dropped to 73.62% in 1973. The difference of 78.20 − 73.62, or 4.58%, has a "composition component" of .66%. In relative terms, the difference in crude rates 1969–1973 is .66/4.58, or a full 14.4% of the difference is due to the changing age distribution of the labor force. These are remarkabe figures indeed.

It could be of interest to project this "age effect" into the future. With the pure age effect evidenced in the analysis of adequate employment ratios, projection by statistical means is unwarranted because the age distribution is, in the short run, unfolding in ways that are determined by fertility already completed. It might be of use, however, to project the age component resulting from the age distribution of the labor force into the future. The assumptions for such a projection are that *participation* patterns by age and population *age structure* change in the near future as it did in this span of 5 years. Since 1969 is our base year (i.e., time = 0), we merely fit a regression line constrained to pass through the origin. The slope coefficient from that regression is a measure of the "annual rate of change" in the composition component. The estimate of this quantity is .15%, which implies that we expect a *decrease* in the rate of adequate employment of .15% each year, or, alternatively, an *increase* in the rate of underemployment of .15% each year. If the observed pattern of age change in the labor force continued to operate into the future, by 1980 we would expect a rate of adequate employment of 1.71% less than in 1969. This projection is, of course, highly conjectural, based upon the assumption that the labor force of the near future continues to change as markedly as it did in these 5 years.

These results have shown that by virtue of the changing age distribution of the population and of the labor force, time-period measures of underemployment in this time span are considerably distorted from their intended meaning. Since frictional underemployment varies with age, the crude rates and ratios that are the standard labor market indicators will overestimate the true level of *structural* underemployment. Indeed, the age distortion in the indicators might well be linked directly to the *rise* in frictional underemployment, although we are currently unable to propose a functional relationship for measurement of it. But there has surely been a rise in frictional underemployment. This is empirical documentation of the need to consider the age variable in any serious study of the U.S. labor force in this peculiar era. The sample sizes upon which the above estimates were based are large enough that we can be confident that sampling error is no factor in the interpretations. Detailed consideration of each of Hauser's underemployment forms by the above procedures shows much the same thing as the above, so we do not present those results here. The implication of this empirical result is that the age variable should be taken into account in underemployment indicators; the technique of direct standardization is one approach by which this task could be carried out, or the method of adjustment used in the previous section might be employed. Of course, for comparisons across time intervals of short duration, the age composition cannot change enough to distort the ordinary measures appreciably. However, for time intervals as long as 4 or more years, unadjusted measures will be very misleading indeed.

These results should be compelling for the following reasons:

1. The analysis was restricted to the prime working ages 20–64, a procedure that here tends to *understate* the variability in underemployment resulting from changing age composition.
2. The analysis was conducted with 5-year age groupings, an aggregation that actually attenuates the degree of age-distribution changes.
3. The analysis pertained to both the labor force and the total population, showing nearly identical results.
4. The analysis was carried out for each of the underemployment forms separately, by sex–race group, with the same or even more marked effects being uncovered.

(Using different "standard populations," we obtained the following estimates of the annual rate of deterioration in adequate employment: .17–.20%, .11–.15%, .21–.28%, and .25% for white males, nonwhite males, white females, and nonwhite females, respectively. To save space, the detailed analyses of each of the underemployment forms by sex–race group will not be presented here, but the results are available on request from the writer.)

4.5 CONCLUSION

Frictional underemployment can be defined as the underemployment that is intrinsic to a labor force at a given point in time. It is the underemployment that is functionally necessary and that occurs even in the presence of adequate total demand for labor. Each underemployment form (including unemployment) possesses its own frictional component, the exact level of which critically depends on the operational criteria used to measure the total incidence of that form. Frictional underemployment levels are not constant over time but instead change as the labor force changes. A variety of factors, as much social–structural (i.e., sociological) in origin as economic in character, determine the level of and trend in frictional components to the underemployment forms. Perhaps chief among these factors is the demographic composition of the labor force, because each particular demographic group (namely, age–race–sex group) has its own intrinsic level of risk to underemployment that cannot change rapidly in the short run. In Section 4.1, this point of view was adopted to partition labor force variability over time into three sources: (a) across-time change in underemployment measured in the T–U interaction; (b) across-time change in demographic composition, measured by the D–T interaction; and (c) across-time change in the relationship of the demographic groups to underemployment, measured by the D–T–U interaction. A series of models were fit to the data showing a decomposition into these three sources, and other models were fit that further specified the components of variability in each distinct source. It was shown that a large part of the overall variability in the labor force across time, around 50% in proportionate terms, involved demographic structure; the proper inference was that the trend in observed underemployment could not provide a clear-cut picture of "true" labor market variability. In Section 4.2, the across-time variability in underemployment (actually, in the rate of adequate employment) was adjusted to remove the effects of the D–T and the D–T and D–T–U interactions, showing in different terms how great the demographic influence actually was. Finally, in Sections 4.3 and 4.4, the analysis was further restricted to an examination of the effects of age-distribution changes per se, and a rationale for considering age distortions in underemployment was proposed. It was shown that even for the four time intervals considered in this work, the changing age distribution of the labor force (and the population of working ages) operates to moderately increase the level of underemployment, principally because the proportion of the labor force at intrinsically high risk to underemployment—including frictional underemployment—increased markedly.

In conclusion, it must be stated that examining the effect of changing demographic composition on underemployment is only a small step toward sharpening our description of the changing mix between frictional and structural underemployment. Surely a host of other factors should be brought into the analysis, and the rather negative conclusions reached here would have to be formulated in a new light. We are presently in a quandary over how other factors might be brought into a framework for estimating the trend in frictional underemployment. In restricting ourselves to simple demographic variables it was hoped that a conservative estimate of the upturn in frictional underemployment would result. Surely it would be difficult to question the vital role that demographic compositional factors have in the interpretation of observed crude rates. Sociologists, in our view, should be encouraged to bring their special analytic skills into an analysis of frictional underemployment; the approach presented here, which focused entirely on demographic composition, is a proper beginning for this endeavor.

5

latent class structure in the
distribution of
labor market rewards

This chapter is concerned with the empirical observation that several underemployment forms often occur simultaneously to the same worker. Parsimonious models that account for the observed pattern of multiple underemployment will be developed. The methods utilized in this chapter are derived from the modified latent structure approach elaborated by Goodman (1974a, b, 1975a), but they are also related to similar methods of Haberman (1974, 1977) and to more conventional latent structure techniques surveyed by Lazarsfeld and Henry (1968).[1] These methods will be used to examine specific hypotheses about the class structure of underemployment or, alternatively, about the class structure of the distribution of the labor market rewards of employment, income, and skill utilization. We believe that the approach advocated here allows a more succinct and theoretically meaningful characterization of labor force class structure than previous approaches have.[2] For reasons that will become apparent

[1] The numerical algorithms presented by Lazarsfeld and Henry (1968) are inadequate as judged by modern statistical criteria; however, these methods are still sometimes used (compare Fielding, 1977). Moreover, some of the models considered in this chapter are different in kind from the ones considered by Lazarsfeld and Henry. A computer program for maximum likelihood latent structure analysis is discussed in Appendix C, and a comprehensive manual describing its use is also available (Clogg, 1977).

[2] Other approaches to characterizing the class structure of the labor force will be discussed later. Some of the more relevant of these are studies by Bonacich (1972, 1976), emphasizing the factor of race; Bluestone (1968), emphasizing the role of low-wage, "marginal" indus-

77

when the empirical data are presented, our analysis is necessarily restricted to the four main underemployment forms discussed in prior chapters: unemployment, involuntary part-time unemployment, low-income underemployment, and mismatch. Let us begin by discussing the importance of multiple underemployment, as it can be conceived using the Hauser-Sullivan approach to labor force measurement.

Multiple underemployment, in the first instance, presents serious problems concerning the manner in which the various underemployment combinations are to be summarized in the form of a social indicator. The problem can be posed in this way: When two or more underemployment forms occur together empirically, it is questionable whether logically distinct *types* of underemployment exist at all. That the several forms of underemployment were distinct from one another, and therefore could not be measured—even indirectly—by standard measures of the time form, is a working hypothesis universally held by those proposing new measurement procedures. When four different forms are purportedly measured, as with the Hauser-Sullivan approach, a natural way to summarize the multidimensional contingency that results is to appeal to scaling methods commonly associated with Guttman (1950; compare Torgerson, 1962). However, the four forms of underemployment have no necessary ordering, a feature that is necessary to establish Guttman scalability, and therefore, when two or more of the forms occurred together, it was necessary to apply admittedly arbitrary criteria in order to produce the five-class underemployment variable used previously.[3] We have implicitly *scaled* (or ordered) the four dichotomous variables, each of which denoted the presence or absence of a given form of underemployment without actually providing the necessary statistical justification for doing so. The observed pattern of association among the underemployment forms can be used to assess scalability, as in the fashion of scalogram analysis (Guttman, 1950), and certain probabilistic generalizations of scaling models can be used to test statistically the distinctness of the underemployment forms (compare

---

tries; and Doeringer and Piore (1971), emphasizing "internal labor markets" restricting interoccupation and interindustry mobility. These are surveyed in part by Gordon (1972) and also by Cain (1976). A recent treatise on the *sociology* of the labor market (Montagna, 1977) describes much of the empirical evidence thus far amassed on the class organization of labor market opportunity. Averitt (1973) also presents a discussion of dualism that is pertinent here.

[3] The four dichotomous variables about which the five-class underemployment variable of Hauser was constructed imply *16* possible response patterns. Actually, since the combination unemployment–part-time unemployment is impossible, there are only *12* possible response patterns. These 12 responses were arbitrarily combined to produce the five-class variable used previously.

Goodman, 1975a). This issue is far from academic, since the observed association among the underemployment forms changes dramatically with economic fluctuation. The extent of multiple underemployment—the association among the forms—is clearly pertinent to the construction of a labor force indicator, since changes in the distributions of the individual variables, or in the distribution of the five-class variable used hitherto, are in part influenced by this changing association.

Hauser suggested one rationale for scaling the underemployment variable that was based on usual policy priorities concerning the perceived importance of the various forms. Gauging the aggregate volume of unemployment is usually of first importance to policymakers, and so it was suggested that all persons who were unemployed should be considered in one distinct class. All unemployed persons were placed in the category denoting unemployment, but this category also included some persons who experienced the low-income form, some persons who were mismatched, and some persons who suffered both low income and mismatch. The low-income and/or mismatch facet of these multiple underemployed persons was ignored. Policy endeavor has usually considered part-time unemployment as less severe than unemployment, and so Hauser's suggestion was to include all the part-time unemployed persons in a second distinct category. But this category also contained some who experienced low income, some who were mismatched, and some who were both low-income underemployed and mismatched. The low-income and/or mismatch facet of these multiple underemployed persons was also ignored. Labor force policy has only recently been concerned with the invisible forms—low income and mismatch—and so these were dealt with in Hauser's scheme only after the visible forms were measured. The low-income status, for example, contained only those who had low income but who were not at the same time unemployed or part-time unemployed. It did contain some who were mismatched, but since the mismatch form has a low priority for policymakers, the joint occurrence of the low-income and mismatch forms was singly designated as a low-income type, disregarding completely the mismatch facet of this kind of multiple underemployment. Finally, the mismatch status was considered, but this category was determined in such a way that it contained persons who were mismatched but who experienced *no* other kind of underemployment. It was hoped that a small amount of overlap of the several forms would in fact be observed, so that the categories of Hauser's five-class indicator would fairly represent the *distinct* forms of underemployment that were presumed to exist. But in the event of multiple classification, the implied hierarchy of underemployment was, in the order of "severity," (*a*) unemployment, (*b*) hours (i.e., part-time employment), (*c*) income (i.e., low income), and (d) mismatch. Before describing the techniques used to assess the conformity of observed patterns of underemployment to the theory that had posited *distinct* underemployment forms, we first consider the special meaning that attaches to the income form as it has been determined in this study.

The income form of underemployment, unlike the other three forms, was constructed on the basis of workers' *entire year's* labor force experience, so that the dichotomous income variable approximately separated the labor force into a portion below the poverty line during the past year and into a portion above the poverty line during the past year.[4] Since the income variable is based upon the range of labor force experience for an entire year, and therefore separates the labor force into a segment that is marginal (with respect to income) and a segment that is not marginal (with respect to income), we might use this basic dichotomous income variable to discuss in quantitative terms the theory of the dual labor market. As might be expected, when we view the income variable as an explanatory control, the unemployment and part-time unemployment rates are dramatically different between the low-income and the adequate-income portions of the labor force. This view of the income variable as an indicator of marginality is pertinent to the dual labor market theory, because that theory is built upon the presupposition of the existence of a fairly homogeneous marginal labor force segment, and part of the marginality of that segment is income marginality. The income variable, as we have measured it, is thus both the indicator of one kind of underemployment and a measure that bifurcates the labor force into two distinct parts corresponding roughly to the two ideal types of dual labor market theory (see, e.g., Gordon, 1972; Cain, 1976). We will show later that the income measure we have used is, in certain respects, preferable to other indicators of marginality that are implicitly used in the dual labor market literature (e.g., race, sex, age, occupation, or industrial sector criteria).

Some available evidence suggests that the low-income part of the labor force, in addition to maintaining approximately the same numerical level over time, is also fairly stable in its composition over time. That is, we may presume that many of the *same persons* in the low-income form at year t will also be in the low-income form at year $t + 1$, and so even in the absence of panel data, we can make some inference about the persistence of underemployment characteristics in the low-income part of the labor

---

[4] That is, average weekly work-related income (adjusted for weeks worked) was below the poverty threshold for the past year for the low-income part and above the poverty threshold for the adequate-income part. This, of course, disregards the impact of income received by illicit means, income received through various welfare mechanisms, etc.

force (see Morgan *et al.*, 1974; or Levitan and Taggart, 1974). If the low-income part of the labor force has a 20% rate of unemployment at time t and a 25% rate of unemployment at time $t + 1$, we may assume—because of the relatively unchanging composition of the low-income part of the labor force—that unemployment increased approximately 5% for the part of the labor force that was below the poverty line at time t. Similar inferences cannot be made on the basis of the other three dichotomous variables, since (a) these other three underemployment forms were defined with respect to labor force experience of 1 week, (b) these other forms are known to be much more subject to time-period variation, and (c) these other forms are known to change their composition over time; for example, the pool of unemployed persons is not the same at time $t + 1$ as at time t. This unique information attaching to the dichotomous income variable will be used to considerable advantage later.

5.1 THE LATENT CLASS PERSPECTIVE IN THE ANALYSIS OF UNDEREMPLOYMENT

Much labor force theory posits the existence of different "ideal types" of workers who contribute differentially to the observed structure of current underemployment and changes therein over time. These ideal types of workers are largely of a conjectural nature and are based upon the conceptualization of an unobservable qualitative variable (namely a *class* variable), which, if properly specified, would explain the observed rates of underemployment. Labor force theory built about ideal typologies of the labor force lends itself to empirical test within the framework of the latent class model developed some 30 years ago by the late Paul Lazarsfeld and his co-workers. Several problems that will be at least partly resolved by the latent class approach are as follows.

1. The problem of the *scalability* of underemployment is important whenever several different, not necessarily mutually exclusive, underemployment forms are given simultaneous consideration. At issue is the *distinctness* of the several underemployment types and the implications of same for the feasibility of measurement. Since, in fact, multiple underemployment occurs, we wish to determine if the pattern of multiple underemployment is consistent with a model that contains distinct "scale types" corresponding to each of the several underemployment forms. In order to examine the scalability of underemployment (in the above sense), we will adopt a probabilistic formulation of the scaling problem recently proposed by Goodman (1975a) that is related to but different from com-

mon Guttman scaling. This approach will force us to conclude that (*a*) the unemployment and part-time unemployment forms are distinct underemployment forms, (*b*) the mismatch form is also distinct, (*c*) the income form is not distinct from unemployment and part-time unemployment, and (*d*) a very large part of the labor force (some 25%) has underemployment patterns that are not scalable at all (i.e., they are "intrinsically unscalable").

2. The labor force can be thought of as being composed of distinct parts, each of which are at different levels of *risk* to the various underemployment forms. In the case where the labor force is not homogeneously exposed to the risks of underemployment, it is no longer meaningful to compute unrefined rates of underemployment and attribute probabilistic meaning to them.[5] We will show that a large part of the labor force (some 65% of the total) can be thought of as not being exposed to the risk of underemployment at all. Also, we will show that about 1% of the labor force can be thought of as being at *perfect* risk of unemployment or part-time unemployment, that another 9% can be thought of as being at perfect risk of mismatch, and that another 25% may be thought of as being at very high risk (but not perfect risk) of all the underemployment forms. For the part of the labor force at very high (but not perfect) risk of underemployment, we will provide a statistically justified method that will predict the occurrence or nonoccurrence of any pattern of multiple underemployment. An alternative interpretation of some models will be similar in that we will separate the labor force into two parts, the first of which is composed of 20–25% of the labor force and is at very high risk (but not at perfect risk) of underemployment, and the second of which is composed of 75–80% of the labor force and is at very low risk (but not at zero risk) of underemployment.

3. Some of the underemployment forms considered here may be connected to one another through similar socioeconomic mechanisms. Other underemployment forms may be unrelated to these and unrelated to the socioeconomic mechanisms "causing" them. Two or more of the underemployment forms might be presumed to have common causes, but other underemployment forms might be presumed to have different "causes."

---

[5] This point of view, we believe, has wide ramifications. For example, in the abundant literature on status attainment over the life cycle (compare Blau and Duncan, 1967), the assumption is made, albeit implicitly, that the labor force is a homogeneous aggregate. If, however, the labor force is heterogeneous, in the sense that different parts have vastly different risks to unemployment, low income, and mismatch, then the models of status attainment that ignore this feature will be seriously misspecified. The difficulty in conceptualizing occupational status for those who are underemployed requires a rethinking of the idea of status "attainment."

In certain respects, this conjecture is at the basis of proposals to measure invisible, as opposed to only visible, underemployment. We will show that it is plausible to assume that mismatch must have a different set of causes from the others but that the other three forms have common causes.[6] This inference is based on the observation that most workers experiencing the first three underemployment forms have been drawn from a fairly homogeneous subpopulation and that therefore the "causes" that affect only this subpopulation are pertinent to locating the "causes" of these three forms. This one subpopulation will contain *all* persons having low work-related income, giving us a clue that the causes of low work-related income are generally the same as the causes of unemployment and part-time unemployment.

4. When association among the underemployment forms exists, and when this association itself changes over time, it can be misleading to summarize underemployment by reference to information based only upon the five-class variable used previously or only upon the distribution observed in each of the four dichotomous underemployment variables. We will devise a model that *explains* the observed association among the underemployment forms, and we will find that this same model will also explain the changing association across time. Since the association among underemployment types is accounted for by this model, it will only be necessary to summarize changing underemployment over time in terms of the structural parameters of this model. These structural parameters will take into account both the changing distribution in the four dichotomous underemployment variables and the changing association among them.

5. The theory of the dual labor force or dual labor market, about which some comment has already been made, involves the assumption that two inherently "unobservable" classes in the labor force exist, the first of which has very high risk of underemployment and the second of which has very low risk of underemployment. (Other considerations also enter into the dual labor market theory, e.g., specifying the kinds of work force marginality that characterize the high-risk part of the labor force.) The very nature of that theory, and of the labor force data now available, demands that the two main labor force classes of that theory be characterized by the *indirect* observation of a latent or unobservable class variable on data such as will be discussed here. We will treat the observed pattern of multiple underemployment as if it were generated from the

---

[6] That mismatch levels are "caused" by different forces than those that "cause" unemployment levels might at first seem rather tautological. However, persons who are mismatched—that is, have *too much* skill for the job they are in—have unemployment risks that are very high. See Clogg (1979b) for a fuller discussion of this phenomenon.

underemployment experience of two (or more) latent labor force classes corresponding to the ideal types of the theory of the dual labor force. This latent structure perspective will provide us with parameters of the dual labor force model and will also provide a basis from which to enrich that theory.

These five different kinds of inference pertain to (*a*) the scalability or distinctness of the several underemployment forms, (*b*) meaningfully summarizing the varying levels of risk to underemployment in the distinct structural parts of the labor force, (*c*) the "causal analysis" of underemployment, (*d*) the construction of underemployment indicators taking into account multiple underemployment, and (*e*) the indirect observation of ideal labor force types corresponding to dual labor market theory. Outwardly, these problems might appear unrelated to one another. However, we will show how only a few models will bring them all into joint play.

5.2 THE 1970 DATA

We first consider the March 1970 data in some detail. Let U, H, I, and M denote the four dichotomous underemployment variables referring to unemployment, part-time unemployment (or low hours), underemployment by income, and mismatch, respectively. For each variable, let Class 1 denote presence of that type of underemployment and let Class 2 denote absence of that type of underemployment. The raw cross-classification of the labor force 14 years of age and over recorded on the March 1970 CPS with respect to these four variables is given in Table 5.1. This four-way cross-table has four missing entries owing to the mutual exclusiveness of unemployment and part-time unemployment. A person who is unemployed cannot be part-time employed, and a part-time employed person cannot be unemployed. These cell zeros are not the result of sampling variability but instead are the result of the prior constraint that the combination where $(U, H) = (1, 1)$ is impossible. Table 5.1 is thus an *incomplete* cross-table in the sense that it has "structural zeros" (Goodman, 1968; Bishop *et al.*, 1975, Chapter 5). The "scale types" corresponding to those set forth earlier are also designated in Table 5.1. These are the cells corresponding to persons experiencing no multiple underemployment. If the four underemployment forms were completely distinct from each other, then these cells would contain all the observations. We see that these "scale types" are indeed the largest in magnitude, which could itself be an a posteriori rationale for considering these as distinct underemployment forms.

The 16-fold cross-table of Table 5.1 can be collapsed by combining the

TABLE 5.1
Sixteenfold Cross-classification of the Types of Underemployment,
United States Labor Force, March 1970

Cell U-H-I-M	Frequency	Scale types
1 1 1 1	—[a]	
2 1 1 1	46	
1 1 1 1	83	
2 2 1 1	378	
1 1 2 1	—	
2 1 2 1	70	
1 2 2 1	154	
2 2 2 1	5560	Mismatched only
1 1 1 2	—	
2 1 1 2	451	
1 2 1 2	890	
2 2 1 2	3742	Low income only
1 1 2 2	—	
2 1 2 2	987	Low hours only
1 2 2 2	1713	Unemployed only
2 2 2 2	45299	Not underemployed, or adequately "utilized"
Total	59373	

[a]Denotes cells with "structural zeroes," since the combination where U is 1 and H is 1 is impossible. That is, unemployment and part-time unemployment are mutually exclusive.

Variables: U = unemployment; H = involuntary part-time employment (Hours); I = underemployment by low work-related *I*ncome; M = underemployment by skill level (*M*ismatch).

Variable values: 1 = underemployment; 2 = not underemployed.

U and H variables into one joint variable, say UH. Since the (1, 1) combination of (U, H) is impossible, it suffices to consider the joint variable UH with three classes where there is a one-to-one correspondence between $UH = \{(1), (2), (3)\}$ and $(U, H) = \{(1, 2), (2, 1), (2, 2)\}$. Thus the first category of the joint variable UH refers to unemployment, the second category refers to low hours (or part-time unemployment), and the third category refers to "not low hours and not unemployment." Table 5.1 where the (1, 1) category of (U, H) is ignored can be collapsed into a *complete* $3 \times 2 \times 2$ cross-table because the set of cells where $(U, H) \neq (1, 1)$ is *separable* from the set of cells where $(U, H) = (1, 1)$.[7] This complete cross-table is presented in Table 5.2. All subsequent analysis is based upon the complete cross-table of Table 5.2 or upon others like it, but it

[7] For the concept of separability, see Goodman (1968).

also pertains to the incomplete cross-table of Table 5.1 or to ones like it, where it is understood that the structural zeros are taken into account. Assume now that the four main underemployment forms were *distinct* from one another. This would imply that apart from random disturbances to be specified later, there would be no multiple underemployment. Considering the three-way cross-table presented in Table 5.2, we would then expect the cells corresponding to $(UH, I, M) = \{(1, 2, 2), (2, 2, 2), (3, 1, 2), (3, 2, 1), (3, 2, 2)\}$ to contain all the observed responses, since all other combinations denote multiple underemployment. These five scale types would correspond to the distinct underemployment types of unemployment, hours, income, and mismatch and to a distinct scale type corre-

TABLE 5.2
Twelvefold Cross-classification of the Types of Underemployment,
United States Labor Force, March 1970

Cell UH-I-M	Frequency	Percent	Meaning	Scale type[a]
1 1 1	83	.1		0
2 1 1	46	.1		0
3 1 1	378	.6		0
1 2 1	154	.3		0
2 2 1	70	.1		0
3 2 1	5560	9.4	Mismatched only	4
1 1 2	890	1.5		0
2 1 2	451	.8		0
3 1 2	3742	6.3	Income only	3
1 2 2	1713	2.9	Unemployed only	1
2 2 2	987	1.7	Hours only	2
3 2 2	45299	76.2	Adequately utilized	5
Total	59373	100.0		

Percentage correctly allocated into the scale types: $57301/59373 = 96.5\%$
Percentage of underemployed correctly allocated: $11944/14002 = 85.3\%$
Percentage of unemployed who are unemployed only: $1713/2840 = 60.3\%$
    % of unemployed who are low income: $973/2840 = 34.3\%$
Percentage of low hours who are hours only: $987/1554 = 63.5\%$
    % of low hours who are low income: $497/1554 = 32.0\%$
Percentage of low-income who are low income only: $3742/5590 = 66.9\%$
Percentage of mismatched who are mismatched only: $5560/6291 = 88.4\%$

Source: Table 5.1, this volume.
[a]Scale types: 0 = unscalable; 1 = unemployed; 2 = underemployed by hours; 3 = underemployed by income; 4 = mismatched; 5 = adequately utilized, or fully employed.
    Variables: UH = unemployment and hours; I = underemployment by income; M = underemployment by skill level (mismatch).

sponding to adequate employment. By considering those cells in Table 5.2, it is found that a full 96.5% of the labor force are located in the cells corresponding to these cell types and that only 3.5% of the labor force are located in the cells not corresponding to our scale types. By ignoring the adequately employed cell [i.e., the (3, 2, 2) cell], we see that a full 85.3% of the underemployed are found in the cells corresponding to the distinct underemployment types (see Table 5.2). At first sight, this seems to represent a remarkable degree of scalability in the observed table and seems to imply that we have indeed measured four truly distinct underemployment forms. However, a closer look reveals substantial departures of the observed data from the scale types corresponding to distinct underemployment forms.

Beneath Table 5.2, we also present various percentages of persons who are underemployed with respect to *only one* type of underemployment relative to all persons who are underemployed with respect to that same type of underemployment. We see that 60.3% of the unemployed are unemployed only, that 65.5% of the low-hours persons are hours only, that 66.9% of the low-income persons are low income only, and that a full 88.4% of the mismatched are mismatched only. Apparently, the mismatch form is distinct from the other types, since there is not a marked tendency for a mismatched worker to be simultaneously underemployed by the other kinds of underemployment considered in this study.[8] (But even for those workers experiencing mismatch, the occurrence of other kinds of underemployment is alarmingly high. We expect a priori that the most skilled workers in an occupation would have only negligible risk to the other forms.)

The joint occurrence of unemployment and low income especially, and of low hours and low income, seems to occur with a frequency that cannot be ignored. Of the unemployed persons, 34.3% also have low income; of the low-hours persons, 32.0% also have low income. The overlap of these three forms, when viewed in the above perspective, seems to suggest that possibly the income form is *not* distinct from the visible underemployment forms. This is not a consequence of the definitions at all, since the income form was measured with respect to the *entire previous year's* work experience, whereas the other forms were measured with respect to the *current week's* experience, and there is no necessary connection between the two. That is, there is no necessary relationship between low work-related income over the entire year (when this income is adjusted to reflect the

---

[8] Readers familiar with Guttman scalogram analysis will recognize the resemblance of this analysis to the calculation of error responses in the conventional scalogram. The reader should note that those who are mismatched—those who are ''overskilled''—have almost a 12% chance of being underemployed by time or income.

weeks worked in the past year) and temporary unemployment or part-time unemployment during the survey week in March. The joint occurrence of these three underemployment forms therefore casts doubt upon the distinctness of the income form of underemployment.

The other way to view the dichotomous income variable I is as an exact indicator of labor force marginality, where that marginality is determined on the basis of the past year's "average" experience. Table 5.3 shows the rates of unemployment, low hours, and mismatch for the two labor force types corresponding to the low-income part (or marginal labor force) and to the adequate-income part. The 9.4% of the labor force that is marginal with respect to income for the previous year had current unemployment rates almost *five* times that of the other part. The hours form was over *four* times as great in this low-income segment, and quite surprisingly, mismatch was only *slightly smaller* in the low-income segment. We have therefore located an *observable* marginal segment of the labor force that has very different rates of unemployment and part-time unemployment than an *observable* nonmarginal part. In addition, the work force making adequate income has levels of visible underemployment that are low enough to be frictional in character and need not indicate "structural" underemployment for this type at all. We are not aware of another single indicator of labor force marginality (e.g., age, race, sex, occupation, or industry), approximate in meaning to the concept of marginality, that does as well as the I variable in predicting the current risk to underemployment. In sum, these results show that it is unclear how to *measure* underemployment without taking into account the association among the underemployment types, particularly the association among the income form and the visible forms unemployment and low hours.

TABLE 5.3
Underemployment Risks in the Low-Income and the Adequate-Income Parts of the Labor Force

Type of underemployment	Low-income labor force		Adequate-income labor force	
	Number	Percent	Number	Percent
Unemployment	973	17.4	1867	3.5
Low hours	497	8.9	1057	2.0
Mismatch	507	9.1	5784	10.8
Total	5590	9.4	53783	90.6

Source: Table 5.2, this volume.

5.3 THE BASIC MODEL

We conceive of a labor force that is composed of six distinct "intrinsic types" or "latent classes" of individuals. For convenience, we label these as types 0, 1, . . . , 5. The zeroth type corresponds to labor force members who are "intrinsically unscalable" with respect to underemployment. For these persons, the underemployment forms are not distinct at all, and any possible combination of the underemployment forms may occur. Some persons in this intrinsic class will be found in every cell of the twelvefold cross-table represented in Table 5.2. For members of this class, however, the responses to variables UH, I, and M are assumed to be mutually independent, so that we can predict the pattern of underemployment solely upon the basis of knowledge concerning the *marginal* distributions of UH, I, and M for this class. The first through the fifth intrinsic types correspond to individuals who are intrinsically scalable with respect to the distinct scale types of underemployment. The first class corresponds to persons who are intrinsically unemployed, the second to persons who are intrinsically underemployed by low hours, the third to persons who are intrinsically underemployed by low income, the fourth to persons who are intrinsically mismatched, and the fifth to persons who are intrinsically adequately employed. For members of these intrinsic scale types, their response to the variables UH, I, and M will correspond to a distinct underemployment form with probability 1. For example, an intrinsically unemployed person, a member of the first latent class, will be observed as being unemployed with certainty and will not be observed in any other kind of scale type with certainty. An intrinsically scalable individual is one who is at 100% risk of the given *distinct* kind of underemployment. A person in the fifth latent class, corresponding to the intrinsically adequately employed, is observed as being adequately employed with certainty. That is, persons in this fifth ideal labor force type have zero risk of underemployment.

Using a model very similar to the above, Goodman (1975a) recently proposed new probabilistic models and statistical methods for the scaling of response patterns.[9] Most of the models to be used here derive from the class of models he developed in that fundamental work. They can be viewed, with certain exceptions, as special kinds of quasi-independence models for cross-classifications and also as certain special cases of the latent class model (Goodman, 1975a). For ease of exposition, we treat these models here within the latent class perspective, since that approach lends

---

[9] This new concept of scaling is different from that implied by Guttman scaling because it posits a *probabilistic* model underlying the observed response patterns.

itself most easily to substantive interpretation in the present context (see Section 5.1). The notation and structural parameters of our basic model will now be described.

Denote the population proportions in the twelvefold cross-classification of underemployment types as π_{ijk}, $i = 1, 2, 3$; $j = 1, 2$; $k = 1, 2$. Let π_0^X denote the proportion of the labor force that is intrinsically unscalable with respect to the underemployment variables *UH*, *I*, and *M*. Similarly, let π_1^X, π_2^X, π_3^X, π_4^X, π_5^X denote the proportions in the labor force who are intrinsically unemployed, intrinsically part-time unemployed, intrinsically underemployed by income, intrinsically mismatched, and intrinsically adequately employed, respectively. Now define $\pi_{it}^{\overline{UH}X}$ for $i = 1, 2, 3$, $t = 0$, $1, \ldots, 5$, to be the conditional probability that a member of the *t*th latent class is in the *i*th class of the *UH* variable. Let $\pi_{jt}^{\overline{I}X}$, $\pi_{kt}^{\overline{M}X}$, $j = 1, 2$; $k = 1, 2$; $t = 0, 1, \ldots, 5$ be defined accordingly. These parameters describe the risk to particular underemployment forms for members of the particular latent classes; they are merely "rates" of underemployment for members of the six latent classes. The model relates the population proportions π_{ijk} to the structural parameters by the following equation:

$$\pi_{ijk} = \sum_{t=0}^{5} \pi_t^X \, \pi_{it}^{\overline{UH}X} \, \pi_{jt}^{\overline{I}X} \, \pi_{kt}^{\overline{M}X} \tag{5.1}$$

Equation 5.1 says that (*a*) there are six mutually exclusive and exhaustive labor force types in the population, and (*b*) within each of these classes responses to *UH*, *I* and *M* are mutually independent. Restrictions on the parameters of the right-hand side of Equation 5.1 that are always imposed are

$$\sum_t \pi_t^X = \sum_i \pi_{it}^{\overline{UH}X} = \sum_j \pi_{jt}^{\overline{I}X} = \sum_k \pi_{kt}^{\overline{M}X} = 1$$

These are the usual restrictions that probabilities and conditional probabilities must sum to unity.[10] Equation 5.1 defines an unrestricted six-class latent structure model. Additional restrictions that take account of the distinct scale types corresponding to $(UH, I, M) = \{(1, 2, 2), (2, 2, 2), (3, 1, 2), (3, 2, 1), (3, 2, 2)\}$ are the following:[11]

---

[10] The computer program described in Appendix C guarantees that these restrictions are always satisfied and in addition, that the estimates of probabilities will always be in the proper range [0, 1]. See Goodman (1978).

[11] These are different scale types than are implied by, say, usual Guttman scaling. With four dichotomous variables indicating a single cumulative underlying scale, the cells (1, 1, 1, 1), (1, 1, 1, 2), (1, 1, 2, 2), (1, 2, 2, 2), (2, 2, 2, 2) are the scale types acceptable to a Guttman scale, and Guttman scalability is assessed by examining the conformity of observed re-

$$\pi_{11}^{\overline{UHX}} = 1; \pi_{1t}^{\overline{UHX}} = 0, \qquad t = 2, \ldots, 5 \qquad (5.2)$$

(intrinsically unemployed are observed as unemployed with certainty)

$$\pi_{22}^{\overline{UHX}} = 1; \pi_{2t}^{\overline{UHX}} = 0, \qquad t = 1,3,4,5$$

(intrinsically part-time unemployed are observed as part-time unemployed with certainty)

$$\pi_{13}^{\overline{IX}} = 1, \pi_{1t}^{\overline{IX}} = 0, \qquad t = 1,2,4,5$$

(intrinsically low income are observed as low income with certainty),

$$\pi_{14}^{\overline{MX}} = 1, \pi_{1t}^{\overline{MX}} = 0, \qquad t = 1,2,3,5$$

(intrinsically mismatched are observed as being mismatched with certainty), and

$$\pi_{35}^{\overline{UHX}} = \pi_{25}^{\overline{IX}} = \pi_{25}^{\overline{MX}} = 1$$

(intrinsically adequately employed are observed as being adequately employed with certainty).

From Equation 5.1, and by taking account of the restrictions of Equation 5.2, we see after straightforward algebraic manipulation that the proportions of the labor force in each *distinct* underemployment type are related to the structural parameters as follows:

$$\pi_{122} = \pi_1^X + \pi_0^X \pi_{10}^{\overline{UHX}} \pi_{20}^{\overline{IX}} \pi_{20}^{\overline{MX}} \qquad (5.3)$$

(unemployed only)

$$\pi_{222} = \pi_2^X + \pi_0^X \pi_{20}^{\overline{UHX}} \pi_{20}^{\overline{IX}} \pi_{20}^{\overline{MX}}$$

(hours only)

$$\pi_{312} = \pi_3^X + \pi_0^X \pi_{30}^{\overline{UHX}} \pi_{10}^{\overline{IX}} \pi_{20}^{\overline{MX}}$$

(income only)

$$\pi_{321} = \pi_4^X + \pi_0^X \pi_{30}^{\overline{UHX}} \pi_{20}^{\overline{IX}} \pi_{10}^{\overline{MX}}$$

(mismatch only)

$$\pi_{322} = \pi_5^X + \pi_0^X \pi_{30}^{\overline{UHX}} \pi_{20}^{\overline{IX}} \pi_{20}^{\overline{MX}}$$

(adequately employed)

---

sponses to these scale types. Obviously, that type of Guttman scale model is inappropriate in the present context. We here have a $3 \times 2 \times 2$ table, and the prior selection of "scale types" does not conform to the Guttman pattern. In addition, our model here is probabilistic; that is, it specifies an underlying probabilistic structure generating the observed pattern of responses, thereby accounting for "error responses."

The proportions observed in any other cell (i, j, k) in the twelvefold table are determined by

$$\pi_{ijk} = \pi_0^X \pi_{10}^{\overline{UH}X} \pi_{j0}^{IX} \pi_{k0}^{\overline{M}X} \qquad (5.4)$$

or are solely due to the random assignment of intrinsically unscalable individuals according to an assumption of independence among UH, I, and M. From Equation 5.3, we see that the proportions in the cells corresponding to the distinct types will overestimate the population proportions in the intrinsic scale types, since, for example, $\pi_{122} - \pi_1^X = \pi_0^X \pi_{10}^{\overline{UU}X} \pi_{20}^{IX} \pi_{20}^{\overline{M}X}$ is a positive quantity. The *observed* proportion in a distinct scale type (e.g., the type corresponding to unemployment only) is composed of a part arising from intrinsically unemployed individuals but also of a part that results from the random assignment of persons from the intrinsically unscalable class. In general, the observed proportion in the distinct scale types, estimated for Table 5.2 as .965, will therefore overestimate the true proportion of scalable respondents, given by our model as $1 - \pi_0^X$. The basic parameter π_0^X is therefore a summary index of the scalability of underemployment and provides us with a means of assessing the distinctness of the four underemployment forms. The parameters π_1^X, π_2^X, . . . , π_5^X also provide information concerning the distinctness of the respective underemployment forms. If $\hat{\pi}_i^X$, $i = 1, . . . , 5$, is found not significantly different from zero, we would be forced to conclude that the ith scale type is not distinct, since when π_i^X is zero, all the individuals who are observed in the corresponding cell type can be thought of as being drawn from an unscalable class where no distinct underemployment types exist at all. With the notation introduced above and with the meaning attaching to the structural parameters, we now see how this basic model provides very compelling answers indeed to the basic questions outlined in Section 5.1.

5.4 LATENT CLASS MODELS FOR THE 1970 DATA, INCLUDING PROBABILISTIC SCALE MODELS

A sequence of models, most of which are based upon the above general formulation of intrinsic labor force types and which are related to one another in ways that are meaningful in the present context, are now presented. A summary of some of the models actually tested, the goodness-of-fit, and the descriptive level of significance corresponding to each model are presented in Table 5.4.[12]

---

[12] All of the latent class models of this chapter were tested with a computer program adapted by the writer partly for this purpose. This program, denoted as MLLSA (Maximum

TABLE 5.4
Chi-square Values for Some Latent Class Models Applied to the 1970 Data, Including Scale Models for Underemployment

Hypothesis	Likelihood-ratio χ^2, L^2	Goodness-of-fit χ^2	Degrees of freedom, df	P-value of L^2
H_0	2233.05	3274.92	7	.000
$H_1 (=H_2)$	1.01	1.00	3	$> .5$
$H_3 (=H_4)$	10.28	10.01	5	.072
$H_4	H_2$	9.27		2	.010
H_5	1853.44	2119.02	6	.000
H_6	1.26	1.25	4	$> .5$
H_7	1442.60	1451.33	5	.000
H_8	3978.01	4183.81	6	.000
H_9	2218.27	3260.16	3	.000
$H_{10} (=H_{11})$	5.50	5.45	3	.153
H_{12}	6.77	6.67	4	.242
$H_{13} (=H_4)$	10.28	10.01	5	.072
H_{14}	36.75	33.11	4	.000

Consider first the hypothesis that all individuals are intrinsically unscalable and that consequently it would be unjustified to speak of distinct underemployment types at all. That is, $\pi_0^X = 1$ and $\pi_t^X = 0$ for $t = 1, \ldots,$ 5. Such a circumstance would be the case if there were no latent class structure to the distribution of labor market rewards, and if this were true, it would be appropriate to view the labor force as an homogeneous aggregate. In order to predict the pattern of multiple underemployment, we assume that for members of this intrinsically unscalable class (i.e., for all individuals), the responses to UH, I, and M are mutually independent. This hypothesis is actually equivalent to the independence hypothesis for the complete cross-table in Table 5.2. Under this hypothesis, we find a likelihood-ratio χ^2 (L^2) of 2233.05 and a Pearson goodness-of-fit χ^2 (X^2) of 3274.92, each of which would be distributed as a χ^2 variate on 7 df if the model H_0 were true. These data obviously contradict this simple hypothesis, as informal inspection of the data has indicated earlier. A model of labor force "monism" is simply not congruent with these data.

Likelihood Latent Structure Analysis), is able to estimate general latent class models with polytomous observed variables. Other latent class programs described in Lazarsfeld and Henry (1968) are inappropriate for these models and are inferior to the maximum likelihood methods presented in Goodman (1974a) or in Haberman (1974). The table analyzed here is a $3 \times 2 \times 2$ table, necessitating the use of this modified program. See Appendix C for a description of that program and some additional comments.

Model H_1 is the full-scale model discussed in the previous section, with all the restrictions of (5.2) imposed. After many iterations with the latent structure program, we find that $\hat{\pi}_3^X$, the proportion intrinsically underemployed by income, is approaching zero.[13] Model H_1 modified such that π_3^X = 0 is the next model to be discussed, model H_2.[14]

Model H_2 says that H_1 is true and that the proportion intrinsically underemployed by low income is zero. Thus, model H_2 would say that the income form of underemployment is not distinct, since there are not "intrinsic" types of workers in a distinct low-income form. For this hypothesis, we find L^2 = 1.01 and X^2 = 1.00 on 3 df. This model contains four additional parameters over H_0, and we see that inclusion of these parameters produces a dramatic improvement in goodness-of-fit. In fact, using $X^2(H_0)$ as a measure of variation in the data, we see that H_2 accounts for 99.99% of that variation, and this with only four additional parameters over H_0. This is all the more dramatic given the extremely large sample size, N = 59,373. Contrary to expectations, and contrary to the literature that dictated the need to consider a *distinct* income form of underemployment, we find that in terms of a relatively simple model, it is not necessary at all to posit an income form distinct from the others. Model H_2 says that the income form is so intertwined with the usual visible underemployment forms that we can not isolate them from each other. For purposes of illustration, the observed and expected frequencies under H_2 are presented in Table 5.5. Clearly all possible combinations of the underemployment types are predicted well by the model; a simple and parsimonious explanation of the pattern of multiple underemployment has been obtained.

Estimates of the structural parameters from H_2, including the risk parameters, are particularly illuminating and will provide one basis for characterizing the labor force according to the perspectives set forth in Section 5.1. These estimates are presented in Table 5.6. From Table 5.6, we see that whereas the observed proportion of scalable persons estimated directly from Table 5.2 was .965, the *intrinsically scalable* proportion is estimated by our model as .748 (1 − $\hat{\pi}_0^X$ or 1 − .252). The joint occurrence of unemployment and low income and of low hours and low income is chiefly responsible for this substantial difference. We also see the very low proportions intrinsically unemployed and intrinsically low hours ($\hat{\pi}_1^X$ = $\hat{\pi}_2^X$ = .004). And we see the relatively large proportion intrinsically mismatched ($\hat{\pi}_4^X$ = .083); at least the mismatch form seems to emerge as a distinct one in this analysis. Of similar interest is the estimate

---

[13] It is actually zero to three decimal places.
[14] H_2 can be described as the condition where H_1 is true *and* π_3^X is zero.

TABLE 5.5
Observed and Expected Frequencies and Standardized Residuals for Modified Scale
Model H_2

UH-I-M	Meaning	Observed	Expected	Standardized residual
1 1 1		83	88.72	−.61
2 1 1		46	44.64	.20
3 1 1		378	373.75	.22
1 2 1		154	148.95	.41
2 2 1		70	74.94	−.57
3 2 1[a]	Mismatch only	5560	5559.99	.00
1 1 2		890	889.27	.02
2 1 2		451	447.41	.17
3 1 2[a]	Income only	3742	3746.21	−.07
1 2 2[a]	Unemployed only	1713	1713.06	.00
2 2 2[a]	Hours only	987	987.01	.00
3 2 2[a]	Adequately employed	45299	45299.04	.00

[a]Denotes cells that should be fitted perfectly by H_2. Additional iterations would have made observed and expected frequencies identically equal for these cells.

of the proportion of the labor force intrinsically adequately utilized, given by our model as .657. That is, within the context of this probabilistic model of the labor force, we can think of 65.7% of the labor force as being at zero risk of underemployment. The observed proportion in the adequately utilized scale type was .761 (obtained from Table 5.2), and the difference between .761 and $\hat{\pi}_5^X = .657$ is due to the random assignment of persons in the intrinsically unscalable (or zeroth) latent class. We will now see that this intrinsically unscalable part of the labor force that we have indirectly observed in these data is a very special part of the labor force, one that is, on the whole, very marginal with respect to the risk of being adequately employed.

Table 5.6 also presents the conditional probabilities (e.g., $\hat{\pi}_{10}^{\overline{UH}X}$) pertaining to the marginal distributions of UH, I, and M within the unscalable class, and these enable us to infer the special underemployment structure of this intrinsically unscalable class. Since the income form did not emerge as a distinct underemployment form, this unscalable class contains all persons whose work-related income for the past year placed them below the poverty level. That is, all persons who are marginal with respect to the income indicator are included in this class, and they in fact constitute 37.3% of this class as a whole (since $\hat{\pi}_{10}^{\overline{I}X} = .373$). This part is also at very high risk of unemployment ($\hat{\pi}_{10}^{\overline{UH}X} = .175$), at very high risk of part-time unemployment ($\hat{\pi}_{20}^{\overline{UH}X} = .088$), and at high risk of mismatch ($\hat{\pi}_{10}^{\overline{M}X} = $

TABLE 5.6
Parameter Estimates for Scale Model H_2 Applied to March 1970 United States Labor Force

Scale type	Meaning	Observed[a]	Expected under H_2
	A. Proportions in the scale types		
0	Unscalable	.035	$.252 = \hat{\pi}_0^X$
1	Unemployed	.029	$.004 = \hat{\pi}_1^X$
2	Hours	.017	$.004 = \hat{\pi}_2^X$
3	Income	.063	$.000 = \hat{\pi}_3^X = \pi_3^X$
4	Mismatch	.094	$.083 \tilde{n} \hat{\pi}_4^X$
5	Adequate	.761	$.657 = \hat{\pi}_5^X$

B. Risk characteristics of the "intrinsically unscalable"

$\hat{\pi}_{10}^{\overline{UHX}} = .175$ (17.5% of the "intrinsically unscalable" are unemployed)

$\hat{\pi}_{20}^{\overline{UHX}} = .088$ (8.8% of the "intrinsically unscalable" are underemployed) by hours)

$\hat{\pi}_{30}^{\overline{UHX}} = .737$

$\hat{\pi}_{10}^{\overline{IX}} = .373$ (37.3% of the "intrinsically unscalable" are underemployed by income)

$\hat{\pi}_{20}^{\overline{IX}} = .627$

$\hat{\pi}_{10}^{\overline{MX}} = .091$ (9.1% of the "intrinsically unscalable" are mismatched)

$\hat{\pi}_{20}^{\overline{MX}} = .909$

[a]Observed proportions in the scale types obtained directly from Table 5.2, this volume.

.091). By comparing these rates with the ones presented earlier in Table 5.3 pertaining to the underemployment rates for the low-income segment of the labor force, we see that the rates are virtually identical for the two groups (i.e., for the *unobservable* intrinsically unscalable class of model H_2 and for the *observed* low-income class). The unscalable class is not so unobservable as might be first imagined, since besides containing all persons whom we observe in the low-income status, it also contains other persons who also have rates of underemployment like those in the observable low-income status.

A further characterization of the intrinsically unscalable part of the labor force is contained in Table 5.7, where the risks to underemployment of that part are compared with the *apparent* risks to underemployment in the total aggregate labor force. Since 37.3% of the intrinsically unscalable are marginal with respect to income, 37.3% of the underemployment rates for the intrinsically unscalable labor force type are due precisely to persons who are low income. Thus, while the intrinsically unscalable part is not completely homogeneous with respect to income (since 62.7% have adequate income), and we know that some skilled workers are contained in this class (since mismatch can only occur to skilled workers), it is nevertheless a fairly homogeneous subpopulation, since all persons in this class are at very high risk to underemployment and, in fact, contribute excessively to the apparent rates that we observe for the aggregate labor force. Further evidence for the *marginality* of this class is obtained by noting that only 41.9% of the class will be expected to be adequately employed. In view of the above characterization of this intrinsically unscalable class, it seems warranted to assume that this class is composed of the marginal labor force spoken of in dual labor market theory. We see that this class is *larger* than the low-income class alone, implying that to locate the true marginal labor force type of dual labor market theory we must look beyond the low-income segment alone in order to explain the observed pattern of underemployment.

The model H_2 just described has brought into joint play many of the

TABLE 5.7
A Characterization of the "Intrinsically Unscalable" Labor Force (in Percentages)

Labor force characteristic	Risk for the "intrinsically unscalable"	Risk in the aggregate labor force[a]
Unemployed	17.5	4.8
Low hours	8.8	2.6
Low income	37.3	9.4
Mismatch	9.1	10.6
Adequate	41.9[b]	76.1
Percentage of total labor force	25.2	100.0

[a]Obtained directly from Table 5.2, this volume. Rows 1 to 5 do not sum to 100.0 because in the aggregate labor force, multiple underemployment is possible, that is, the categories are not mutually exclusive.

[b]The quantity 41.9 is obtained from the independence assumption. This figure was calculated to more significant digits than are reported in this table.

guiding research questions with which this chapter began. We can think of the labor force as being composed of five intrinsic types. The first includes those who are at very high risk of underemployment but has underemployment patterns that do not produce distinct underemployment forms. The joint occurrence of any kind of underemployment for this type can be predicted solely on the basis of the marginal distributions of UH, I, and M within this class. Two types are at perfect risk of visible underemployment. Another type corresponded to persons intrinsically mismatched, and another part, 65.7% of the total labor force, can be thought of as being at zero risk to underemployment. Since we have found unemployment, hours, and the income forms to be confounded with one another, one additional inference to make is that the same set of causal factors influencing one of these types influences the others as well, since most observed underemployment of this kind may be thought of as being drawn from a fairly homogeneous subpopulation. Also, we have gone a long way toward characterizing the marginal class—denoted here as the unscalable class—of dual labor market theory. In order to validate the compelling statistical results corresponding to model H_2 and to bring additional insight into the parameters of H_2, a series of other models is now considered.

In the set of parameters for H_2, we note that the estimate for π_2^X is close to zero. By deleting the intrinsic low-hours category, we arrive at model H_3. In estimating this model, however, we find that the estimate $\hat{\pi}_1^X$ of the proportion intrinsically unemployed also approaches zero. Consideration of the model H_3 then forces us to consider an additional model (model H_4) in which the intrinsic income, the intrinsic hours, and the intrinsic unemployment proportions are nil. We note that H_3 and H_4 are approximately equal to each other as H_1 and H_2 were approximately equal to each other.[15]

Model H_4 with only three latent labor force types is simpler than H_1, H_2, or H_3 and yields an L^2 of 10.28 on 5 df of freedom. This is also an acceptable fit to these data and indicates that *all* the underemployed by hours, income, and unemployment can be thought of as being drawn from a single class. This does not say that unemployment, low hours, or low income cannot be regarded as distinct scale types, but instead it gives us additional understanding of the confounding of the income form with the other two. Actually, by definition, we know that unemployment and low

---

[15] Because the next model to be considered (H_4) assumes that the second and third latent classes are nil, whereas H_3 assumes only that the third latent class is nil, and because when estimating H_3 we found that the proportion in the second latent class was nil, H_3 and H_4 are approximately equal.

hours are distinct from each other and are evidently distinct from the mismatch form. However, the hypothesis that π_1^X and π_2^X are jointly zero is questionable, since $L^2(H_4) - L^2(H_2) = 9.27$ on 2 df. For this reason we sometimes prefer to maintain the detail of model H_2, even though it is not as parsimonious as H_4.

Model H_5 tests the necessity of including an intrinsic mismatch category, that is, it tests the distinctness of the mismatch form. When deleting the intrinsic mismatch category (i.e., setting $\pi_4^X = 0$), we find that the estimates of π_1^X, π_2^X are also approaching zero, so, strictly speaking, we cannot test this modification of H_2 without imposing further restrictions on the parameters. As an expedient, π_1^X and π_2^X were constrained to equal the respective values obtained as final estimates in H_2, producing model H_5, and this expedient allows us to assess the approximate contribution of the intrinsic mismatch class. With these restrictions imposed, we find an L^2 of 1853.44, which is striking evidence of the distinctness of the mismatch form.

In order to examine in more detail the special structure of the intrinsically unscalable part of the labor force, itself accounting for most of the observed underemployment excepting mismatch, several other hypotheses were entertained. Model H_6 imposes on H_2 the additional restriction that hours and mismatch are equally likely for the unscalable class, and with an $L^2(H_6)$ of 1.26, we see that these data support this hypothesis. Model H_7 says that H_6 is true and that, in addition, unemployment and income are equally likely. $L^2(H_7)$ is 1442.60 on 5 df, giving us a clue to the statistical differences in the unemployment and low income risks in this class. Model H_8 says that within the unscalable class, all underemployment forms are equally likely, and with an $L^2(H_8)$ of 3978.01, we are also given further insight into the very special structure of the intrinsically unscalable class.[16] These models are presented by way of illustration; they show, among other things, that the very high risk to the low-income form in this very marginal segment of the labor force is a characteristic critical to defining this class.

Dual labor market theory posited the existence of only *two* ideal labor force types, whereas model H_2 contained five ideal types and model H_4 contained three ideal types. If we consider the manifest responses to UH, I, and M as being the result of the indirect observation of characteristics of the *two* latent types of dual labor market theory, then this suggests fitting an unrestricted two-class latent structure to these data rather than the

---

[16] At first sight, this value of L^2 seems disconcerting, since the L^2 for the "baseline" model H_0 is *less* than $L^2(H_8)$. H_0 does not imply this particular kind of restricted latent structure, so it is not impossible to have such a result.

probabilistic scale models proposed earlier. (We will show later that the *five-class* model H_2 and the *three-class* model H_4 may also be given *two-class* interpretations, and so these models will also allow us to characterize the *dual* labor force.)

The unrestricted two-class latent structure (model H_{10}) was also fit to the 1970 data, but unfortunately, we find that $\hat{\pi}_{11}^{\overline{UH}X} = 0$ for this model. (As before, we let class $X = 1$ refer to the *second* latent class.) The restricted two-class model (restricted so that $\pi_{11}^{\overline{UH}X} = 0$) is denoted as H_{11}, and the two models yield identical parameter estimates and expected frequencies. We assign 3 *df* to both these models, although that number would only be appropriate for the restricted model. We see that $L^2(H_{11})[=L^2(H_{10})]$ is 5.50, which is also a very good fit for these data. Thus, only two latent classes, corresponding to the ideal types of dual labor market theory, are necessary to explain the pattern of underemployment. With such a large sample size, such a fit is, of course, quite compelling. This is a remarkable validation of the classical theory based upon a statistical method (latent structure analysis) that easily lends itself to testing that classical theory.

That the reader may see how marginal is the marginal labor force type and how nonmarginal is the nonmarginal labor type, the parameter estimates (expressed in percentages) corresponding to H_{11} are presented in Table 5.8. Under the truth of this model, 20.2% of the labor force can be thought of as being marginal, and 79.8% can be regarded as nonmarginal. We see, for example, that the unemployment rate is 23.6% in the marginal type, that the rate of low income is 34.0%, and that it is only expected that 38.9% of the marginal labor force type will be adequately employed. In the nonmarginal type the rates of visible underemployment and low in-

TABLE 5.8
Underemployment Risks for the Marginal and the Nonmarginal Latent Labor Force Classes under Two-Class Unrestricted Model H_{10} or Two-Class Restricted Model H_{11} (in Percentages)[a]

Type of underemployment	The risk to underemployment for each class	
	Marginal class	Non-marginal class
Unemployment	23.6	.0
Low hours	12.3	.2
Low income	34.0	3.2
Mismatch	8.0	11.2
Adequate employment	38.9	88.8
Percentage of labor force in class	20.2	79.8

[a]Likelihood-ratio χ^2 = 5.50, and goodness-of-fit χ^2 = 5.45.

TABLE 5.9
Assignment of Respondents into Latent Labor Force Classes, Based upon Restricted
Two-Class Model $H_{11}{}^a$

Underemployment pattern UH-I-M	Assign to latent class[b]	Modal P^c	Rank	Error rate ϵ $(= 1 - P)$
1 1 1	0	1.00	1	.00
2 1 1	0	.99	2	.01
3 1 1	0	.55	6	.45
1 2 1	0	1.00	1	.00
2 2 1	0	.90	4	.10
3 2 1	1	.93	_d	.07
1 1 2	0	1.00	1	.00
2 1 2	0	1.00	1	.00
3 1 2	0	.64	5	.36
1 2 2	0	1.00	1	.00
2 2 2	0	.93	3	.07
3 2 2	1	.90	_d	.10

[a]Percent of workers correctly assigned = 88.78, and λ = .45. The λ is a measure of association between the latent variable X and the manifest joint variable $UHIM$. It is an additional measure of modal adequacy, being a proportional-reduction-in-error measure showing how well the classes of X can be predicted from the observed responses.
[b]Latent class 0 = marginal class; latent class 1 = nonmarginal class.
[c]This is the modal conditional probability of the tth latent class given the observed response (i,j,k). The "error rate" for any observed response pattern is $\epsilon = 1 - P$.
[d]This response pattern pertains to the nonmarginal type and so is not ranked.

come are low enough to be frictional in character, and, as we might expect, the rate of mismatch is quite high (11.3%). We see that a full 88.8% of the nonmarginal type is expected to be adequately employed. These are indeed quite revealing estimates of the dualistic structure of the labor force.

For purposes of inferring the latent labor force class in which a worker with a given pattern of underemployment is most likely to be in, Table 5.9 is presented. Table 5.9 assigns workers into the latent classes based upon observed labor force characteristics. We see that persons who are mismatched only [where $(UH, I, M) = (3, 2, 1)$] and the adequately employed [where $(UH, I, M) = (3, 2, 2)$] would be predicted as being in the nonmarginal class and that all others would be predicted as being members of a marginal class. The error in prediction would be greatest for the combination where $(UH, I, M) = (3, 1, 1)$, with an error rate of .45, and for the combination where $(UH, I, M) = (3, 1, 2)$, with an error rate of .36. We would make the most errors in predicting the latent class of the worker, then, for persons who have low income only or for persons who have both low income and mismatch. We might use the error rates ϵ (or their complement $1 - \epsilon$) to rank the underemployment combinations in terms of severity, since they show us the relative likelihood of a person in a given response pattern being in the marginal labor force class, and this marginal labor force class is presumably a subpopulation characterized by severe socioeconomic conditions. This ranking is also contained in Table 5.9, and it might be used to construct an ordinal-level (or possibly an interval-level) underemployment scale. For the ranking of underemployment combinations corresponding to the marginal latent type, we see that the ranking in terms of ability to predict marginality is, in fact, much in accord with the ordering in terms of "severity" that Hauser used to infer the five-class underemployment indicator. We see also that latent class membership can be predicted moderately well with knowledge of the response patterns since, for example, 88.8% would be "correctly assigned" to the latent classes.

The results of H_{11} (or H_{10}) lend themselves to representation in a path diagram. Following procedures developed by Goodman (1974b) in the latent class context and taking into account the special meaning of the UH variable, we can calculate path coefficients appropriate to the X–U, X–H, X–I, and X–M effects in a model in which the observed variables are thought to be indicators of (or thought to be "caused" by) the latent variable X. The corresponding path diagram is presented in Figure 5.1, with the additive effects drawn in on the respective arrows. We see that the X–U path is infinity (since all unemployed persons are in the marginal latent type) and that the U–H path is negative infinity (since unemployment and part-time unemployment cannot occur together, i.e., they are perfectly negatively associated). The other paths show a descending order of effect as we proceed from the X–U, X–H, X–I, to the X–M paths, and we might also use these relative magnitudes to infer the order of severity and the *distance* among the four respective underemployment forms. We see that unemployment and hours are *apparently* very far apart (infinity relative to 2.20), that low hours and low income are close together (2.20 and 1.39), and that mismatch is very distant from the others (the X–M path is $-.19$). Beneath the path diagram we also present (*a*) multiplicative effects, which enable assessment of effects on a geometric scale, and (*b*) normed effects with range $[-1, +1]$, which show the effects on a scale that is somewhat easier to interpret. These normed effects are analogous to the familiar Yule's Q measure of association (see, e.g., Yule, 1912; Reynolds, 1977), and their use is justified by comments contained in Appendix E. The normed effects also show mismatch to be a form that is very distant (i.e., very distinct) from the other three forms. Figure 5.1 and the struc-

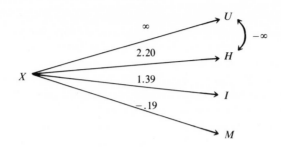

Path	Multiplicative effect	Additive effect	Normed effect
X-U	∞	∞	1.00
X-H	9.0626	2.2042	.9759
X-I	3.9686	1.3784	.8806
X-M	.8288	$-.1878$	$-.1856$

Figure 5.1. Path model showing the relationship between the latent variable X and the observed variables UH, I, and M (two-class model H_{11}). Normed effects are analogous to Yule's Q for the 2 × 2 table. See Appendix E for the justification for these normed effects and some further comments.

tural parameters therein may be regarded as a model of the labor force, showing the structural relationships between the latent variable X denoting labor force marginality and the observed indicators of underemployment.

In the two-class model H_{11} (or H_{10}), the conditional distribution of the observed variables within each latent class was one of independence. Strictly speaking, since $\pi_{11}^{\overline{IH}X} = 0$ in H_{11}, the responses to H, I, and M are mutually independent for the nonmarginal (i.e., the second) latent class. In the nonmarginal type (as well as for the marginal type), any combination of responses to H, I, and M can occur. We see from Table 5.8 that $\hat{\pi}_{21}^{\overline{IH}X}$ is close to zero, and so it is natural to test whether the low-hours form can be regarded as nil for the nonmarginal latent type. The hypothesis testing this assumption is H_{12}, and with an $L^2(H_{12})$ of 6.77, we see that we cannot reject this hypothesis, that is, we can regard all observed unemployment and part-time unemployment as having been drawn from the marginal class of the labor force. Under H_{12}, however, the relationship between I and M is still one of independence for the nonmarginal labor force type.

Hypothesis H_{13} imposes the restriction $\pi_{11}^{\overline{I}X} = 0$, that is, it tests the plausibility of the assumption that all the low-income persons can be regarded as belonging to the latent marginal class. We see that with an $L^2(H_{13})$ of 10.28 on 5 df, we would not be seriously misled by assuming that all persons experiencing the low-income form are drawn from the latent marginal type.

Model H_{13} is apparently a two-class restricted model where the relationship among UH, I, and M is one of independence in each latent type and where certain constraints *restrict* the independence relationship in the nonmarginal latent type. In view of the basic equations for the latent structure model, we see that the observed response patterns corresponding to mismatch only and to adequate employment can be denoted as

$$\pi_{321} = \pi_0^X \pi_{30}^{\overline{UHX}} \pi_{20}^{\overline{IX}} \pi_{10}^{\overline{MX}} + \pi_1^X \pi_{11}^{\overline{MX}}$$

and

$$\pi_{322} = \pi_0^X \pi_{30}^{\overline{UHX}} \pi_{20}^{\overline{IX}} \pi_{20}^{\overline{MX}} + \pi_1^X \pi_{21}^{\overline{MX}}$$

This shows that under H_{13}, the proportion in each of these two cells is partly a result of the random assignment of persons in the marginal labor force type (namely $\pi_0^X \pi_{30}^{\overline{UHX}} \pi_{20}^{\overline{IX}} \pi_{10}^{\overline{MX}}$) and is partly a result of the "random" assignment of persons in the nonmarginal labor force type (namely $\pi_1^X \pi_{11}^{\overline{MX}}$). By letting $\tilde{\pi}_1^X = \pi_1^X \pi_{11}^{\overline{MX}}$ and $\tilde{\pi}_2^X = \pi_1^X \pi_{21}^{\overline{MX}}$, we see that these same equations can be rewritten as

$$\pi_{321} = \pi_0^X \pi_{30}^{\overline{UHX}} \pi_{20}^{\overline{IX}} \pi_{10}^{\overline{MX}} + \tilde{\pi}_1^X$$

and

$$\pi_{322} = \pi_0^X \pi_{30}^{\overline{UHX}} \pi_{20}^{\overline{IX}} \pi_{20}^{\overline{MX}} + \tilde{\pi}_2^X$$

and these are seen to correspond identically to a special case of the probabilistic scale models proposed in Section 5.3. The quantity $\tilde{\pi}_1^X$ can be regarded as the proportion who *intrinsically* belong in the (3, 2, 1) scale type, and $\tilde{\pi}_2^X$ may be regarded as the proportion who *intrinsically* belong in the (3, 2, 2) scale type. This model was considered from the scaling point of view earlier as model H_4, and this shows why the two models H_4 and H_{13} are equivalent to each other. That particular kind of scale model used earlier (H_4) is actually a kind of two-class model (H_{13}), and this two-class model *appears* more isomorphic with the dual labor market theory. The scaling interpretation posited *certainty* for *two* types of individuals and *uncertainty* for only *one* type of individual, whereas the usual latent class interpretation posits *uncertainty* for *two* types of individuals. We see here then that the *three-class* model H_4 used earlier in the scaling context can be regarded as a *two-class* model, with the above interpretation.

We now show how the corresponding scale model H_2 with *five* latent classes can also be regarded as a special kind of two-class model and so will have more direct bearing upon the dual labor market theory. We recall that the five-class model was a modification of a six-class model, with one class (the zeroth class) pertaining to unscalable individuals and with the other five classes pertaining to scalable individuals. In this model the underlying mechanism X divides the labor force into an unscalable part, in which any underemployment combination can occur but in which the relationship among the underemployment indicators was one of independence, and a *single* scalable part, in which the underemployment types cannot occur together. Define $\tilde{\pi}_1^X = 1 - \pi_0^X$ as the proportion "scalable." The quantities $\pi_i^X/\tilde{\pi}_1^X$, $i = 1, \ldots, 5$ can be regarded as the *conditional* probability of the ith underemployment form in a *single* scalable class, since

$$\sum_{i=1}^{5} \pi_i^X/\tilde{\pi}_1^X = 1$$

For example, the quantity $\pi_1^X/\tilde{\pi}_1^X$ can be regarded as the rate of unemployment in the scalable part and so forth. For this scalable part, the underemployment forms cannot occur together, and so for the scalable part (composing a proportion $\tilde{\pi}_1^X$ of the total labor force) the responses to the underemployment indicators UH, I, and M are *conditionally quasi-independent*. This kind of two-class interpretation of the probabilistic scale models used earlier is therefore very much similar to the two-class interpretation of models H_{10} through H_{13}, where *conditional independence* among the variables in the scalable class is replaced by *conditional quasi-independence* in the scalable class. We see from $L^2(H_2)$ of 1.01 presented earlier that this conditional quasi-independence hypothesis is a better fit than $H_{10}(=H_{11})$, and it is somewhat more simple, since in the scalable class we have not found it necessary to permit *multiple* underemployment of any kind. This different interpretation of the scale model is brought out in Table 5.10.

We see in Table 5.10 that the unscalable part corresponds to the latent marginal class and that the single scalable part corresponds to the latent nonmarginal class of dual labor market theory. If we interpret the scalable part as the nonmarginal class, then the restriction that multiple underemployment cannot occur at all for this type is not unrealistic. (Perhaps in the nonmarginal class underemployment is so transitory or frictional that only one form can occur at a given time.) We see from Table 5.10 that for the 25.2% of the labor force in the marginal part, it is expected that only 41.9% will be adequately employed, but for the 74.8% of the labor force in the nonmarginal (i.e., scalable) part, a full 87.8% are expected to be adequately employed. It should be noted that H_2 says that 25.2% of the labor force can be regarded as marginal, whereas H_{11}, discussed earlier,

TABLE 5.10
Two-Class Interpretation of Five-Class Scale Model H_2: Underemployment Risks for the
Marginal and the Nonmarginal Latent Labor Force Classes (in Percentages)

Type of underemployment	Risks for the marginal class	Risks for the nonmarginal class[a]
Unemployment	17.5	.5
Low hours	8.8	.5
Low income	37.5	.0
Mismatch	9.1	11.1
Adequate employment ·	41.9	87.8
Percent of labor force in class	25.2	74.8

[a]The underemployment forms are *quasi-independent* in the nonmarginal class. Multiple underemployment is impossible for this class.

said that 20.2% of the labor force can be regarded as marginal. The substantial difference results from the fact that with H_2, *all* the persons experiencing the low-income form are included in the marginal part, whereas this was not the case in the alternative model H_{11}. It seems plausible to consider H_2 as the more tenable model, owing to the special meaning that attaches to the income indicator of this study. Since the *observed* income measure pertained to *observed* income adequacy based upon an entire year's experience, it is plausible to regard persons in the low-income status (as well as some others) as being entirely in the marginal part of the labor force.

The introduction of Goodman's probabilistic scale model and the general latent structure perspective has, for the 1970 data, brought insight into the problem of inferring structure to the underemployment forms. We showed that it was tenable to assume that distinct underemployment forms corresponding to unemployment, hours, and mismatch existed but that it is not tenable to speak of a *distinct* income form of underemployment. The low-income form was so confounded with the visible forms that a simple model without an intrinsic low-income type could explain the occurrence or nonoccurrence of the income form. For a large part of the labor force, some 20–25% of the total, we have shown that the various underemployment combinations could be the result of a random mechanism that generates the various underemployment combinations solely on the basis of certain marginal distributions exogenously determined. This part of the labor force is characterized by being at extremely high risk of all the underemployment forms, and most of the observed underemployment (excepting mismatch) could be thought of as being the result of the underemployment structure of this very marginal labor force type. The complementary 75–80% of the labor force has adequate income and has rates of underemployment (excepting mismatch) that are low enough to be frictional in character. The labor force can then be regarded as being composed of two latent types, each of which are at *very different* characteristic levels of risk to the various underemployment forms. Across-time comparisons of these structural models are also illuminating, since new indicators of underemployment emerge from them. Before turning to across-time comparisons, we consider some other models for the 1970 data that will add further meaning to the ones presented above and that will further corroborate the preceding results.

5.5 OTHER MODELS FOR THE 1970 DATA

One conception of dual labor force theory is that labor force marginality could be indicated exactly by an income measure (see Bluestone *et al.*, 1973). Taking account of the special meaning that attaches to the dichotomous income measure of this study (i.e., variable I dichotomizes the labor force into a low-income and an adequate-income part based upon an average of the past year's experience), we can test the adequacy of this conception of labor force marginality. By enforcing restrictions on the latent class model such that the "latent variable" X *exactly* indicates the observed variable I, this kind of hypothesis can be tested. The model with this restriction if H_{14}, and we see that with $L^2(H_{14})$ of 36.75 on 4 *df*, this model—although doing admirably well for such a large sample size—does not do as well as the previous models that did not make this assumption. We conclude that income marginality alone is *not* sufficient to indicate the ideal types of dual labor market theory and, at the same time, account for the pattern of multiple underemployment.[17]

Proctor (1970) introduced a scaling model that could also be meaningful in the present context. His model is a special case of the latent class model, and when that model is appropriately modified for the $3 \times 2 \times 2$ cross-table here, it can also be tested with the latent class program used above. Proctor's model is equivalent to the full-scale model H_1 introduced earlier, with *all* individuals intrinsically scalable and certain additional modifications on the conditional probabilities. Instead of assuming that a

---

[17] This model is equivalent to the hierarchical hypothesis fitting marginals (UHI) and (MI), which is interpreted that UH and M are mutually independent, given the levels of I. Since $I = X$ in this context, this model is therefore equivalent to the two-class latent structure with the necessary restrictions imposed.

member of an intrinsic scale type is observed in that scale type with certainty, Proctor's model assumes that uncertainty exists but that this uncertainty is the same for any intrinsic type of individual. In the present context, Proctor's model would hypothesize a labor force composed of distinct types, each of which are at high risk (but not perfect risk) of a distinct underemployment form, and the risk to any particular underemployment form is the same as for any other.[18] Proctor's model is designated as H_9, and we see that with an $L^2(H_9)$ of 2218.27, his model is simply not tenable for these data. Various modifications of Proctor's model could have also been tested, but they were not, because the substantive interpretation of Proctor's model does not appear as compelling in the present context as Goodman's probabilistic scale models. Goodman's models allowed us to say that certain types of individuals are at *perfect risk* to particular underemployment forms, which is a more parsimonious interpretation of the labor force (since it postulates *un*certainty with respect to only a small part of the labor force), and his models fit our data.

Various hierarchical log-linear models were also applied to the 1970 data. These results, along with the margins fit under the respective models, are presented in Table 5.11. These models do not, on the whole, fit these data as well as do the latent class models H_1, H_2, H_3, H_4, H_6, H_{10}, H_{11}, H_{12}, and H_{13}, and the best-fitting model (M_2) is not as parsimonious as many of those latent class models. More importantly, the substantive interpretation of some of those models is difficult to assess from the point of view of this chapter. Model M_6, however, does show the extreme dependence of UH and I, since the UH–I interaction alone accounts for $[L^2(M_0) - L^2(M_6)]/L^2(M_0) = 97.6\%$ of the variation in these data. Model M_6 shows directly the confounding of visible underemployment and low

---

[18] Proctor's model modified for the present circumstance is equivalent to a five-class latent structure with the following restrictions:

$$\pi_{11}^{\overline{U}HX} = \pi_{22}^{\overline{U}HX} = \pi_{13}^{\overline{I}X} = \pi_{14}^{\overline{M}X} = \pi_{35}^{\overline{U}HX} = \pi_{25}^{\overline{I}X} = \pi_{25}^{\overline{M}X} = \pi; \pi_{21}^{\overline{U}HX} = \pi_{12}^{\overline{U}HX} = 0.$$

The parameters $\pi_{it}^{\overline{U}HX}$, $i = 1, 2; t = 3, 4, 5$ were left unrestricted in H_9. It may be more appropriate to constrain $\hat{\pi}_{1t}^{\overline{U}HX} = \hat{\pi}_{2t}^{\overline{U}HX}$, $t = 3, 4, 5$ in the present context. The latent class program used in this chapter can also deal with this latter kind of restriction. The rescaling of relevant conditional probabilities after each cycle of iteration, necessary in the estimation of the general latent class model with polytomous observed variables, is no longer a trivial matter for these more general kinds of equality restrictions. (Rescaling will destroy some kinds of equality constraints if care is not taken.) The program MLLSA referred to above will deal with the case where, for a given manifest variable and fixed latent class, there are two conditional probabilities constrained to be equal to each other (namely $\hat{\pi}_{1t}^{\overline{U}HX} = \hat{\pi}_{2t}^{\overline{U}HX}$). Thus the restriction that $\hat{\pi}_{1t}^{\overline{U}HX} = \hat{\pi}_{2t}^{\overline{U}HX}$ could have been imposed here, but since the model without that restriction did not fit these data, there was little point in doing so.

TABLE 5.11
Hierarchical Log-Linear Models Applied to the 1970 Data

Hypothesis	Margins fit	Likelihood-ratio χ^2, L^2	Goodness-of-fit χ^2	Degrees of freedom, df	P-value of L^2
$M_1 (=H_0)$	UH,I,M	2233.05	3274.92	7	.000
M_2	$UHI,UHM,$				
	IM	8.74	9.04	2	.013
M_3	UHI,UHM	16.13	15.68	3	.001
$M_4 (=H_{14})$	UHI,IM	36.75	33.11	4	.000
M_5	UHM,IM	2180.84	3235.99	4	.000
M_6	UHI,M	52.49	48.66	5	.000
M_7	UHM,I	2196.65	3240.23	5	.000
M_8	UH,IM	2217.26	3247.53	6	.000

income together, as we have also found with certain other models discussed previously.

Several other models for the 1970 data were also tested, and these additional models were similar to ones found in Goodman's fundamental papers on the newer latent class methods.[19] To save space, we will not discuss those results here. We note, however, that those other models did not, on the whole, fit these data as well as the models presented here, they were not generally as parsimonious as some of the simpler models that we have found to impute a plausible structure to the U.S. labor force, and their interpretation would require a point of view different from that which we have outlined in Section 5.1.

5.6 TIME-PERIOD HETEROGENEITY IN STRUCTURAL PARAMETERS OF A DUAL LABOR FORCE MODEL, AND NEW INDICATORS OF UNDEREMPLOYMENT

Part of the rationale for introducing the latent class perspective was hopefully to account for the association among underemployment forms in a way that other methods could not. For the 1970 data, this perspective has been very advantageous and has lent itself to substantive interpretation from several different points of view. We will now see that one basic model (the five-class scale model previously denoted as H_2) will explain these data at each of the several time points. Comparisons of parameters

[19] In addition to references previously cited, see Goodman (1974c).

TABLE 5.12
Twelvefold Cross-classification of the Types of Underemployment, United States Labor Force, 1969–1973

A. Raw cross-classifications

Underemployment type UH-I-M	1969 Number	1969 %[a]	1970 Number	1970 %	1971 Number	1971 %	1972 Number	1972 %	1973 Number	1973 %
1 1 1	80	.1	83	.1	135	.2	140	.2	123	.2
2 1 1	35	.1	46	.1	58	.1	74	.1	60	.1
3 1 1	393	.6	378	.6	459	.8	595	1.0	570	1.0
1 2 1	111	.2	154	.3	232	.4	256	.4	206	.4
2 2 1	72	.1	70	.1	115	.2	126	.2	103	.2
3 2 1	5640	9.1	5560	9.4	6219	10.3	6363	10.8	6766	11.7
1 1 2	738	1.2	890	1.5	1167	1.9	1194	2.0	1001	1.7
2 1 2	426	.7	451	.8	520	.9	483	.8	455	.8
3 1 2	4090	6.6	3742	6.3	3486	5.8	3639	6.2	3691	6.4
1 2 2	1304	2.1	1713	2.9	2340	3.9	2087	3.6	1791	3.1
2 2 2	943	1.5	987	1.7	1126	1.9	997	1.7	837	1.4
3 2 2	48017	77.7	45299	76.2	44373	73.6	42811	73.0	42350	73.0
Total	61849	100.0	59373	100.0	60230	100.0	58765	100.0	57953	100.0

B. Crude indicators of scalability

	1969	1970	1971	1972	1973
Percentage correctly allocated	97.0	96.5	95.5	95.1	95.7
Percentage of underemployed correctly allocated	86.6	85.3	83.1	82.0	83.9
Percentage unemployed who are unemployed only	58.4	60.3	60.4	56.8	57.4
Percentage low hours who are low hours only	63.9	63.5	61.9	59.3	57.5
Percentage low-income who are low-income only	71.0	66.9	59.8	59.4	62.6
Percentage mismatch who are mismatch only	89.1	88.4	86.2	84.2	86.4

C. Percent low-income

1969	1970	1971	1972	1973
9.3	9.4	9.7	10.4	10.2

[a]Percentages adjusted to ensure total of 100.0.

of this model applied at successive points in time are meaningful because this model *explains* the association among the underemployment types. Since the association among the underemployment forms is explained, and since the changing association over time is also explained by changing the basic parameters of the model, we can suggest new indicators of underemployment that take account of the changing prevalence of *multiple* underemployment.

The time × underemployment cross-table is presented as Table 5.12, and this table shows how underemployment varied over time for the U.S. labor force. Both the changing association among the underemployment forms and relative changes in the incidence of the forms may be obtained from that table. We note a steady decrease in the percentage of hours that are hours only, a decrease of about 5% for this 5-year time span. From the indexes presented beneath Table 5.12, it is also apparent that the relationship between low income and low hours, and between low income and unemployment, changes appreciably. By considering the "percentage correctly allocated" and the "percentage of the underemployed correctly

TABLE 5.13
Latent Class Model H_2 Applied to Labor Force Data, 1969–1973

Year	Likelihood-ratio χ^2, L^2	Goodness-of-fit χ^2	P-value of L^2
1969	2.55	2.57	.47
1970	1.01	1 00	> .5
1971	3.20	3.23	.38
1972	13.52	13.16	.002
1973	5.88	5.81	.13
Total	26.16[a]	—	.17

Proportions in the intrinsic scale types

	1969	1970	1971	1972	1973
Unscalable	.244	.252	.256	.264	.252
Unemployed	.002	.004	.007	.006	.006
Hours	.004	.004	.004	.004	.003
Income	.000	.000	.000	.000	.000
Mismatch	.081	.083	.091	.094	.103
Adequate	.669	.657	.641	.633	.636

[a]Each L^2 will be distributed as χ^2 on 3 degrees of freedom if H_2 is true. The sum of L^2 across all 5 years will be distributed as χ^2 on 15 degrees of freedom if H_2 is true for each year.

allocated,'' we find that the ability to discern distinct underemployment forms seems to deteriorate with the intensity of economic recession. Also, by considering the percentage with low income, it is clear that the absolute level of the low-income form of underemployment (or the proportion of the labor force marginal with respect to income) remains fairly constant over time, changing by only about 1%, whereas the levels observed in the other underemployment forms changed by much more than 1%. (See similar comments in Chapter 2.) It appears reasonable to assume that 10% of the labor force in this income form are relatively stable in composition over time, since some studies have documented the persistence of poverty status (i.e., low-income status) for certain parts of the labor force. This latter assumption will make plausible certain across-time inferences to be formulated later in this section.

Table 5.13 presents the fit of model H_2 applied successively to each of the five time-periods. The model fits very well for each year except 1972, and the total likelihood-ratio χ^2 summed over all years is 26.16 with 15 df. These models therefore provide remarkable fit for these data, given that the total sample size is nearly 300,000. All the inferences made earlier pertaining to differential risks to underemployment in different structural parts of the labor force, to the dual labor market theory, and to the distinctness of the underemployment forms also pertain to each year of the study.[20] The parameters themselves change appreciably over time. In order that this time-period heterogenity can be inferred, Table 5.13 also contains estimates of proportions in each of the six intrinsic scale types for each time-period. Table 5.14 presents a time-series comparison of the intrinsically unscalable (i.e., marginal) labor force type and the intrinsically scalable (i.e., nonmarginal) labor force type. We see that in the class that we have designated as the scalable class (i.e., the nonmarginal class), visible underemployment is relatively constant at each time point, but the rate of mismatch is increasing substantially over time. On the other hand, the intrinsically unscalable (i.e., the marginal) labor force type has rates of underemployment that vary substantially and that fluctuate much more than do the aggregate rates of underemployment for the total labor force.

---

[20] Even for year 1972, the *substantive* conclusions are not greatly affected by the statistical considerations, which force us to cast some doubt upon this model for that year. We find by examining the standardized residuals that the larger share of the moderately large value of χ^2 for 1972 is due to the overprediction of the unemployment–income–mismatch cell, which is not itself substantively very important, since this is a type of very small occurrence in the labor force. The full model H_1 was also applied to the 1972 data in the anticipation that an ''intrinsic low-income'' class would emerge in that recession year. The lack of fit was not due to the omission of an intrinsic scale type for income. Inclusion of an ''intrinsic unemployed–low-income'' class *would* have improved the fit for this year, however.

TABLE 5.14
A Characterization of the "Intrinsic" Parts of the Dualistic Labor Force, 1969–1973

	1969	1970	1971	1972	1973
Intrinsically unscalable					
(i.e., marginal latent class)					
% unemployed	14.1	17.5	22.2	21.6	19.0
% low hours	8.1	8.8	10.0	9.3	8.8
% low income	38.2	37.3	37.7	39.5	40.4
% mismatch	8.8	9.1	11.2	13.2	12.8
% adequate	43.9	41.3	37.5	36.3	37.6
% of labor force	24.4	25.2	25.6	26.4	25.2
Intrinsically scalable					
(i.e., nonmarginal latent class)					
% unemployed	.2	.5	1.0	.8	.8
% low hours	.5	.5	.6	.6	.4
% low income	.0	.0	.0	.0	.0
% mismatch	10.7	11.1	12.3	12.7	13.8
% adequate	88.5	87.9	86.2	85.9	85.1
% of labor force	75.6	74.8	74.4	73.6	74.8
Total labor force					
(i.e., marginal and nonmarginal latent classes confounded)					
% unemployed	3.6	4.8	6.4	6.3	5.4
% low hours	2.4	2.6	3.0	2.9	2.5
% low-income	9.3	9.4	9.7	10.4	10.2
% mismatch	10.2	10.6	12.0	12.9	13.5
% adequate	77.6	76.1	73.7	72.9	73.1

We see, for example, that the total increase in unemployment from 1969 to 1971 of 6.4% − 3.6% = 2.8% was coexistent with an increase in unemployment of 22.2% − 14.1% = 8.1% in the marginal class of the labor force. It would of course be important to know if the persons marginal at time t were also the same persons who are marginal at times $t + 1, t + 2$, etc., since in that event, we would have traced most across-time variation to changing risks occurring in a fixed 25% of the labor force. We cannot, of course, document this with such data as we now have at our disposal, but note that in view of some evidence at least, this inference appears plausible. That all low-income persons are in the marginal class at each time point suggests the possiblity that this class might be composed of nearly the same persons at each time point. It would require panel data to provide a fuller test of this assumption and to make more precise the

TABLE 5.15
"Intrinsic" Indicators of Underemployment, 1969–1073

Year	All underemployment except mismatch	Mismatch only	Adequate
1969			
Observed	.122	.091	.776
Nonmarginal class	.006	.081	.669
Marginal class	.116	.010	.107
1970			
Observed	.145	.094	.761
Nonmarginal class	.008	.083	.657
Marginal class	.137	.011	.104
1971			
Observed	.160	.103	.737
Nonmarginal class	.011	.091	.641
Marginal class	.149	.012	.096
1972			
Observed	.163	.108	.729
Nonmarginal class	.010	.094	.633
Marginal class	.153	.014	.096
1973			
Observed	.152	.117	.731
Nonmarginal class	.009	.103	.636
Marginal class	.143	.014	.095

Source: Tables 5.12, 5.13, and 5.14, this volume.

statements concerning the time-period change in underemployment risks in the two different structural parts of the dualistic labor force.[21]

Since this model explains the association among the underemployment forms, indicators based upon its parameters can be suggested that will not be distorted by the changing association among the underemployment forms. Table 5.15 presents a breakdown of the observed rates of underemployment into a portion resulting from rates in the nonmarginal labor force class and a portion resulting from the rates of underemployment in

[21] Such data might be derived from the National Longitudinal Survey (the "Parnes data"), the Michigan Panel Study of Income Dynamics, or other panel-type studies of labor market characteristics. We are currently attempting an extension of the results of this chapter to these other data. Strictly speaking, the analysis here only permits us to say that a dualistic conception of the labor force provides a compelling explanation of the *cross-sectional* data.

the marginal labor force class. The reader, by following the columns downward across time in the table, can examine the change in underemployment as we have indirectly observed its behavior in the two latent labor force classes. A graph of those results appears in Figure 5.2, showing the time-trend more forcibly. These results summarize the labor of this chapter and show how *aggregate* underemployment over time can be understood from the perspective of labor force dualism. Most of the time-period variation in underemployment other than mismatch is due to changing risk in a latent marginal labor force class, a class that is characterized by being at especially high risk of underemployment at every time-period. Most of the time-period change in mismatch is the result of changing risk in the nonmarginal class. Although the route that we have taken to obtain these summary results has been laborious, the benefits derived from this relatively parsimonious view of underemployment seem well worth the effort.

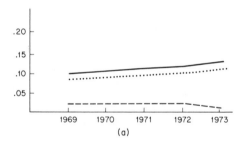

(a)

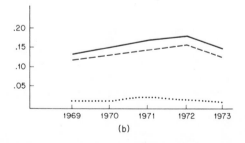

(b)

Fig. 5.2. Across-time fluctuation in underemployment for the marginal and the nonmarginal labor force classes. Solid line = Underemployment in the total labor force; dotted line = underemployment in the nonmarginal class; broken line = underemployment in the marginal class. (a) Trend in mismatch. (b) Trend in economic underemployment.

5.7 DIFFERENTIALS IN LATENT CLASS STRUCTURE FOR THE RACE–SEX GROUPS, 1970

The model designated as H_2 has proven compelling when applied to the 1970 data, and in the previous section, it was demonstrated that this single model could describe the changing pattern of underemployment observed across time. Before concluding this chapter, we provide additional results that break down the data by race–sex group. This analysis will indicate the degree to which marginality, as it is conceived within the latent class framework, can be said to characterize each of the race–sex groups. In addition, the analysis will show the differentials in the class organization of labor market opportunity evidenced across the race–sex groups, thereby giving us some insight into the question of whether, for example, "marginal" white males are different from "marginal" nonwhite females.

Model H_2 was applied separately to four race–sex-specific cross-classifications corresponding to Table 5.2, analyzed at length earlier.[22] The fit of this model was remarkably good for each race–sex group, with a likelihood-ratio χ^2 of 4.04, 1.40, 1.42, and 7.75 for white males, nonwhite males, white females, and nonwhite females, respectively. The parameter estimates, expressed so that they conform to the dual labor force orientation developed previously, are provided in Table 5.16. The estimated proportions in the latent marginal class range from a low of 18.5% for white males to a high of 39.2% for nonwhite females. As would be implied by the literature on split labor markets (see Montagna, 1977), nonwhites and females are overrepresented in the marginal class, and so in this sense, those results add somewhat to the face validity of H_2 as a plausible model of dualism. A distinctive feature of these results is the observation that *over half* of the females in the marginal class experience the low-income form, as compared to a corresponding fraction of about one-quarter to one-third for males. The extreme differentials in underemployment risks in the marginal class among the race–sex groups indicate that race–sex criteria have an impact on underemployment risks. (Indeed, a model assuming homogeneity of these underemployment risks would woefully fail to fit these data.) This result will probably surprise few but will hopefully show how the latent class perspective can enrich current attempts to understand the role of race and sex as factors in the distribution of labor market rewards. If the structural parameters in Table 5.15 were found to adequately describe the across-time experiences of the race–sex groups, as would properly be determined from an analysis of

---

[22] To save space, the cross-tables will not be reproduced here, but they are available on request from the writer.

TABLE 5.16
The Dual Labor Force Model H_2 Applied to Each Race Sex Group, 1970

	White males	Nonwhite males	White females	Nonwhite females
Marginal latent class				
Percentage in class	18.5	26.4	30.8	39.2
Percentage unemployed	17.0	26.9	16.0	21.8
Percentage low hours	6.5	15.6	8.0	16.2
Percentage low income	24.0	31.3	52.5	51.6
Percentage mismatch	11.6	7.2	7.8	10.8
Percentage adequate	51.4	36.6	33.3	26.7
Nonmarginal latent class				
Percentage in class	81.5	73.6	69.2	60.8
Percentage unemployed	1.1	.1	.2	.2
Percentage low hours	1.0	.8	.4	.1
Percentage low income	.0	.0	.0	.0
Percentage mismatch	11.5	8.7	10.0	12.5
Percentage adequate	86.4	90.5	89.5	87.2

panel data, then much study of the labor market now undertaken through the perspectives of "dual" or "segmented" labor market theorists would reduce to an explanation of those quantities.

5.8 CONCLUSION

The compelling statistical results of this chapter bring the several problems that we outlined in Section 5.1 into joint play. A plausible structure to the labor force and to time-period change in the labor market has been made quantitatively explicit. From the scaling perspective adopted early in this chapter, we were able to show that (*a*) mismatch is very distinct from the other forms of underemployment, and (*b*) low-income is *not* distinct from the visible underemployment forms. In spite of this latter result, however, the income measure of this study is instrumental to the analysis of labor force structure, since it can be used as a rough indicator of labor force marginality. Hauser's low-income measure predicts the risk to unemployment better than any other single socioeconomic variable with which we are familiar.

It was also shown how the labor force could be regarded as being composed of distinct parts and how hypotheses of dualism could be easily tested. One structural part of the labor force, having all the characteristics of the marginal labor force of dual labor market theory, makes up 20–25% of the labor force and is at extremely high risk of all underemployment forms. Another part, having rates of underemployment (excepting mismatch) low enough to be purely frictional in character, made up 75–80% of the labor force. Several of the models that have been found to fit these data could serve as structural models isomorphic to dual labor market theory.

Using across-time comparisons of parameters of one attractive model, we were able to infer that most time-period variation in *aggregate* unemployment was due to variation in unemployment risks in a marginal part of the labor force. Since 40% of the marginal part was, by our definition, marginal with respect to income, we were led to believe that a "causal" analysis of the determinants of across-time variation in unemployment and part-time unemployment could profitably focus upon this very special subpopulation with severe economic conditions that are reflected in its low wage income.

It could be argued that the substantive interpretation of these compelling statistical results is somewhat strained owing to the absence throughout of panel data that would establish the persistence of underemployment risks over time. The across-time comparisons would, of course, have been much more convincing if we could say with certainty that the persons in the marginal class at time t remained in that class at successive points in time. We have, however, made suggestions as to why this assumption appears reasonable. Panel data of the kind necessary to establish the veracity of our conclusions are available, but here we have contented ourselves with inferences about dualism that can be made with cross-sectional data. The statistical methods, the computer program used in the calculations, and the specific application to the labor force context are also quite new.

6

the dependence of labor force status on age, time-period, and cohort

The forms of underemployment divide the population of working ages into distinct labor force statuses, and the distribution of persons among these statuses will depend on age, time-period, and cohort. The distribution depends on age because the labor force and the rewards of the labor market are *age-graded,* that is, organized in distinctive ways about the age of the individual. The distribution likewise depends on the time-period in which it is observed, because labor market fluctuation changes the risk to underemployment for the labor force and even changes the risk to labor force participation itself. The distribution will also depend on cohort, because socialization patterns of the past produce cohorts that are unique in their risks to the several forms of underemployment.

Three labor force statuses of special importance are obtained by combining certain of the statuses considered in this study. One status is here referred to as "economic underemployment" because it is defined with reference to time spent in employment or the wages of work for economically active or marginally economically active persons. All sub-unemployed, unemployed, part-time unemployed, and low-income persons are included in this status; it denotes subproductive economic activity, because loss of work time or low wages both indicate low productivity. A second status in the population of working ages is the "not-in-labor-force" status, where this status does not now contain the marginally active sub-unemployed persons. (Sub-unemployed persons are contained in the "economic underemployment" status.) This status denotes economic inactivity, albeit in a slightly different manner from the usual labor force approach. Finally, a third status is the one corresponding to persons who are mismatched or adequately employed. By collapsing mismatched persons into a single status with the adequately employed, we thereby create a status that denotes productive employment. It is clear that the mismatched—the most skilled—can nevertheless be productive, and this fact justifies our collapsing mismatched persons together with the adequately employed. The analysis of this chapter is focused on the influence of age, time-period, and cohort category upon the distribution of persons among the three statuses corresponding to

1. Not in the labor force (or economic inactivity)
2. Economic underemployment (or subproductive economic activity)
3. Adequate employment, including mismatch (or productive economic activity)

The last two categories, when combined, denote the *modified* labor force spoken of in earlier chapters. By observing the relationship of this threefold qualitative variable to the master variables of demography— age, time-period, and cohort—we will be able to infer (*a*) the dependence of labor force participation upon these master demographic variables and (*b*) the dependence of (economic) underemployment within the labor force upon these master demographic variables. This single trichotomous labor force status variable reflects productivity in a way that is quite different from that obtained from the more usual labor force indicators, and so a cohort analysis of it promises to be provocative.

   In Chapters 2, 3, and 4, the age effects and the time-period effects upon underemployment and upon labor force participation were considered, but those results were limited because of the crudity of age measurement (e.g., in 5-year or even 15-year age intervals) and in their omission of the potentially confounding influence of the cohort variable logically intertwined with the age and time-period variables. This chapter brings into joint consideration the three variables—age, time-period, and cohort—by reference to special kinds of log-linear models for qualitative data (Goodman, 1972c, 1975b; Pullum, 1977; Fienberg and Mason, 1978). Of primary interest is the effect of *cohort category* upon the age–time-specific distribution of persons among the labor force statuses, and the way that cohort effect conditions the observed age distribution and time-period fluctuation. To our knowledge, this topic has not been given full consideration in the analysis of underemployment (e.g., unemployment), in the analysis of labor force participation, or in the analysis of more general kinds of labor force dynamics. A rigorous analysis of the joint influence of age, time-period, and cohort on labor force status requires methods and a general approach similar to that of the present chapter.

The discussion here is restricted to the five time-period observations on the labor force history of the age group 20–34 and the cohort experience that this age range implies. The age variable is here measured in single years, enabling us to infer the cohort pattern of progression through the labor force statuses with time. The rationale for restricting attention to the age group 20–34 is that a very large share of the overall time variation in labor force participation and underemployment results from fluctuations that occur in this 15-year age group. The age variation in labor force status is also greater in this 15-year interval than in any other broad age interval we might consider. The implied assumption is that our ability to discern cohort effects will also be the greatest when we focus entirely on this interval of age.

By the observation of the partial experience of several cohorts for the 5 years of this study, it will be shown that introducing the cohort variable and the cohort concept into the analysis of labor force dynamics enriches our understanding of both labor force participation and underemployment. We will document the hypothesis that different cohorts in this era of quickening social change in the labor force have markedly different patterns of distribution throughout the labor force statuses and that these cohort differences themselves are quite different among the race–sex groups. The cohort approach of this chapter will also provide us with insight into (a) the "true" time-period variation in the distribution among the labor force statuses and (b) the "true" age distribution of employment opportunity. These perspectives will add further meaning to our understanding of current underemployment and will suggest new methods for the measurement of labor market change that are consistent with the cohort approach of demography (compare Wunsch and Termote, 1978, Chapter 1).

6.1 THE DATA

The cross-tables to be analyzed here are too bulky to be presented in the text but are available upon request from the writer. Our discussion, however, will be more lucid if a description of the data is provided. The cross-tables subject to analysis were arranged so that three variables were explicit, as is customary in demographic tabulations. These were the row variable (variable A) with categories $i = 1, \ldots, 15$ corresponding to ages 20–34 in single years of age; the column variable time-period (variable T) with classes $j = 1, \ldots, 5$ corresponding to years 1969–1973; and the dependent variable labor force status (variable U) with classes $l = 1, 2, 3$ corresponding to not in labor force, economic underemployment, and adequate employment (including mismatch), respectively.[1] Implicit in the $15 \times 5 \times 3$ ($A \times T \times U$) cross-tables is a cohort variable (variable C), marking the chronological cohort category in which a given individual is located. The C variable is implicit in these tables, but the data can easily be rearranged to make the cohort variable explicit and one of the other variables age or time-period implicit (see, e.g., Bishop, Fienberg, and Holland, 1975, for the technique of "unfolding" complete cross-tables).

There are $k = 1, \ldots, 19$ cohort categories, corresponding to the number of diagonals in a cross-table with 15 age categories and five time-periods. As a convention, we label the cohorts from $k = 1$, corresponding to the extreme upper right diagonal, to $k = 19$, corresponding to the extreme lower left diagonal. The cohorts (i.e., the diagonals) are thus labeled according to the time of "entry" into age 20. Persons most recently entering this age are denoted as cohort 1, cohort 2, etc. As can easily be ascertained, only the partial experience of any given cohort is recorded. For cohorts 5–15 only 5 year's experience is provided, while for the other cohorts the recorded history is even more incomplete.

Demographic analysis of age × time-period × cohort tables usually begins with an analysis of marginal distributions of the dependent variable in respect to each of the three variables A, T, and C. Informal analysis of these marginal distributions here *apparently* shows considerable cohort differentiation in labor force status and also *apparently* shows that this cohort differentiation is of a markedly different character for each of the race–sex groups. These informal comparisons can be misleading, however, owing to the functional dependence of the cohort variable on the age and time-period variables. The usual demographic practice of examining marginal distributions on the age, time-period, or cohort variables with respect to the dependent variable of interest and then claiming that these marginals indicate age, time-period, or cohort effects is incorrect. Each marginal with respect to one of these three variables is generally confounded by the influence of the other two, and it is not possible to disentangle the age, time-period, and cohort effects by the usual informal methods because of the linear dependence among these three variables. That is, if age i and time-period j are known, then the cohort category k is also known and is given in the present context by

$$k = i - j + 5 \tag{6.1}$$

---

[1] A "not-in-labor-force" category is included in the labor force status variable U in part so that the population sampled at each time point is essentially the same one. Because of net immigration and military service for males in these ages, the civilian population being sampled at each successive survey is not exactly the same one but will be *approximately* the same one with this convention.

An exact linear relationship exists among A, T, and C of the form $C = A - T + 5$; it would be impossible to estimate the parameters in a linear model of the form $U = a + b_1A + b_2T + b_3C$, and it would likewise be impossible to estimate a regression relationship where each of these variables were broken down into component "dummy variables." In contingency table terms, the joint variable (ATC) is equivalent to the joint variable (AT), or to the joint variable (AC), or to the joint variable (TC). The linear constraint on the independent variables of cohort analysis imposed by Equation 6.1 leads to an identification problem, as has been recently discussed in the sociodemographic literature (Mason *et al.*, 1973). That same restriction led, in the fertility context (and in some other contexts), to the process that Ryder has referred to as the "demographic translation" of time-period rates into cohort rates, and vice versa (Ryder, 1964). The constraints in Equation 6.1 will accordingly force us to impose an "identifying restriction" on the *parameters* of the cohort model. Unlike in the context of the linear model, however, we will be able to examine the overall effect of a cohort variable in terms of additional variation explained by a model including the cohort variable relative to variation explained by a model excluding the cohort variable, without reference to the problem of identification of parameters. In this context the log-linear model can be tested even though the parameters are not identified, whereas in the linear model the nonidentifiability of parameters necessarily implies that the model cannot be tested. A complete discussion of the identification problem in cohort analysis is taken up in Appendix F, and readers unfamiliar with the identification problem in cohort analysis are referred to this appendix for material that will only be touched upon here.

6.2 MULTIPLICATIVE MODELS FOR COHORT ANALYSIS BASED UPON SUCCESSIVE SAMPLE SURVEYS

For the kind of trichotomous dependent variable of interest here (variable U), the more usual linear models (namely multiple classification analysis) should not be used.[2] A multiplicative or log-linear model is appropriate, however, and more nearly takes into account the actual statistical

---

[2] The linear model that might be used here would correspond to a bivariate regression where both of the dependent variables were dichotomous. The corresponding univariate regressions would violate the homoscedasticity assumption in a way that could not be ignored, and the situation would become much more complicated by consideration of the corresponding bivariate regression (see Goodman, 1975c). For a discussion of some of the pitfalls of cohort analysis through successive sample surveys in the fertility context, see Ryder (1975a).

distribution of these data. The frequency data that we are analyzing here are multinomially distributed (disregarding the complex sampling design of the CPS); the nominal labor force status variable itself is definitely not normally distributed. Let f_{ijkl} denote the observed frequency in the ith age category, the jth time-period, and the kth cohort category (with $k = i - j + 5$), and the lth class of the dependent variable referring to labor force status. A ratio that conveniently describes the chances that U takes on the value 1 relative to class l' ($l' > 1$) is

$$\omega_{ijkl'} = f_{ijk1}/f_{ijkl'}, \qquad l' = 2, 3 \tag{6.2}$$

Given some particular hypothesis or model let F_{ijkl} denote the expected frequency in the (i, j, k, l) cell. The ratio corresponding to that in Equation 6.2 expressed in terms of the expected frequencies F_{ijkl} is

$$\Omega_{ijkl'} = F_{ijk1}/F_{ijkl'}, \qquad l' = 2, 3 \tag{6.3}$$

We will consider a series of models relating $\Omega_{ijkl'}$ to parameters that denote the main multiplicative effects of age, time-period, and cohort. For a full discussion of these models, the reader is referred to Goodman (1975b), as well as to related discussions by Pullum (1977) and Fienberg and Mason (1978). Every model to be considered is actually a special case of the "full" model

$$\Omega_{ijkl'} = \gamma_{l'}^{U}\gamma_{il'}^{AU}\gamma_{jl'}^{TU}\gamma_{kl'}^{CU} \qquad \begin{aligned} i &= 1, \ldots, 15; \\ j &= 1, \ldots, 5; \quad k = 1, \ldots, 19 \end{aligned} \tag{6.4}$$

The parameters on the right-hand side of Equation 6.4 (disregarding the $\gamma_{l'}^{U}$ parameters) represent main multiplicative effects of age i, time-period j, and cohort category k, respectively, upon the trichotomous variable U. The $\gamma_{il'}^{AU}$ parameters denote the main effect of the ith age category upon the particular ratio (e.g., $\Omega_{ijkl'}$) pertaining to variable U, and other parameters are interpreted similarly. Because this full model allows the main effects of all three independent variables, we denote this model as $H_{(A,T,C)}$.

An alternative and equivalent way to view model $H_{(A,T,C)}$ is suggested in the following equation relating the expected frequencies F_{ijkl} to other multiplicative parameters related to the ones on the right-hand side of (6.4):

$$F_{ijkl} = \tau_{l}^{U}\tau_{ij}^{AT}\tau_{il}^{AU}\tau_{jl}^{TU}\tau_{kl}^{CU} \tag{6.5}$$

From the definition $\Omega_{ijkl'} = F_{ijk1}/F_{ijkl'}$ ($l' = 2, 3$), we see that the parameters on the right-hand side of (6.4) can be reexpressed as ratios of the τ parameters in (6.5). We have, for example, $\gamma_{il'}^{AU} = \tau_{il'}^{AU}/\tau_{il}^{AU}$, with similar expressions for $\gamma_{il'}^{TU}$ and $\gamma_{kl'}^{CU}$. These ρ parameters are actually the ones used to estimate the expected frequencies under the various models in the computer program described in Appendix G. In that program, we have rescaled the τ parameters so that

$$\prod_l \tau_{il}^{AU} = \prod_l \tau_{jl}^{TU} = \prod_l \tau_{kl}^{CU} = 1$$

but other kinds of restrictions could also be imposed. Model 6.5 and model 6.6 are equivalent to each other, and it is easy to go back and forth from one formulation to the other.

The other models to be tested for the data of this chapter are

$$\Omega_{ijkl'} = \gamma_{l'}^{U} \gamma_{il'}^{AU} \qquad (H_{(A)}) \qquad (6.6)$$

$$\Omega_{ijkl'} = \gamma_{l'}^{U} \gamma_{jl'}^{TU} \qquad (H_{(T)}) \qquad (6.7)$$

$$\Omega_{ijkl'} = \gamma_{l'}^{U} \gamma_{kl'}^{CU} \qquad (H_{(C)}) \qquad (6.8)$$

$$\Omega_{ijkl'} = \gamma_{l'}^{U} \gamma_{il'}^{AU} \gamma_{jl'}^{TU} \qquad (H_{(A,T)}) \qquad (6.9)$$

$$\Omega_{ijkl'} = \gamma_{l'}^{U} \gamma_{il'}^{AU} \gamma_{kl'}^{CU} \qquad (H_{(A,C)}) \qquad (6.10)$$

$$\Omega_{ijkl'} = \gamma_{l'}^{U} \gamma_{jl'}^{TU} \gamma_{kl'}^{CU} \qquad (H_{(T,C)}) \qquad (6.11)$$

in an obvious notation. Model $H_{(A)}$ expresses the odds $\Omega_{ijkl'}$ in terms of only the main effects of age, setting the γ^{TU} and γ^{CU} parameters at 1, and similar comments pertain to the other models. These models may also be represented in terms of certain τ parameters, as in Equation 6.5. For additional meaning that attaches to each of the models $H_{(A)}$ through $H_{(A,T,C)}$, the reader is once again referred to the paper by Goodman (1975b) on these models.[3]

A special problem with models of the kind $H_{(C)}$, $H_{(A,C)}$, $H_{(T,C)}$, and $H_{(A,T,C)}$, including the main effects of cohort category upon the dependent variable of interest, results from the general kinds of systematic errors that are known to occur with age data in general. Systematic biases in recorded age data on sample surveys (as well as in the "complete enumerations" of population censuses) are known to occur. Some of these biases are "age heaping" and "digit preference" and are discussed in several standard texts on demographic methods (see, e.g., Shryock and Siegel, 1973). Systematic biases in age data of this kind will produce an impression that models like $H_{(C)}$, $H_{(A,C)}$, $H_{(T,C)}$, or $H_{(A,T,C)}$ are false even if they were true; the γ^{CU} parameters (or the τ^{CU} parameters) will be attenuated toward one. We have examined the consequences of this problem in a kind of Monte Carlo experiment, the results of which do not need to be detailed here. It should be noted that for the *single-year* data considered here, these

---

[3] Also see Goodman (1972c). The full model $H_{(A,T,C)}$ is analogous to the "diagonals parameter" model described in this article and is used there to analyze social mobility.

kinds of age errors can be important and that, in fact, we will *underestimate* the magnitudes of cohort effects in general and will therefore have a somewhat dimmed perception of real differentiation among cohorts.[4] Accuracy of age data is thus a prerequisite to cohort analysis; some comments concerning the accuracy of single-year age data used in this chapter are contained in Appendix D.

Because of the restriction that cohort category $k = i - j + 5$, a special problem arises with the full model $H_{(A,T,C)}$, since the parameters of this model will not be identified even if the usual restrictions are imposed. The actual identifying restrictions used to identify the parameters of $H_{(A,T,C)}$, and the substantive rationale for them, will be presented as they are needed. The models presented above are identified, however, and we can use the χ^2 statistics of each model to assess the overall contributions of the γ^{AU}, γ^{TU}, and γ^{CU} parameters in a relatively unambiguous manner. Before examining the fit of these log-linear cohort models for the four contingency tables of this chapter, we first discuss the theoretical rationale used here for interpreting the various cohort models.

6.3 THE CONCEPT OF A COHORT EFFECT: STATISTICAL DIFFERENTIATION AMONG COHORTS AND THE TEMPO OF SOCIAL CHANGE

We know that the age variable and the time-period variable must exert strong influence upon labor force status, and it is of course important to estimate the magnitude of those effects. The age variable, for example, can be viewed from the perspective of human capital economics as an indicator of experience (compare Weiss and Lillard, 1978), or it can be viewed as an indicator of position in social structure broadly conceived (compare Hughes, 1958), and these twin conceptions of the role of age justify its importance. Time-period variation in labor force status (i.e., time-period effects) is usually taken as an indicator of purely economic forces, such as changing demand for labor or other kinds of labor market fluctuation (compare Farkas, 1977). Therefore, an attempt to estimate age

---

[4] If cohorts are statistically distinct from each other, then inaccuracy in the recording of age will imply that the cohort category of a person will not be known accurately at each successive survey. Members of different cohorts will be observed as being in the same cohort, at a given point in time, thereby dulling our perception of true cohort differences. Winsborough (1975) applied linear model analogues to the log-linear models here in a cohort analysis of income differentials among whites and nonwhites, but his analysis focused upon age data in *2-year* categories, and so would perhaps be less subject to this special kind of age inaccuracy.

and time-period effects is nothing less than an attempt to summarize in empirical terms the role of age structure and labor market change in characterizing the aggregate labor force. Age and time-period are variables with a clear meaning, and the underlying phenomena that they measure are theoretically and substantively meaningful. Age effects and time-period effects may thus be assigned an ostensibly important role in any discussion of the labor force.

But the primary research question here pertains to effects of a *cohort* variable, so some preliminary comments are in order to establish the approach by which a cohort effect should be discerned and the perspective through which the cohort effects (if they exist) should be interpreted. The reason for such preliminary comment pertains partly to the *nonidentifiability* of parameters in models allowing the dependence of labor force status upon all three of the variables age, time-period, and cohort. Although we may estimate the fit of models involving the simultaneous influence of all three of these master variables and can therefore assess the overall contribution of a cohort variable to our understanding of labor force status, there is an inherent ambiguity over how the distinct effects of each cohort can be identified. Another ambiguity in the interpretation of cohort effects results from the theoretical perspective within which such cohort effects are to be interpreted. The point of view adopted here is that the cohort variable should play an explanatory role that is logically subservient to the age and time-period variables. In the remainder of this section, we outline the rationale for this theoretical position.

The importance of age and time-period upon labor force status hardly requires documentation. Utopian considerations aside, the risk of labor force participation and the risk of underemployment will normally depend upon the age of the individual. The age distribution of the labor force statuses, when purged of the possible distortion of transitory time-period influence and of the confounding of cohort effects (both of which will be explicitly discussed later), could indeed be regarded as depicting the "true" institutionalized age stratification of employment opportunity. The time-period variation in labor force status, when purged of the confounding of age and cohort, is (in a sense to be discussed later) a truer gauge of the impact of the transitory economic exigencies than are the ordinary crude rates and ratios that do not take into account the cohort effect. The concept of a cohort variable and the effects of such a variable upon labor force status is much more subtle, however, and requires justification in the present context of "explaining" variation in the distribution of the population of working ages among the labor force statuses.

Motivated by Ryder's general account of the concept of a cohort in the study of social change, we will view the *persistence* of labor force characteristics over time for a given cohort as a "cohort effect" indicating *indirectly observable* social change if the following two conditions are met.

1. The various cohorts can be *statistically* distinguished from one another by virtue of different patterns of distribution among the labor force statuses, each pattern of which seems to be characteristic to a particular cohort. This condition is to be inferred from inspection of the γ^{CU} parameters described in the previous sections.

2. The statistical "cohort effect" cannot be attributed to the effects of aging and/or time-period fluctuation. This concept of a total "cohort effect" is thus a *partial effect* of cohort category, "controlling" for the effects of the age and time-period variables. That is, the γ^{CU} parameters will only be discussed in the context of the full model $H_{(A,T,C)}$, where age and time-period effects are statistically controlled.

Loosely speaking, the cohort variable will be associated with labor force status if different chronological cohorts differ with respect to their across-time progression through the labor force statuses in a manner that *cannot* be attributed to mere aging (reflecting cohort progression through age-graded social structure) or to time-period variation (reflecting the exposure of cohorts to the momentary economic exigencies). In the interests of parsimony, we have assigned a logical priority to the age and time-period variables over the cohort variable. Correspondingly, we have assigned *theoretical* priority to the age and time-period variables, since there is little ambiguity here over the logical distinctness of these respective variables or over the interpretation of their effects. Cohort effects themselves, since they are properties of cohorts that are invariant across time, are taken as indicators of the force of socialization as it operates to produce truly distinct cohorts. In this view, the γ^{CU} parameters, as well as the differences among them, reflect the tempo of social change.

As in the general cohort approach to the study of social change espoused by Ryder, the examination of statistical differentiation among cohorts is one point of reference for a more general analysis of social change in the labor force. Since in this conception of a cohort effect we have *controlled* for the effects of time-period, social change that occurs uniformly to all age groups over time will be confounded with the economic effects of time-period, but the cohort effects so defined nevertheless permit us to infer the social change in the labor force wrought by the entry of new cohorts with each succeeding year. The constant renewal of the labor force, and of the population of persons of working age, by fresh cohorts with intrinsically unique patterns of distribution throughout the labor force statuses allows the inertia of past history to shape current labor force experience. That is, succeeding cohorts differ from one another by unique socialization patterns, levels of human capital endowment, relative size in numbers, and so forth, and these factors, as imbedded as they are in past history, according to this view produce real cohort differentiation and allow a particular kind of social change in the labor force to occur. To summarize, cohort effects that are estimated in the context of the full model $H_{(A,T,C)}$, and hence are "partial" effects controlling for age and time-period, are regarded here as indicators of the force of past history. Cohort effects are produced by the working of past history, and at any given cross section in time, several different cohort effects must be reckoned with in order to describe the observed distribution among the labor force statuses. The unobservable force of past history carries over as a type of social inertia in the cohort effects, and estimation of these cohort effects allows inference about the strength of past history in the shaping of current experience.

6.4 THE GOODNESS-OF-FIT OF COHORT MODELS ACCOUNTING FOR THE AGE–TIME-PERIOD–COHORT-SPECIFIC DISTRIBUTION AMONG THE LABOR FORCE STATUSES, FOR MALES AND FEMALES BY RACE

Each of the cohort models discussed previously were estimated separately for the race–sex groups. Two different computer programs were used, the first of which provided only the χ^2 statistics of the respective models and the second of which provided both χ^2 statistics and identified parameter estimates.[5] The goodness-of-fit and likelihood-ratio χ^2 statistics associated with these models are presented in Table 6.1. Since the sample sizes differ dramatically from sample to sample (with the white to nonwhite sample ratio being about 5.5 to 1), and since the overall unexplained variation in the data [given by $X^2(H_0)$ or $L^2(H_0)$] is also dramatically different from sample to sample, these statistics by themselves are difficult to

---

[5] The models of this section were estimated first using the ECTA program of Leo A. Goodman and Robert Fay. Parameter estimates cannot be obtained from this program when the cross-tables contain structural zeros, and estimating many of the models input data with structural zeros was necessary. We could have estimated these models with computer programs based upon a modified Newton–Raphson-type algorithm but did not do so here. If the tables are entered as tables with all variables explicit with the necessary structural zeros, then estimating the full model $H_{(A,T,C)}$ (and some other models) would have required successive inversions of a matrix of very high order and would therefore have been prohibitively expensive. In contingency table problems as complicated as those of this chapter, the ECTA program and its iterative proportional scaling algorithm appear to be the most appropriate. Fienberg and Mason (1978), however, used the Newton–Raphson algorithm in estimation, and it is presently unclear (at least to this author) which is to be preferred in the cohort context.

TABLE 6.1

Goodness-of-Fit and Likelihood-Ratio χ^2 Statistics for Log-Linear Cohort Models Applied to White Male, Nonwhite Male, White Female, and Nonwhite Female Data

Model	Degrees of freedom df	White X^2	White L^2	White L^2/df	Nonwhite male χ^2	Nonwhite male L^2	Nonwhite male L^2/df
		White female					
H_0	148	8682.83	7938.09	53.64	726.49	714.77	4.83
$H_{(A)}$	120	369.97	372.71	3.01	131.74	138.11	1.15
$H_{(T)}$	140	8429.04	7719.27	55.14	698.83	681.51	4.87
$H_{(C)}$	112	1142.46	1132.57	10.11	150.15	151.07	1.35
$H_{(A,T)}$	112	166.35	165.17	1.47	104.15	110.60	.99
$H_{(A,C)}$	84	187.42	185.88	2.21	86.33	90.29	1.07
$H_{(C,T)}$	104	352.41	336.91	3.24	116.62	118.31	1.14
$H_{(A,T,C)}$	78	82.26	82.61	1.06	71.95	75.19	.96
		Nonwhite female					
H_0	148	1787.93	1775.86	12.00	292.72	304.55	2.06
$H_{(A)}$	120	322.49	324.96	2.71	109.82	110.22	.92
$H_{(T)}$	140	1655.73	1639.52	11.71	295.04	300.49	2.15
$H_{(C)}$	112	336.26	339.58	3.03	120.02	120.05	1.07
$H_{(A,T)}$	112	181.55	183.52	1.64	104.67	105.38	.94
$H_{(A,C)}$	84	144.62	145.36	1.73	75.98	75.69	.90
$H_{(C,T)}$	104	290.14	292.55	2.81	93.26	93.34	.90
$H_{(A,T,C)}$	78	123.63	124.51	1.60	72.31	72.30	.93

interpret. We see with $L^2(H_0)/df(H_0)$ as an index of total variation in these data that the variation is 53.64, 4.83, 12.00, and 2.06 for the white male, nonwhite male, white female, and nonwhite female samples, respectively. Since L^2 varies with sample size, a correction factor should be used to adjust the variation in the nonwhite data. Since the white samples were approximately five and one-half times as large as the nonwhite samples, the nonwhite indexes should be multiplied by 5.5 to make these statistics comparable. Carrying out this multiplication, we see that these indexes of variation are 53.64, 25.57 ($=4.83 \times 5.5$), 12.00, and 11.33 ($=2.06 \times 5.5$), respectively, showing that the relative ordering of the sex–race groups as regards total variation in labor force status is now considerably different. Males exhibit the largest variation, and white males exhibit the largest variation of all. White and nonwhite females exhibit about the same order of total variation in labor force status.

A preliminary gauge of the adequacy of the models in explaining the data is provided by the likelihood-ratio χ^2 statistic divided by its degrees of freedom. By examining the progression in this quantity from the simpler to the more complex models for each sex–race group, we are able to note the following:

1. The fit of the full model $H_{(A,T,C)}$ is very good for white males, for nonwhite males, and for nonwhite females, but it is not so good for white females (L^2/df is 1.06, .96, .93, and 1.60, respectively, for these groups).

2. For virtually *all* the sex–race groups, progression from the simple models ($H_{(A)}, H_{(T)}, H_{(C)}$) to the more complex models ($H_{(A,T)}, H_{(A,C)}, H_{(T,C)}$) to the full model ($H_{(A,T,C)}$) produces moderate to substantial improvement in L^2/df. The exception is for nonwhite females, where we apparently do better for $H_{(A,C)}$ or $H_{(T,C)}$ than for the full model. But even for nonwhite females the cohort variable seems important, since two of the models that are plausible contain cohort effects. Were it not for the uneasiness in interpreting the effects of a cohort variable without first controlling for the age and time-period variables, we might be led to conclude that *apparent* time-period variation for nonwhite females is purely spurious, since $H_{(A,T,C)}$ does not contribute substantially to explaining the variation in labor force status over the model $H_{(A,C)}$.

3. Given the overall sample sizes, $H_{(A,T,C)}$, allowing for the main effects of age, time-period, and cohort, does admirably well for the four race–sex groups. In fact, if we consider the sum of $L^2(H_{(A,T,C)})$ over all four samples, then the resulting χ^2 statistic on $4 \times 78 = 312$ df, equal to 354.61, produces $L^2/df = 1.14$ and a descriptive level of significance of approximately .09.

From these considerations, it is fair to conclude that the full model is an acceptable model for each of these samples, with the possible exception of the white female sample. In the remainder of this section, we provide additional comment about the overall adequacy of fit of these models and the contribution of the cohort variable to that fit. Even without examining parameter estimates, over which there is the inherent ambiguity in choosing suitable identifying restrictions, it will still be possible to make statements about the total contribution of a cohort variable to our understanding of labor force dynamics.

In order to gauge more fully overall goodness-of-fit, coefficients analogous to the unadjusted and adjusted multiple R^2 statistics of regression analysis are presented in Table 6.2.[6] Although these measures do not depend on sample size, they do depend on the extent of unexplained varia-

---

[6] Indexes somewhat analogous to the usual multiple and partial R^2 statistics of regression analysis were presented by Goodman (1971a) for use with log-linear models. On the adjusted coefficients, see Theil (1971). The use of both unadjusted and adjusted coefficients in the process of model selection is discussed by Hocking (1976). Wiorkowski (1970) presents a critique of the usual procedures for obtaining adjusted coefficients, observing that the adjusted coefficients can occasionally become negative. Rather than use his suggested adjustments, the usual adjusted coefficients were used for simplicity.

TABLE 6.2
Multiple R^2 and Adjusted Multiple R^2 for Cohort Models of Table 6.1

Model	Degrees of freedom, df	White males	Nonwhite males	White females	Nonwhite females
		Multiple R^2			
$H_{(A)}$	120	.953	.807	.817	.638
$H_{(T)}$	140	.028	.047	.077	.013
$H_{(C)}$	112	.857	.789	.809	.606
$H_{(A,T)}$	112	.979	.845	.897	.654
$H_{(A,C)}$	84	.977	.874	.918	.751
$H_{(C,T)}$	104	.958	.834	.835	.694
$H_{(A,T,C)}$	78	.990	.895	.930	.763
		Adjusted multiple R^2			
$H_{(A)}$	120	.942	.796	.774	.554
$H_{(T)}$	140	$.00^a$	$.00^a$	.024	$.00^a$
$H_{(C)}$	112	.811	.721	.747	.479
$H_{(A,T)}$	112	.973	.796	.863	.457
$H_{(A,C)}$	84	.959	.777	.856	.562
$H_{(C,T)}$	104	.940	.764	.766	.564
$H_{(A,T,C)}$	78	.980	.800	.867	.550

^{a}Adjusted R^2 was negative.

tion in the baseline model H_0. (The variation in these data was quite different among the sex–race groups.) In terms of the unadjusted measures, however, we see that the full model does better for whites regardless of sex ($R^2 = .990$ for white males, and $R^2 = .930$ for white females), than for nonwhite males ($R^2 = .895$) or for nonwhite females ($R^2 = .763$). The unadjusted coefficients show much the same pattern but highlight the very remarkable fit for white males (adjusted $R^2 = .980$), and the relatively poor fit for nonwhite females (adjusted $R^2 = .550$). These adjusted coefficients increase in magnitude from the simpler to the more complicated models, in every case except for nonwhite females. This should be the case if additional parameters are contributing more than would be expected merely on the basis of chance. It is striking that for the subpopulation with the highest overall variation [white males with $L^2(H_0)/df$ of 53.64], the variation explained by simple main effects of these demographic variables is the *greatest*.

In Section 6.3, we presented a rationale that assigned logical priority to the age and time-period variables over the cohort variable and defined a total cohort effect only as a *partial* effect of the cohort variable, *controlling* for the effects of age and time-period. This perspective implies that certain *partial* coefficients should be calculated in order to examine the influence

TABLE 6.3
Partial R^2 Controlling for Age, for Some Age, Time-period, and Cohort Models

	White male	Nonwhite male	White female	Nonwhite female
	Partial R²			
$T \mid A$	.557	.199	.435	.044
$C \mid A$	.502	.346	.553	.313
$C,T \mid A$	.778	.456	.617	.344
	Adjusted partial R²			
$T \mid A$	.525	.142	.395	.00[a]
$C \mid A$	.288	.066	.361	.019
$C,T \mid A$	.659	.162	.411	.00[a]

[a]Adjusted partial R^2 was negative.

of the cohort variable. Table 6.3 presents unadjusted and adjusted squared partial correlation coefficients between the labor force status variable and time-period, between the labor force status variable and cohort, and between the labor force status variable and both the variables age and time-period, each of which control for the effects of age. We see once again the negligible effects for nonwhite females, the moderate effects for nonwhite males, and the very substantial effects for white males (especially) and for white females. Thus, even though on statistical grounds the fit for non-whites was generally better than that for whites, in terms of proportion of variation explained by the models, the converse is true.

Table 6.4 presents in summary form the total or overall cohort effect, where this is understood as a *partial* effect of the cohort variable controlling for *both* age and time-period. We see that cohort differences that cannot be attributed to aging and/or to time-period must exist for these

TABLE 6.4
Total Effect of Cohort, Controlling for Age and Time-period

Sex–race group	Partial R^2	Adjusted partial R^2
White male	.500	.282
Nonwhite male	.320	.024
White female	.322	.026
Nonwhite female	.314	.00[a]

[a]Adjusted partial R^2 was negative.

TABLE 6.5
Summary of the Goodness-of-Fit of the Full Model $H_{(A,T,C)}$ for Each of the Sex–Race Groups

Sex–race group	L^2 $H_{(A,T)}$ (1)	L^2 $H_{(A,T,C)}$ (2)	(1)–(2) (3)[a]	(3)÷(1) (4)[b]	Index of dissimilarity (percent) (5)	P-value of L^2 (6)	$\dfrac{L^2(H_{(A,T,C)})}{df}$ (7)
White males	165.17	82.61	82.56	.500	.95	.36	1.06
Nonwhite males	110.60	75.19	35.41	.320	3.01	> .5	.96
White females	183.52	124.51	59.01	.322	1.54	< .001	1.60
Nonwhite females	105.38	72.30	33.08	.314	3.29	> .5	.93

[a]To be compared with 34, the additional number of parameters in $H_{(A,T,C)}$ relative to $H_{(A,T)}$.
[b]Equivalent to the unadjusted "partial R^2" coefficients in Table 6.4.

TABLE 6.6

Indexes of Time-Period Variation and of Age Variation, Showing the Distortion Resulting from the Cohort Variable

Controls	White male	Nonwhite male	White female	Nonwhite female
A. Indexes of time-period variation in labor force status[a]				
Age	.556	.199	.435	.044
Age and cohort	.556	.167	.143	.314
B. Indexes of age variation in labor force status[a]				
Time	.979	.838	.888	.649
Time and cohort	.755	.364	.574	.225

[a]"Squared partial correlation coefficient" between labor force status and time-period or age, with the given controls.

sex–race groups, and we also see that the cohort effect (in this partial sense) must be strongest overall for white males and less strong for the other sex–race groups. For nonwhite females, we see once again that cohort differentiation (in the sense in which we have defined it) must be small, since the adjusted squared partial correlation coefficient is negative. For nonwhite males and for white females, the *overall* cohort effect is nearly identical.

In Table 6.5, a summary of the results is presented, providing additional documentation that the full model $H_{(A,T,C)}$ is acceptable on the whole and that this model provides some evidence of marked cohort differentials when compared with model $H_{(A,T)}$ for some groups. An additional index of fit, the index of dissimilarity between observed and expected frequencies for $H_{(A,T,C)}$ [i.e., $\Delta = (\Sigma |f_{ijkl} - F_{ijkl}|/2n) \times 100$] shows in different terms the goodness-of-fit of this model. When sample size is taken into account, as with the index of dissimilarity, we see that the full model does admirably well overall, since the index of dissimilarity ranges from .95 to 3.29%.[7]

Another point of view from which to interpret the results presented in the preceding tables is contained in Table 6.6. One way to view the effect of the cohort variable is to examine the degree to which it distorts our

[7] The index of dissimilarity used here will not have an upper bound of 100%, implying that this index should be normed in some way. We present this index, even though it is not properly normed, in order to evaluate further the adequacy of fit apart from the influence of sample size. Pullum (1975, Appendix 6) demonstrates the calculation of the maximum index of dissimilarity for some cases, but his formulas would not apply in the present context. Related comments are also contained in Cortese *et al.* (1976), although the formulas presented by these authors to "standardize" the index of dissimilarity would also be difficult to apply in the present context.

perception of time-period variation in labor force status or our perception of age variation in labor force status. Indexes of time-period variation—the "squared partial correlation coefficients," used earlier—are presented in Table 6.6 with this objective in mind. When the effects of the age variable are controlled, we see that these indexes of time variation in labor force status are .556, .199, .435, and .044 for white males, nonwhite males, white females, and nonwhite females, respectively. After controlling for effects of age *and* cohort these same indexes are .556, .167, .143, and .314. This shows that *overall variation* in time-period change in labor force status remains constant when the cohort variable is taken into account for white males, but it changes markedly for the other sex–race groups. For nonwhite males the total time-period variation is somewhat dampened (.199–.167), for white females the total time-period variation is greatly dampened (.435–.143), and for nonwhite females the total time-period variation is greatly *increased* by controlling for the effects of the cohort variable (.044–.314). These results suggest that it might be plausible to assume that apparent time-period variation is somewhat distorted by the confounding of the cohort variable. Also presented in Table 6.6 are corresponding indexes of age variation, first controlling for the effects of time-period and then controlling for the effects of both time-period and cohort. We see that the apparent age variation is greatly dampened by controlling for the cohort variable for all the sex–race groups. An attempt will be made later to see how dramatic the cohort distortion really is.

The results presented in this section show that the full model $H_{(A,T,C)}$, involving the main effects of age, time-period, and cohort, provides an acceptable model for these data. No interactions among these three variables are necessary, apart from the special kind of interaction among age and time-period that is implicitly contained in a model with all three main effects. We have shown that strong cohort differences are apparent for white males and that moderate to strong cohort differences are apparent for white females and for nonwhite males. The statements we have made about the strength of cohort effects are not limited by the identification problem of cohort analysis, given the conception of a cohort effect as a *partial* effect of the cohort variable only after the age and time-period variables are controlled. The model $H_{(A,T,C)}$ is identified, and coefficients presented in Tables 6.1–6.6 are therefore unambiguous. These results by themselves are evidence for the need to consider the cohort variable, and the cohort concept, in the analysis of work force dynamics in this time span for the U.S. population aged 20–34. In the next section, we will present *identified* parameter estimates corresponding to $H_{(A,T,C)}$, showing the tempo of social change in the labor force, but because of the ambiguity over the nature of the identifying restrictions, there is some ambiguity over their interpretation.

6.5 IDENTIFIED COHORT PARAMETERS, SHOWING THE TEMPO OF SOCIAL CHANGE IN THE LABOR FORCE

The computer program described in Appendix G was used to estimate parameters for the full model $H_{(A,T,C)}$ involving main effects of age, time-period, and cohort. We tried several different kinds of restrictions in order to identify the parameters, but in every instance, we restricted only the relationship between the *two oldest cohorts*.[8] Our assumption was as follows: In an era of quickening social change in the labor force and in the social institutions that influence the future labor force experience of youth, it is probably least damaging to assume that the oldest cohorts are negligibly different from each other with respect to their "intrinsic" (i.e., cohort) pattern of labor force participation or of underemployment. Presumably, our error in assuming equality between the effects of the two oldest cohorts will have the least deleterious influence upon our perception of age, time-period, and cohort effects. With these assumptions in mind, one set of identified cohort effect parameters will be presented.

Because the dependent variable of this chapter is a trichotomy, it is necessary to formulate an approach through which the model parameters can be substantively interpreted. To take account of the special meaning that attaches to the dependent variable, effects will be coded in a way analogous to the coding of effects in analysis of variance (compare Ott, 1977; or Bock, 1975). The specific "contrasts" used here are actually analogous to "Helmert contrasts," which are often used in analysis of variance. Since we have $F_{ijkl} = \tau_{ij}^{AT}\tau_{il}^{AU}\tau_{jl}^{TU}\tau_{kl}^{CU}$, we can define effects by taking the ratios

$$\frac{(F_{ijk2}F_{ijk3})^{1/2}}{F_{ijk1}}$$

and

$$\frac{F_{ijk2}}{F_{ijk3}}$$

[8] To verify identification of parameters in the full model $H_{(A,T,C)}$, given the several kinds of identifying restrictions that we imposed, we can alter start values for the parameters in that algorithm used in the computer program of Appendix G and see if different start values produce the same final estimates. This technique was used to verify that the restrictions actually imposed would identify the parameters.

and examining the relationship of the model parameters to these quantities. The first ratio is a measure of tendency for a member of the ith age, in the jth time-period, and the kth cohort to be participating in the labor force. Corresponding to this measure, we find that $(\tau_{k2}^{CU}\tau_{k3}^{CU})^{1/2}/\tau_{k1}^{CU}$ will describe the effect of membership in the kth cohort on that measure. The logarithm of this function of the parameters will accordingly be designated as a *labor force participation effect*. The second quantity above (i.e., F_{ijk2}/F_{ijk3}) is a measure of the tendency for a member of the relevant age–time-period–cohort category to be underemployed. Corresponding to this measure we find that $\tau_{k2}^{CU}/\tau_{k3}^{CU}$ will describe the effect of membership in the kth cohort on that measure. The logarithm of this function of the parameters will be designated as an *underemployment effect*. Other techniques could certainly be used to code the τ^{CU} parameters for substantive interpretation, but the approach just suggested certainly seems reasonable. Note that in the definition of the underemployment effect the not-in-labor-force category is not directly relevant, since, for example, the quantities F_{ijk1} and τ_{k1}^{CU} have been ignored.

Table 6.7 presents the cohort effects on labor force participation, where these are defined as in the previous paragraph. Since the full model $H_{(A,T,C)}$ has been used to calculate them, they can be interpreted as partial effects of cohort, controlling for the effects of age and time-period. Because these models were applied separately to each race–sex group, comparisons across rows in Table 6.7 are inappropriate, since each set of parameters depends on the different restriction used for each group to identify parameters. (See the note to Table 6.7.) To interpret these quantities, it is imperative that the concept of a cohort effect be borne in mind; in Section 6.3, it was suggested that these be regarded as "intrinsic" cohort characteristics—since the age and time-period effects are controlled—and that further they should be interpreted as indicators of the social forces that operated in past history to produce distinct cohorts. Cohort differentiation, as judged by differences among these cohort effects, is to be regarded as an indicator of the tempo of social change in the labor force wrought by the entry of new cohorts. The following general observations can be made on the basis of results in Table 6.7.

1. Younger cohorts of white males have a greater intrinsic tendency to participate in the labor force than do older cohorts. The average amount of change in the cohort effects (disregarding the two oldest cohorts, which, by assumption, have identical effects) is .42; that is, the effect of cohort on participation is .42 greater on the average for a given cohort relative to the next oldest cohort. We might take this mean change in

TABLE 6.7
Identified Cohort Parameters, Showing the Tempo of Social Change in Labor Force Participation

Cohort category	Participation effect			
	White male	Nonwhite male	White female	Nonwhite female
1	9.61	−13.78	−4.16	−7.01
2	9.04	−13.44	−4.03	−6.64
3	8.36	−12.80	−3.85	−6.16
4	7.88	−11.88	−3.67	−5.89
5	7.44	−11.16	−3.45	−5.38
6	7.00	−10.27	−3.25	−5.16
7	6.53	− 9.17	−3.08	−4.65
8	6.07	− 8.46	−2.97	−4.39
9	5.82	− 7.38	−2.80	−3.98
10	5.47	− 6.16	−2.61	−3.54
11	4.93	− 5.46	−2.53	−3.33
12	4.81	− 4.66	−2.33	−2.91
13	4.21	− 3.39	−2.17	−2.52
14	4.13	− 2.76	−1.93	−2.26
15	3.95	− 2.09	−1.73	−2.10
16	3.35	− 1.10	−1.71	−1.56
17	3.05	+ .26	−1.35	−1.13
18	2.49[a]	+ 1.75[a]	−1.20[a]	− .45[a]
19	2.49[a]	+ 1.75[a]	−1.20[a]	− .45[a]

[a]Parameters restricted to equal observed participation effect for the nineteenth cohort category for relevant sex–race group.

effects as a summary measure of the tempo of social change; for white males the tempo of social change is very great indeed.

2. Younger cohorts of nonwhite males have a *lesser* intrinsic tendency to participate in the labor force than do older cohorts. The tempo of social change is −.91, or in other words, the average change from one cohort to the next oldest is −.91. We can infer that there has been very marked social change in regard to the labor force participation of nonwhites here, with the result that newer cohorts are much less likely to participate than are older cohorts. The decline in labor force participation for nonwhite males has been noted in many contexts; here, the cohort trend is consistent with the general time-trend and can serve in part to explain that time-trend.

3. Younger cohorts of white females have a *lesser* intrinsic tendency to

participate in the labor force than do older cohorts. The tempo of social change, measured as before, is $-.17$ and is not nearly so large as for males. This observation would seem to contradict popular understanding of the intrinsic participation patterns of younger cohorts of white women in this era. But here it is once again necessary to revert to the interpretation of these cohort effects in the context of the model at hand. These cohort effects are partial effects, controlled for time-period effects, and much of the rise in labor force participation for white women across this time span can be attributed to time-period effects.[9] Since the differences among cohort effects are slight, perhaps it would even be prudent to suspend judgment concerning their substantive interpretation.

4. Younger cohorts of nonwhite females also have a *lesser* intrinsic tendency to participate in the labor force than do older cohorts. The tempo of social change is $-.39$ which, on the scale used here, is over twice that for white females. The tempo of social change is approximately of the same magnitude as for white males—although in an opposite direction.

Perhaps the best way to summarize the above general observations is with the average change in effect across cohorts. These figures were .42, $-.91$, $-.17$, and $-.39$ for white males, nonwhite males, white females, and nonwhite females, respectively. As will be apparent to the reader, some of these conclusions about the intrinsic labor force participation tendencies of successive cohorts run somewhat counter to prior expectations. Results for white males and females, especially, run counter to our prior expectations and therefore beg further explanation.

Table 6.8 presents the cohort effects on underemployment, $\log(\tau_{k2}^{CU}/\tau_{k3}^{CU})$. Because of the nature of the identifying restrictions, again these quantities cannot be directly compared across the sex–race groups. But the trend across cohorts can be discussed in the same way as participation effects were discussed previously. The following observations can be made regarding the intrinsic cohort tendencies to be underemployed.

1. Younger cohorts of white males have a *greater* intrinsic tendency to be underemployed than do older cohorts. The average change in the underemployment effect is $+.19$, showing that each cohort has, on the

---

[9] Recall that social change that occurs uniformly to each age group over time will be encompassed in the *time-period* effects. We are suggesting that, for the interval 1969–1973, perhaps this type of social change predominated. A tantalizing theoretical issue arises here, since for white females the cohort effects do not exhibit the same general pattern as do the time-period effects. That is, with the progress of time, there is an increase in the tendency to participate in the labor force for white women, but younger cohorts appear to have an *intrinsic* tendency to participate less when the time-period effects are controlled.

TABLE 6.8
Identified Cohort Parameters, Showing the Tempo of Social Change in Underemployment

Cohort category	Underemployment effect			
	White male	Nonwhite male	White female	Nonwhite female
1	+ .11	−5.19	−3.02	8.85
2	− .06	−5.25	−2.96	8.08
3	− .26	−4.80	−2.81	7.53
4	− .36	−4.60	−2.51	7.06
5	− .54	−4.72	−2.62	6.59
6	− .69	−4.41	−2.46	5.98
7	− .86	−4.36	−2.44	5.52
8	−1.09	−4.51	−2.36	5.08
9	−1.41	−4.16	−2.12	4.33
10	−1.52	−3.81	−2.01	3.89
11	−1.79	−3.73	−1.92	3.09
12	−1.80	−3.67	−1.91	2.46
13	−1.90	−3.27	−1.78	1.96
14	−2.14	−3.28	−1.68	1.58
15	−2.36	−2.90	−1.62	.89
16	−2.56	−2.79	−1.69	.44
17	−2.65	−2.67	−1.37	− .29
18	−3.09[a]	−2.38[a]	−1.35[a]	− .80[a]
19	−3.09[a]	−2.38[a]	−1.35[a]	− .80[a]

[a]Parameters constrained to equal observed underemployment effect for the nineteenth cohort category for relevant sex–race group.

average, a .19 greater underemployment effect than the cohort 1 year older.

2. Younger cohorts of nonwhite males have a *lesser* tendency to be underemployed than do older cohorts. The average change from one cohort to the next is −.17, showing the tempo of social change in underemployment for nonwhite males. Nonwhite males have a lesser intrinsic risk to underemployment with the succession of each new cohort, but previous analysis suggested that they also have lower intrinsic tendencies to participate in the labor force.

3. Younger cohorts of white females have a lesser intrinsic tendency to be underemployed, and the tempo of social change (−.11) is roughly similar to that of nonwhite males.

4. Younger cohorts of nonwhite females have a *greater* tendency to be underemployed, and the tempo of social change in underemployment for this group is a dramatic .57.

As a partial summary of these rather unwieldy results, consider the quantity referred to above as the index of the tempo of social change. For the intrinsic participation effects derived from the cohort parameters, we found that these quantities were .42, −.91, −.17, and −.39, and for the intrinsic underemployment effects, we found that these quantities were .19, −.17, −.11, and .57, respectively, for white males, nonwhite males, white females and nonwhite females. That is,

1. Younger cohorts of white males have a greater tendency to participate but also a greater tendency to be underemployed.
2. Younger cohorts of nonwhite males have a lesser tendency to participate but also a lesser tendency to be underemployed.
3. Younger cohorts of white females have a lesser tendency to participate but also a lesser tendency to be underemployed.
4. Younger cohorts of nonwhite females have a lesser tendency to participate *and* a greater tendency to be underemployed.

We presently have little more than conjecture to explain these features of the data. Perhaps, since these results are based only on 5 years of labor force experience, it would be prudent to avoid serious theoretical generalization here. However, these cohort parameters, as well as the deductions that derive from them, are very provocative. If our cohort model is not seriously misspecified, and if the cohort trends exhibited in these data are suggestive of trends subsequent to 1973, then these intriguing empirical results would be important benchmark figures that a full-fledged theory of across-time change in labor force structure would explain. For nonwhite males, it might be argued that these results indicate a bifurcation in their labor market opportunity. Nonwhite males *as a whole* have an intrinsic tendency to participate less and less with each new cohort, but for those who *do* participate, the intrinsic tendency to underemployment is diminishing.

6.6 THE "TRUE" ACROSS-TIME VARIATION IN LABOR FORCE STATUS: THE CASE OF WHITE MALES

Thus far in this chapter we have alluded several times to the effect that the cohort variable might have on our perception of time-period change (or labor market change). In this section, we provide estimates of the "true" time-period change in the distribution among the labor force statuses. These estimates are developed in a way that is entirely consistent with the cohort perspective. Since cohort effects are conceived (tautologically) as attributes of cohorts that do not change over time, the entry of new cohorts to each cross section in time will have a decided effect on labor force characteristics observed in any cross section. A variety of methods suggest themselves for the examination of this phenomenon, the most direct of which might be a comparison of the γ^{TU} parameters from model $H_{(A,T)}$, where the cohort effects are not controlled, with the γ^{TU} parameters from the full model $H_{(A,T,C)}$, where the cohort effects are controlled. However, it is not directly apparent how the γ^{TU} parameters, which describe effects on certain *ratios* of expected frequencies, should be brought to bear on interpreting the differences in rates. Here we will focus on the manner in which the cohort effects γ^{CU} distort our perception of across-time variation in rates, the approach for which is outlined in Appendix F.

The approach to be followed here can be summarized by reference to the full model presented as Equation 6.5. It will be recalled that this model related expected frequencies F_{ijkl} to parameters denoting main effects of age, time-period, and cohort. We can purge the F_{ijkl} of the cohort effects by taking $F^*_{ijkl} = F_{ijkl}/\tau^{CU}_{kl}$, so that the "purged" frequencies F^* are free of the cohort effects but depend on the (partial) age and time-period effects estimated from the full model. Rates of occurrence of the labor force statuses can be calculated from the F^*, and—given the specification of the model that yielded the parameter estimates—these rates are free of the cohort distortion. These purged rates can be compared to the observed rates to examine the influence of the cohort effects *on the rates,* and this procedure is wholly consistent with the cohort model chosen to explain the data. Here we apply this technique to the data on white males.

Table 6.9 presents the across-time changes in the distribution among labor force statuses. In the upper tier of the table are the changes actually observed. The percentage of persons not in the labor force declined, then rose, and then steadily declined. The percentage of those who are economically underemployed rose through the first three intervals and declined in the fourth. However, when the cohort effects are purged from the data, and the percentage distributions are recalculated, a markedly different perspective emerges. The percentage of persons not in the labor force—if cohort effects are removed—increases steadily over time, and the percentage of those who are economically underemployed declined steadily (although slightly) over time. The overall variability in the observed percentage changes is seen to be much greater than with the purged data. It seems fair to state that the time-period change in the purged data represents a truer gauge of the effects of time-period, implying that transitory labor market fluctuation is best depicted by the entries in the lower tier of Table 6.9. Although we will not take the space to present the purged time-period change for the other race–sex groups, it is clear that a very

TABLE 6.9
Observed Time-period Change in Labor Force Status, and Time-period Change Purged of the Cohort Effects (in Percentages)

	1970–1969	1971–1970	1972–1971	1973–1972
	Observed change			
Not-in-labor force	– .3	+ .9	–.9	– .3
Economic under-employment	+ 1.3	+ 3.3	+ .4	–2.0
Productive employment	–1.0	–4.2	+ .5	+ 2.3
	Change purged of cohort effects			
Not-in-labor force	+ .4	+ .4	+ .2	+ .2
Economic under-employment	– .2	– .1	–.1	– .1
Productive employment	– .2	– .3	–.1	– .1

different empirical summary of time-period change ensues from this approach. In our view, this approach to measuring time-period change free of cohort effects holds much promise for the demographic analysis of the labor market.

6.7 SOME OTHER COHORT MODELS

Since the relatively simple model $H_{(A,T,C)}$ fits our data well, there is little point in estimating other, more complicated models for the data of the present chapter. We here outline some other kinds of log-linear cohort models that might be useful in other contexts. An extensive discussion of these matters is presented by Fienberg and Mason (1978), and so we will concentrate only on some matters that are not brought out fully in their seminal work.

Suppose two or more populations are considered (e.g., males and females) and it is of interest to consider the hypothesis that the cohort effects were homogeneous across the populations. If we have arranged the data in a full age × time-period × cohort × underemployment × population cross-table (say, an $A \times T \times C \times U \times P$ table), where the resulting structural zeros were taken into account, then the model assuming homogeneity of cohort effects (but not age or time-period effects) is obtained by fitting the marginals $(ATCP)(UC)(UTP)(UAP)$. Extensions of this kind of "partial heterogeneity" model (i.e., heterogeneous age and time-period effects but homogeneous cohort effects across the populations) follow trivially from more general models developed by Goodman (1973b) in a different context.

None of the models of this chapter restricted the nature of the relationship between the dependent variable and the independent variables of cohort analysis. They were in this respect analogous to the "dummy variable regression" models (i.e., "multiple classification analysis") used by Mason (1973) and her co-workers. If we were to posit a relationship that more explicitly took into account the *distance* between age categories, the *distance* between time-period categories, and the *distance* between cohort categories (e.g., single years), and if we wished to examine the dependence of the variable in question upon the linear, quadratic, cubic effects etc. of these variables, taking into account the additional information in the distance between variable categories, then log-linear models for ordered classifications presented by Haberman (1974a,b) would be appropriate.[10]

An approach whereby the relative *size* of cohorts were to be considered as the sole explanatory factor attaching to cohort category could also be tested, but as in the above paragraph, this type of model would require use of a Newton–Raphson-type algorithm. An extension of orthogonal polynomial contrasts in the log-linear model for ordered classifications seems well suited to this more restrictive kind of cohort model. If c_k, $k = 1, \ldots, I + J - 1$ are scores such that $\Sigma_k c_k = 0$, which reflect the relative size of the $I + J - 1$ cohorts (say, at age 20), where I is the number of age categories and J is the number of time-periods, then these scores could also be used to generate a vector basis for the full cohort model and could also be estimated with the general methods suggested by Haberman (1974b) for ordered data. This model would satisfy the demographer's wish to examine the influence of cohort size more explicitly than we have done in this chapter.

Sometimes it is of interest to entertain the hypothesis that for certain sets of adjacent cohort categories, the cohort effects are identical within each set but are different when compared among these certain sets. For example, we might wish to entertain the hypothesis that cohorts aged 20

---

[10] In summarizing the cohort effect parameters in the previous section, we calculated the average change in cohort parameters and designated this figure as an index of the "tempo of social change." This quantity is actually similar to a linear effect of cohort category on participation or on underemployment. However, we did not estimate the model in which only a linear effect of cohort was allowed to exist (and where quadratic, cubic, etc. effects were set equal to zero).

after the Vietnam War era are identical but different from cohorts aged 20 prior to the Vietnam War era. This type of model is a direct application of the "triangles parameter" model presented by Goodman (1972c) in a more general context than the cohort context and can also be tested.

Other kinds of cohort models in addition to the ones presented here could also be constructed on the basis of existing statistical techniques. These kinds of models were not considered here because less complicated models were found to fit our data. In view of the central importance of the cohort variable and the cohort concept to modern demography and to sociological study of social change, it would be very fruitful to develop these models further.

6.8 CONCLUSION

This chapter has considered age, time-period, and cohort effects on labor force status for the race–sex subpopulations aged 20–34. A perspective was proposed whereby cohort effects could be substantively discussed. We found significant cohort differentiation among labor force statuses that could not be attributed to aging or time-period variation. An attempt was made to estimate parameters showing that cohort differentiation. If our estimates are correct, then our results contradict the popular view concerning the intrinsic labor force characteristics of successive cohorts in the current experience (e.g., labor force participation tendencies of white men and women). In our view, the perspectives and the log-linear methods used in this chapter will become generally useful in demographic cohort analysis and in sociological study of social change. The methods presented here also suggest new ways to measure, in particular, the time-trend in labor force experience.

7

trending and forecasting underemployment: log-linear models and population projection

Spilerman (1975) has noted the deficiency in social indicator models regarding the forecasting, trending, and prediction of social events. Social events are usually conceived as qualitative characteristics, implying that special statistical methods are required for this task. Most social events partition a relevant population into discrete statuses (such as labor force statuses), implying that standard methods of demography used to project the population into the future can be modified to project the relative size of different statuses into the future, given reasonable assumptions concerning the persistence of the age distribution of those statuses. That is, the population can be classified into discrete statuses reflecting the various social events of interest, and an entire range of statistical and demographic methods can be brought to bear upon the problem of forecasting and prediction. The underemployment variable of this work is a qualitative one, classifying persons into several mutually exclusive and exhaustive categories, and so this chapter is concerned with trending and forecasting this qualitative variable, using methods somewhat different from those associated with Box and Jenkins (1970; compare Nelson, 1973; Vigderhous, 1977).

Until the 1970s, time-series techniques had not attracted the attention of sociologists, primarily because these methods usually provided little *substantive* rationale for the statistical trending and forecasting. The customary methods did not, for instance, do much more than trend past experience into the future, assuming all other things equal; they provided little insight into the underlying process of social change. Concepts of autoregression, moving averages, and certain generalizations thereof have apparently not been convincing as structural models of across-time change. These criticisms also apply to the approaches discussed in this chapter, although perhaps with less severity. However, in view of the extremely complex character of underemployment, we should be content at this stage to provide reasonable statistical forecasts, even if the forecasting techniques that we use do not wholly capture the sociological processes underlying the change in underemployment with time. Such an orientation will be familiar to economists engaged in time-series research. Demographers will also be content with this point of view, since trending and forecasting have always been of vital concern to demographic science.

The first approach used in this chapter is an adaptation of a special kind of log-linear model, suited to the distributional assumptions appropriate for a qualitative variable like the underemployment variable of this study. It is an application of more general methods discussed by Cox (1970), Goodman (1971a), Haberman (1974b), Bock (1975, Chapter 8), and others. The technique can be applied with use of the MULTIQUAL program of Bock and Yates (1973) and can also be applied with similar programs for logit analysis. A fuller exposition of this method, making explicit the matrix formulas involved, is presented by Clogg (1979a), and related but different methods are also discussed by Heckman (1978).

The second method to be discussed is a modification of the population projection matrix and is suggested by material in Keyfitz (1968). It is related to the so-called demographic accounting method of Stone (1971, 1975) and is thus related directly to a significant body of methodology now being considered for the study of social indicators. At the conclusion of the chapter, an approach whereby these seemingly unrelated methods can be merged is suggested. Since we are working with a time series that is already several years out of date, the utility of some of the actual projections of this chapter is somewhat limited. However, the methodological insight that will hopefully be obtained is of considerable interest in itself.

7.1 FORECASTING UNDEREMPLOYMENT BY LOG-LINEAR TIME-TREND MODELS

The usual time-series forecast of a quantitative variable y, observed at each of $t = 1, \ldots , T$ points in time, is based upon trending of past experience in a reasonable way and then "forecasting" y along that trend curve. If y_T represents the vector of observations, the standard approach is to consider a model of the form

$$y_t = f(\mathbf{y}_T) + e_t, \qquad t = 1, \ldots, T$$

where the e_t are normally distributed error terms with constant variance and zero autocorrelation. The functional form f in those applications with which we are familiar is a *linear* function of the observations chosen in such a way to ensure that the e_t have the desired statistical properties (see, e.g., Theil, 1971). When a suitable function f, hopefully as simple as possible, can be found to purge the error term of undesirable properties (e.g., autocorrelation), the forecast into the future for any $t' > T$ is given as the projection along the trend curve fit to the original T observations. That forecast will be ''optimal'' to the extent to which the chosen function f has ensured regular properties to the random distrubance terms e_t and to the extent that time-trend in the past can serve as a prediction of the future.

One kind of log-linear forecast is based upon a time-trending of logits. Suppose, for simplicity, that we are interested in forecasting the logits of a dichotomous underemployment variable. As an example, consider the underemployment variable constructed from the sample of all persons aged 14 and over. Let this variable be denoted as U, with class $i = 1$ corresponding to the number in the sample not underemployed and $i = 2$ corresponding to the number in the sample underemployed. Suppose further that we have samples of this binomial variable at $t = 1, \ldots, T$ points in time. The data for such a problem are laid out in a $2 \times T$ table cross-classifying U by T. (We let T refer both to the time variable and to the number of classes of that variable, but the meaning of T will be clear in the context in which it is used.) Since samples have been drawn at T successive points in time, the table is a set of T binomial samples, and it will therefore be necessary to fit the marginal (T) in any ''time-trend'' model in order not to violate restrictions imposed by our sampling design. We also assume that the T observations are equidistant in time, although we can easily modify our results if this is not the case. Let the observed frequencies be denoted as f_{it} and the expected frequencies, given some model, as F_{it}, $i = 1, 2$ and $t = 1, \ldots, T$. We consider a model for the $U \times T$ table whereby the expected logits of the dependent variable, $\log(F_{1t}/F_{2t})$, are related to the time points $t = 1, \ldots, T$ by the following relationship:

$$\Phi_t = \log(F_{1t}/F_{2t}) = A + B_1 t + B_2 t^2 + \cdots + B_{T-1} t^{T-1} \qquad (7.1)$$

$$= \mathbf{t}^{(T-1)'} \mathbf{B},$$

where $\mathbf{B}' = (A, B_1, \ldots, B_{T-1})$ and $\mathbf{t}^{(T-1)'} = (1, t, t^2, \ldots, t^{T-1})$, for

$t = 1, \ldots, T$. Equation (7.1) is a polynomial of degree $T - 1$ linking the expected logits of U to the time scores, and it will be desirable to find models that fit the data and in which several of the B_i are zero (see Haberman, 1974a,b). In this log-linear approach to time-trending, we have made weaker assumptions about the distribution of our dependent variable (i.e., it is binomial or Poisson) and can appeal to maximum likelihood methods generally associated with log-linear models. If we view the time process in underemployment as a Poisson process, with parameter λ_t possibly changing through time, then the sample at each point t provides us with an estimate of λ_t. It could be of interest to interpolate values of $\lambda_{t'}$ $1 < t' < T$ or to extrapolate values of $\lambda_{t'}, t' > T$, given our sample information. A similar interpretation follows if we assume U to be binomially distributed at each time point with parameter p_t depending upon time. The latter point of view is appropriate in the context of this chapter.

A log-linear forecast is straightforward, given Equation 7.1. To forecast the logits of U for time points $t' > T$, we merely find a suitable representation of the time trend in our observed $U \times T$ table. Suppose that this model is

$$\Phi_t = \log(F_{1t}/F_{2t}) = \mathbf{t}^{(p)\prime}\mathbf{B}^{(p)} \tag{7.2}$$

where $\mathbf{t}^{(p)}$, $\mathbf{B}^{(p)}$ are subsets of $\mathbf{t}^{(T-1)}$, $\mathbf{B}^{(T-1)}$, respectively. The predicted logit is then merely

$$\hat{\Phi}_{t'} = \mathbf{t}^{(p)\prime}\mathbf{b}^{(p)}, \qquad t' = T + 1, T + 2, \ldots, \tag{7.3}$$

where $\mathbf{t}^{(p)}$ is some subset of $\mathbf{t}^{(T-1)}$, where the time scores are now replaced by t', and where $\mathbf{b}^{(p)}$ is the sample estimate of $\mathbf{B}^{(p)}$. The predicted proportions in the ith state of U at time t' are given as

$$\hat{p}_{1t'} = \frac{\exp(\hat{\Phi}_{t'})}{1 + \exp(\hat{\Phi}_{t'})} \tag{7.4}$$

and

$$\hat{p}_{2t'} = 1 - \hat{p}_{1t'}$$

The variance of the $\hat{p}_{1t'}$ can be calculated from manipulation of the variance–covariance matrix associated with the estimated parameters b_i. The variance of the predicted logit would be given by

$$\mathrm{Var}(\hat{\Phi}_{t'}) = \mathbf{t}^{(p)\prime}\mathrm{Var}(\mathbf{b}^{(p)})\mathbf{t}^{(p)} \tag{7.5}$$

and this variance estimate would depend upon t'. That is, the variance of the forecast for time t' would depend upon the distance of t' from the mean of the original time scores. A minor complication arises in the application of formula 7.5 because $\mathrm{Var}(\mathbf{b}^{(p)})$ is not calculated by the MUL-

TIQUAL program of Bock and Yates (1973). The variance of $\hat{\beta}$ in the more general definition of log-linear models,

$$\log(F) = X\beta \qquad (7.6)$$

is computed at each step of the iterative process. The variance of $\hat{\Phi}_t$, a linear combination of elements of $\log(F)$, or the variance of $b^{(p)}$, a linear combination of the elements of $\hat{\beta}$, can be obtained by standard formulas for the variance of linear combinations of random variables. We do not go into those details here but refer the reader to Clogg (1979a), where these matters are discussed.

In sum, the approach advocated here seems well suited to the interpolation of logits (or proportions) between time points on which the original sample was obtained and to the extrapolation or projection of logits (or proportions) into the future. Although this technique has not to our knowledge been previously applied, there is little new in the log-linear forecast model.

As a first example, consider the 2×4 U by T table cross-classifying the sample of persons aged 14 and over into not underemployed– underemployed, for years 1969–1972. That table combines the adequately employed with the ''not-in-labor-force'' category to ensure that the population sampled is essentially unchanged from one time-period to another. The data are presented in Table 7.1, where we consider the problem of forecasting the proportion underemployed in 1973 from the trend observed 1969–1972. Four different logit models for that 2×4 table and the results for each are presented in Part C of Table 7.1. The model H_0 where $\hat{\Phi}_t = a$, equivalent to the usual hypothesis of independence for the 2×4 contingency table, yields a likelihood-ratio χ^2 of 491.79, contradicting this simplest time-trend model. Introducing a linear effect parameter produces model H_1, where $\hat{\Phi}_t = a + b_1 t$. With $L^2(H_1)$ of 13.69, we see that we have achieved a remarkable improvement in fit with the addition of only a single parameter. On such a large sample as this one, such a fit is certainly acceptable, even though the descriptive level of significance for H_1 is approximately .001. We see from some algebraic details that will not be presented here that $a = 1.7374$ and $b_1 = -.0844$, the latter term reflecting the decrease in economic opportunity 1969–1972. Using certain formulas presented in Clogg (1979a), we find that $SE(a) = .0043$, $SE(b_1) = .0039$. The constant term reflects the arbitrariness of our time scale; here we have used time scores -1.5, $-.5$, $+.5$, $+1.5$, for simplicity.

By substituting a value of $t' = 2.5$ corresponding to year 1973 in our time-trend model for the expected logits, we find that

$$\hat{\Phi}_{1973} = 1.5264 \quad \text{and} \quad \hat{p}_{2,1973} = .1785$$

TABLE 7.1
2 × 4 Table Cross-classifying the Population 14 and Over by Presence or Absence of Underemployment, 1969–1972

	1969	1970	1971	1972	1973
	A. Observed frequencies				
Not underemployed	93904	89004	89329	85750	(84035)
Underemployed	14611	14744	16790	16955	(16514)
Total	108515	103748	106119	102705	(100549)
	B. Observed and expected[a] logits				
	$\log(p_{1t}/p_{2t})$ and $\log(\hat{p}_{1t}/\hat{p}_{2t})$				
Observed	1.8605	1.7978	1.6715	1.6209	$(1.6270)^b$
Expected	1.8640	1.7796	1.6952	1.6108	$(1.5264)^b$

C. Goodness-of-fit for time-trend models

Model	L^2	X^2	df
$H_0: B_1 = B_2 = B_3 = 0$	491.79	491.12	3
$H_1: B_2 = B_3 = 0$	13.69	13.71	2
$H_2: B_3 = 0$	12.69	12.95	1
$H_3: B_2 = 0$	.48	.48	1

[a]Expected logits predicted from $\hat{\phi}_t = 1.7374 - .0844(t)$.
[b]$p_{1973} = .1642; \hat{p}_{1973} = .1785$.

where $\hat{p}_{2,1973}$ is the projected proportion underemployed in 1973. We also find that $SE(\hat{\Phi}_{1973}) = .0104$, and $SE(\hat{p}_{2,1973}) = .0015$. The observed logit and observed proportion underemployed in 1973 were 1.6270 and .1642, respectively. We see that by virtue of the upturn in the economy during 1973, we have overestimated the number of underemployed persons by 1.43%.

Model H_2 in Table 7.1, Part C corresponds to $\hat{\Phi}_t = a + b_1 t + b_2 t^2$, and we see that this model does not significantly reduce χ^2.

Model H_3 in Table 7.1, Part C corresponds to a linear and a cubic (but not a quadratic) term in the time-trend model. With an $L^2(H_3)$ of .84 on 1 df, we see that this model fits very well indeed. We find for this latter model that $a = 1.7377$, $b_1 = -.1325$, and $b_3 = .0234$. The predicted logit in 1973 is 1.7726, which is, however, worse than our first prediction by a considerable margin. Given the time trend 1969–1972, the upturn in the economy during 1973 was totally unexpected.

Table 7.2 presents log-linear time trend models for the full 2 × 5 table, including the underemployment experience of 1973. With such a large

TABLE 7.2
Log-Linear Time-Trend Models Applied to the 2 × 5 Underemployment by Time Table, 1969–1973

Model	L^2	X^2	df	$[L^2(H_0) - L^2(H_i)]/L^2(H_0)$
H_0: $B_1 = B_2 = B_3 = B_4 = 0$	619.74	613.70	4	–
H_1: $B_2 = B_3 = B_4 = 0$	69.90	70.02	3	.89
H_2: $B_3 = B_4 = 0$	23.64	23.55	2	.96
H_3: $B_4 = 0$	4.90	4.91	1	.99
H_4: $B_2 = B_4 = 0$	49.26	49.39	2	.92

sample size as the one in this table (N = over 500,000), the χ^2 of 69.90 for the simple linear time trend in logits should be adequate for most purposes. The addition of the quadratic term adds substantially, however, to goodness-of-fit, and we might consider $\hat{\Phi}_t = a + b_1 t + b_2 t^2$ as an acceptable summary of the time trend in our data.

Another example of this method exploits the fuller underemployment detail presented in Table 7.3. In this table, the generalization of the above technique is applied to trend a *polytomous* underemployment variable

TABLE 7.3
Underemployment by Time, Ages 14 and Over, 1969–1973

A. Raw cross-table						
		1969	1970	1971	1972	1973
Adequate	1	48017	45299	44373	42811	42350
Mismatch	2	5640	5560	6219	6363	6766
Economic underemployment	3	8971	9184	10571	10592	9748
Not-in-labor force	4	45887	43705	44956	42939	41685

B. Chi-square for time-trend models applied to above 4 × 5 table

Model (parameters included)	L^2	X^2	df	$[L^2(H_0) - L^2(H_i)]/L^2(H_0)$
H_0: constants	742.90	741.65	12	–
H_1: linear	155.66	155.69	9	.79
H_2: linear and quadratic	41.27	41.19	6	.94
H_3: linear, quadratic, and cubic	11.73	11.73	3	.98
H_4: all parameters	0.0	0.0	0	1.00

over time. We consider a series of models of the form

$$\Phi_{it} = \log(F_{it}/F_{4t}) = A_i + B_{i1}t + \cdots + B_{i4}t^4, \qquad i = 1, 2, 3 \quad (7.7)$$

The proper analogy of this model is to a multivariate regression, the application of which is extremely complex. In this case, the application of the log-linear model is much more simple. By following a kind of hierarchy principle, we might focus upon a subset of the wide variety of models possible where, if $B_{ik} = 0$, then $B_{ik'} = 0$ for $k' > k$, $i = 1, 2, 3$. The χ^2 statistics for such models are also presented in Table 7.3. By restricting our time-trending of the polytomous underemployment variable to models of the general kind in Equation 7.7, extrapolation or interpolation is also straightforward. We do not carry out such calculations, however, since our time series is already out of date. We see from Table 7.3 that the linear time-trend model is adequate (accounting for 79% of the across-time variation in underemployment) and that the quadratic terms contribute substantially to understanding the trend in underemployment. We can actually do better by allowance of only a linear term for the mismatch logits (where $i = 2$ in Equation 7.7), but the simplicity of the present range of models is perhaps more desirable.

These examples are presented to illustrate the trending of qualitative attributes over time by the method of maximum likelihood. It is, of course, disappointing that our time series is not more current, for then the actual forecasts obtained from such models would be of considerable importance.

7.2 FORECASTING UNDEREMPLOYMENT WITH THE POPULATION PROJECTION MATRIX

The population at time t can be arranged into an $I \times 1$ vector $\mathbf{P}(t)$, where the ith entry in that vector, $i = 1, \ldots, I$, would correspond to the number of persons in age interval $(i - 1, i)$. If the population were closed to migration, then the population at $t + 1$ is obtained from the population at t by multiplying $\mathbf{P}(t)$ by the "population projection matrix," the properties of which have been discussed by Leslie and others (see Keyfitz, 1968; Goodman, 1968b). That is, we can project the population to time $t + 1$ by

$$\mathbf{P}(t + 1) = \mathbf{L}\mathbf{P}(t) \qquad (7.8)$$

where L is the Leslie matrix, or "projection operator," taking into account fertility and survivorship.

Now let $D^j(t)$ denote the $I \times I$ matrix with zero off-diagonal elements and with diagonal elements $d_i^j(t)$ referring to the rate of occurrence of the

jth labor force status in age i at time t. Then $\mathbf{P}^j(t) = D^j(t)\mathbf{P}(t)$ is the number of persons age by age in the jth labor force status at time t. If the elements of D^j remain unchanged through time, then the forecasted population in the jth labor force status at $t + 1$ is

$$\mathbf{P}^j(t + 1) = D^j(t)L\mathbf{P}(t) \tag{7.9}$$

The projected population at time $t + 1$ may be arranged into a *projected* $I \times J$ age by labor force status matrix

$$[\mathbf{P}^1(t + 1), \mathbf{P}^2(t + 1), \ldots, \mathbf{P}^J(t + 1)]$$

by repeated application of Equation 7.9. The advantage of the matrix formulation in (7.9) is that it suggests we separate our forecast into three distinct parts, the $\mathbf{P}(t)$ vector representing the initial age distribution, the L matrix representing fertility and survivorship, and the D^j reflecting the age-specific rates of occurrence of the jth labor force status. In the mathematical analysis of population growth, an important step was to analytically separate growth into the two components signified by the Leslie matrix L and the vector of initial age distribution. What we are suggesting here is that an analysis of time-trend in the incidence of various social statuses be analytically separated into the *three* parts on the right-hand side of (7.9).

In forecasting the $\mathbf{P}^j(t)$ into the near future, the L matrix can be assumed to remain fixed, but the $D^j(t)$ will surely *not* remain fixed, since these quantities reflect the impact of the transitory economic exigencies. The techniques presented in the previous section show how we can obtain a reasonable statistical forecast of $\mathbf{P}^j(t')$, t' greater than t, by the time-trending of the $D^j(t)$. The example presented in Table 7.3 shows how time-trend in a fourfold qualitative variable (denoting four different statuses) can be used in a forecast, and it is a straightforward procedure to apply those techniques to project the labor force statuses of interest into the future. The methods presented in the previous section show how we can efficiently estimate the time-trend evidenced in a series of $D^j(t)$ observed in the past, and this information can be incorporated into our demographic projection.

In the special case where age is not distinguished, and where the population grows by $P_{t+1} = P_t(1 + r)$ in each interval of time, we see that the expected population in the jth labor force status at $t + 1$ would be given by $\hat{P}^j_{t+1} = \hat{d}^j_{t+1}P_t(1 + r)$, where $\hat{d}^j_{t+1}$ is the forecasted proportion in the jth labor force status obtained by methods developed in the previous section.

The numerical work required to obtain underemployment forecasts by combining the two approaches of this chapter, although fairly straightforward, would be too tedious to take up here.

8

underemployment in the life history of synthetic cohorts

A particularly attractive model that has received sustained attention in population studies is the current life table. The current life table permits analysis of mortality by allowing the currently observed age-specific mortality rates to reign upon a "synthetic" or hypothetical cohort of persons throughout their life history, producing the central life table indicator of mortality—the expectation of life at birth. It is the simplest formal demographic model worth considering and can be thought of as the stable population model corresponding to an intrinsic growth rate of zero, or the "stationary population."[1] Usual tables of working life are an extension of the life table model, where current age-specific labor force participation rates and current age-specific mortality rates are both assumed to operate upon a hypothetical cohort of persons throughout their lives.[2] In this chapter the life table is modified to take into account the fact that under fairly reasonable assumptions, the years lived by a life table cohort can be partitioned into years lived in any of the labor force statuses considered in this work. There is, given this trivial observation, nothing novel to the approach upon which this chapter is based. However, some of the applications of these modified life-table models are quite illuminating and will suggest meaningful ways to summarize the complicated labor force status

[1] See Keyfitz (1976, 1977) for an account of the importance of the stationary population model, and Ryder (1975b) for a discussion of its underlying assumptions and their ramifications.

[2] See references to Appendix B.

variable of this study. An additional advantage of the life-table approach to be discussed is the tractable manner in which the labor force chances of the race–sex groups are given quantitative expression.

A review of the main functions of the modified life table, taking into account labor force status, is presented in Appendix B. The assumptions that are important for understanding the meaning of functions derived from the modified life table are also presented in Appendix B. Since we are estimating underemployment rates on the basis of sample data, sampling error is important to consider. In Section 8.1, the main functions of the modified life tables for males and females by race for 1970 are presented and briefly discussed. In Section 8.2, comparisons of some of the functions of the modified life table over time are presented. This section presents indicators of underemployment that are more refined in certain respects than the ones presented and criticized earlier in this work. In Section 8.3, the analogy of the modified life table to the usual cause-of-death life table is exploited (compare Spiegelman, 1968; Preston *et al.*, 1972; Preston, 1976), showing the policy relevance of this simple model. In Section 8.4, the consequences of a kind of ''meritocracy'' are analyzed through the modified life-table perspective. We there examine the implications of a kind of ''equity'' in the race–sex-specific underemployment rates by age for the length of ''adequately utilized life'' for each of the race–sex groups, given a socioeconomic constraint upon the total number of ''adequately utilized life years'' that a society can provide to its population of persons of working age. In Section 8.5, the life-table indicators of underemployment developed in previous sections are formalized and given further meaning through a simple relationship that is presumed to exist concerning the manner in which human capital is accumulated. All the methods used in this chapter are suited to the cross-sectional data that we are forced to use. If panel data were available, then we could have used Markov chain methods to calculate expected years to be lived in the labor force statuses from an entirely different approach (see Feller, 1968; Karlin, 1969).

8.1 EXPECTATION OF LIFE IN THE VARIOUS LABOR FORCE STATUSES: UNDEREMPLOYMENT HISTORY FOR MALES AND FEMALES BY RACE GIVEN 1970 CONDITIONS

Tables 8.1, 8.2, 8.3, and 8.4 present expectation of life at each age in each of seven labor force statuses for white males, nonwhite males, white females, and nonwhite females, respectively. The seven labor force statuses considered are (*a*) not in labor force, (*b*) sub-unemployment, (*c*)

TABLE 8.1
Expectation of Life to Be Lived in the Labor Force Statuses for White Males Given 1970 Conditions

Age	Life table $\overset{o}{e}_x$	Not-in-labor force	Sub-unemployment	Unemployment	Hours	Income	Mismatch	Adequate
0	67.993	26.512	.261	1.534	.823	1.292	4.468	33.103
			(.017)	(.042)	(.031)	(.038)	(.071)	(.106)
15	54.896	12.218	.268	1.578	.846	1.329	4.597	34.058
		(.076)	(.018)	(.043)	(.032)	(.039)	(.073)	(.109)
20	50.282	9.629	.215	1.304	.783	1.075	4.559	32.717
		(.069)	(.017)	(.041)	(.032)	(.036)	(.073)	(.106)
35	36.486	8.673	.147	.722	.557	.485	2.795	23.108
		(.061)	(.014)	(.031)	(.027)	(.025)	(.058)	(.088)
50	23.418	8.854	.121	.427	.335	.340	1.192	12.150
		(.060)	(.013)	(.025)	(.021)	(.021)	(.040)	(.073)
65	13.149	9.579	.066	.117	.111	.143	.279	2.853
		(.052)	(.010)	(.014)	(.012)	(.014)	(.019)	(.050)

TABLE 8.2
Expectation of Life to Be Lived in the Labor Force Statuses for Nonwhite Males Given 1970 Conditions

Age	Life table $\overset{o}{e}_x$	Not-in labor force	Sub-unemployment	Unem-ployment	Hours	Income	Mismatch	Adequate
0	61.319	26.094	.550	2.150	1.596	1.482	2.600	26.847
			(.070)	(.137)	(.124)	(.115)	(.159)	(.296)
15	49.214	12.278	.577	2.255	1.673	1.554	2.726	28.152
		(.226)	(.074)	(.144)	(.130)	(.120)	(.167)	(.310)
20	44.738	9.359	.446	1.851	1.577	1.324	2.735	27.447
		(.214)	(.069)	(.138)	(.129)	(.116)	(.168)	(.307)
35	32.467	8.647	.263	1.065	1.091	.514	1.780	19.106
		(.196)	(.055)	(.108)	(.110)	(.075)	(.140)	(.261)
50	21.552	8.917	.207	.563	.567	.363	.709	10.225
		(.193)	(.051)	(.083)	(.084)	(.066)	(.095)	(.220)
65	13.304	9.673	.122	.131	.221	.176	.144	2.837
		(.158)	(.044)	(.039)	(.058)	(.050)	(.050)	(.151)

TABLE 8.3
Expectation of Life to Be Lived in the Labor Force Statuses for White Females Given 1970 Conditions

Age	Life table e_x^o	Not-in labor force	Sub-unemployment	Unemployment	Hours	Income	Mismatch	Adequate
0	75.606	51.758	.316	1.108	.653	2.827	1.889	17.055
			(.018)	(.035)	(.027)	(.055)	(.046)	(.115)
15	62.196	37.835	.323	1.131	.667	2.888	1.930	17.422
		(.123)	(.019)	(.035)	(.028)	(.057)	(.047)	(.117)
20	57.369	34.824	.270	.918	.631	2.646	1.890	16.189
		(.120)	(.018)	(.033)	(.027)	(.055)	(.047)	(.114)
35	42.951	27.503	.161	.548	.445	1.496	1.231	11.567
		(.101)	(.014)	(.026)	(.023)	(.043)	(.039)	(.097)
50	29.257	21.163	.092	.211	.214	.661	.722	6.195
		(.078)	(.010)	(.017)	(.016)	(.030)	(.030)	(.074)
65	17.119	15.495	.031	.034	.046	.080	.194	1.240
		(.037)	(.004)	(.006)	(.006)	(.010)	(.013)	(.034)

TABLE 8.4
Expectation of Life to Be Lived in the Labor Force Statuses for Nonwhite Females Given 1970 Conditions

Age	Life table e_x^o	Not-in labor force	Sub-unemployment	Unemployment	Hours	Income	Mismatch	Adequate
0	69.380	43.407	.712	1.886	1.653	2.928	2.307	16.487
			(.073)	(.118)	(.119)	(.149)	(.139)	(.300)
15	56.957	29.998	.739	1.958	1.716	3.039	2.394	17.113
		(.320)	(.076)	(.122)	(.123)	(.154)	(.144)	(.311)
20	52.188	26.352	.663	1.642	1.665	2.834	2.378	16.654
		(.313)	(.074)	(.116)	(.122)	(.152)	(.144)	(.309)
35	38.457	21.403	.308	.757	1.175	1.405	1.606	11.802
		(.271)	(.053)	(.085)	(.107)	(.113)	(.123)	(.267)
50	26.279	17.461	.137	.288	.648	.420	.793	6.533
		(.223)	(.037)	(.057)	(.085)	(.069)	(.093)	(.215)
65	16.353	14.020	.049	.082	.131	.049	.147	1.876
		(.119)	(.017)	(.029)	(.033)	(.017)	(.037)	(.109)

unemployment, (d) involuntary part-time unemployment, (e) underemployment by low work-related income, (f) mismatch, and (g) adequate employment or utilization. These expectations show in summary form the implications of current mortality and underemployment conditions, where these conditions are assumed to operate upon a hypothetical life-table cohort of persons throughout the life span. Of special interest are the several expectations at birth. We see that for white males the average length of life is 68.0, but only 33.1 years of this total (or 48.7%) will be spent in the labor force and in adequate employment. A full 26.5 years would be spent outside the labor force, and the remaining 8.4 years would be spent in less than optimal employment. In a work-oriented society such as our own, it is indeed striking that less than half of the life years of the most economically productive subpopulation (i.e., white males) are in fact spent in adequate employment as we have defined it in this study.[3]

For nonwhite males, the average length of life implied by 1970 mortality rates was 61.3 years, a full 6.7 years less than for white males. We see that 26.8 years (or 43.8% of the average length of life) would be spent in adequate employment, 26.1 years would be spent outside the labor force, and a full 8.4 years would be spent in suboptimal employment. The life years lived in suboptimal employment are thus equivalent for white males and nonwhite males, owing chiefly to the very different *mortality* risks between the two groups. If nonwhite males had the same survivorship as white males, the apparent difference between these two subpopulations with respect to underemployment would increase, since the expectations given in the preceding tables pertain to a smaller overall length of life for nonwhite males relative to white males.

For white females, life expectation at birth is 75.6, with 17.1 of those years spent in adequate employment within the labor force. That is, approximately 22.5% of the white female life-span is spent in adequate employment, as compared with a figure of about 49% for white males. Only 4.9 years would be spent in suboptimal employment, whereas the remaining 53.6 years would be spent out of the labor force (see Table 8.3). Owing to the longer length of life of white women than of white or nonwhite men,

---

[3] Sociologists of work often point to the centrality of the work role in modern industrial societies. That is, the trend in industrial society has been for more and more of its members to define their life worth in terms of occupational prestige, work-related income, skill utilization, and formal economic productivity. Even with the tremendous growth in leisure, such an orientation to the work role seems to persist. That the most economically advantageous race–sex group (white males) actually spends less than one-half of its average lifetime in "adequate employment" is an important index of the *actual* centrality of the work role. The reader must, of course, bear in mind that these figures are *averages* and that there is much variability among individuals.

the differences between white women and males, in one sense, are considerably more marked than these comparisons show. Nonwhite females present corresponding expectations similar to those of white females. We see from Table 8.4 that 16.5 years, or 23.8% of the total expectation of life 69.4 years, is spent in adequate employment. A full 9.5 years are spent in suboptimal employment, and 43.4 years are spent outside the labor force.

The statistics represented in the above tables are of importance in themselves, apart from meaning that they might have as underemployment indicators for use in comparisons across groups or over time. They demonstrate what is at first sight a remarkably small number of years of life that would be lived in the labor force and that would be lived in adequate employment within the labor force. In a culture such as that of the United States, where the work role is increasingly important as the defining frame of reference for the population at large, it is surprising indeed that only about 23% of the total length of life is spent in adequate employment for women and that only roughly 46% of the total length of life is spent in adequate employment for men. Postponed labor force entry, early retirement, conditions of suboptimal employment, long years of preparation for careers, and the increasing number of years lived after retirement all account for this discrepancy between the cultural value of the primacy of work roles and the actuality of only a fraction of life experience lived in a satisfactory work role. These are then quite surprising indicators of the conditions of work in the postindustrial societies. As will be more apparent later, these indicators are only slightly affected by considering the implications of labor force conditions other than those of 1970.

One technique whereby comparisons among the race–sex groups can be made that do not confound the mortality conditions of the respective subpopulations with labor force chances is to consider the above life expectations assuming that the subpopulations all have the same mortality experience. In the modified life tables so derived, the comparisons among the sex–race groups would also be age-standardized, since mortality is the sole determinant of age structure in the life-table "stationary population." In Table 8.5, the expectations are presented assuming that the mortality schedules of white males applied to each population. If it were the objective to adjust underemployment measures for differing survivorship, then the simple summary statistics of Table 8.5 would be more useful than the ordinary underemployment rates used elsewhere in this study. Even with the moderate sampling errors of the nonwhite figures taken into account, we see in simple terms the "true" differences among the race–sex groups in 1970. Marked differences among these groups, which we noted in Chapters 2, 3, and 4, are all borne out by these summary figures, and the units

TABLE 8.5
Expectation of Life at Birth in the Seven Labor Force Statuses, Assuming 1970 White Male Mortality for All Subpopulations[a]

	Not-in-Labor force (1)	Sub-unemployment (2)	Unemployment (3)	Low hours (4)	Low income (5)	Mismatch (6)	Adequate (7)
White males	26.512	.261	1.534	.823	1.292	4.468	33.103
		(.017)	(.042)	(.031)	(.038)	(.071)	(.106)
Nonwhite males	28.516	.613	2.349	1.795	1.609	2.892	30.219
		(.079)	(.151)	(.139)	(.125)	(.177)	(.336)
White females	45.637	.295	1.061	.611	2.699	1.751	15.939
		(.017)	(.033)	(.026)	(.053)	(.043)	(.108)
Nonwhite females	41.922	.714	1.899	1.664	2.955	2.329	16.530
		(.074)	(.119)	(.120)	(.151)	(.141)	(.304)

[a]Total life expectation = 67.993 (white male e_0^o). Standard errors in parentheses.

involved (years of life) are perhaps more meaningful than the usual crude rates. We see that females spend (in the mortality-adjusted sense) twice as much time out of the labor force as do males, that mismatch is the most prevalent among white males, that the income form of underemployment is the most prevalent among females, and that sub-unemployment (a proxy for the discouraged worker phenomenon) is the most prevalent among nonwhites. It is also interesting to note that even though females are in the labor force approximately half as long as males are, their length of life lived in the forms of underemployment is roughly equal to that of males, except for the mismatch form.

In our view, the measures presented in Tables 8.1 through 8.5 are preferable in most respects to the more usual underemployment rates in terms of (a) the units of measurement involved (years of life), (b) the inclusion of a mortality (and implicitly an age distribution) variable, and (c) the implicit assessment of long-run implications of current rates that the life-table approach provides. In the present social engineering quandary about achieving equity in the labor force for different subpopulations, the life-table approach forces us to consider the usually overlooked differential mortality experience of the respective populations involved. The popular conception of equity in the labor force revolves essentially about the explicit goal of achieving equity in age-specific underemployment *rates* (and labor force participation *rates*) among the race–sex groups. An alternative and altogether different conception of equity in the labor force might be a circumstance wherein the sex–race subpopulations, for example, achieved the same average length of life in adequate employment. Still another conception of equity might be that the proportion of an individual's life spent in the various labor force statuses should be equal for the sex–race groups. These different conceptions of equity involve very different conceptions of differential underemployment, and these different conceptions of differential underemployment produce dramatically different implications, as we shall show later in Section 8.4. We now turn to across-time comparisons of some other quantities derived from the life table modified to take into account labor force history. These will show labor market changes in ways that are also quite meaningful.

8.2 ACROSS-TIME COMPARISONS OF LIFE EXPECTATIONS AND OF OTHER QUANTITIES ASSOCIATED WITH THE MODIFIED LIFE TABLE

Tables 8.6, 8.7, 8.8, and 8.9 present the expectation of life and the expectation of years of life to be lived in the seven labor force statuses at age 15 for white males, nonwhite males, white females, and nonwhite

TABLE 8.6
Expectation of Life at Age 15 in the Seven Labor Force Statuses, White Males, 1969–1973 (1970 White Male Life Table)[a]

	Not-in-labor force (1)	Sub-un-employment (2)	Unem-ploy-ment (3)	Low hours (4)	Low income (5)	Mis-match (6)	Adequate (7)
1969	12.193	.256	1.072	.778	1.385	4.486	34.726
	(.074)	(.016)	(.035)	(.030)	(.039)	(.070)	(.105)
1970	12.218	.268	1.578	.846	1.329	4.597	34.058
	(.076)	(.018)	(.043)	(.032)	(.039)	(.073)	(.109)
1971	12.546	.345	2.170	.944	4.343	4.971	32.577
	(.075)	(.020)	(.049)	(.034)	(.038)	(.075)	(.110)
1972	12.466	.403	2.104	.937	1.475	5.346	32.165
	(.076)	(.021)	(.049)	(.034)	(.040)	(.079)	(.112)
1973	12.702	.364	1.703	.795	1.492	5.672	32.167
	(.079)	(.021)	(.045)	(.031)	(.040)	(.081)	(.114)

[a] e^o_{15} = 54.896. Standard errors in parentheses.

TABLE 8.7
Expectation of Life at Age 15 in the Seven Labor Force Statuses, Nonwhite Males, 1969–1973 (1970 Nonwhite Male Life Table)[a]

	Not-in-labor force (1)	Sub-un-employment (2)	Unem-ploy-ment (3)	Low hours (4)	Low income (5)	Mis-match (6)	Adequate (7)
1969	12.117	.637	1.761	1.464	1.450	2.734	29.052
	(.216)	(.077)	(.126)	(.119)	(.116)	(.165)	(.298)
1970	12.278	.577	2.255	1.673	1.554	2.726	28.152
	(.226)	(.074)	(.144)	(.130)	(.120)	(.167)	(.310)
1971	12.587	.758	2.941	1.652	1.699	3.205	26.372
	(.224)	(.084)	(.161)	(.126)	(.122)	(.175)	(.311)
1972	12.601	.729	2.888	1.518	1.613	3.449	26.416
	(.227)	(.081)	(.163)	(.123)	(.124)	(.185)	(.316)
1973	13.118	.576	2.378	1.142	1.415	3.504	27.081
	(.240)	(.076)	(.150)	(.108)	(.118)	(.191)	(.319)

[a] e^o_{15} = 49.214. Standard errors in parentheses.

TABLE 8.8
Expectation of Life at Age 15 in the Seven Labor Force Statuses, White Females,
1969-1973 (1970 White Female Life Table)[a]

	Not-in-labor force (1)	Sub-un-employ-ment (2)	Unem-ploy-ment (3)	Low hours (4)	Low income (5)	Mis-match (6)	Adequate (7)
1969	38.156	.410	.877	.621	3.055	1.831	17.247
	(.120)	(.021)	(.030)	(.026)	(.056)	(.044)	(.114)
1970	37.835	.323	1.131	.667	2.888	1.930	17.422
	(.123)	(.019)	(.035)	(.028)	(.057)	(.047)	(.117)
1971	37.762	.456	1.451	.818	2.621	2.150	16.937
	(.123)	(.022)	(.040)	(.031)	(.054)	(.049)	(.116)
1972	37.292	.515	1.353	.788	2.897	2.155	17.196
	(.125)	(.024)	(.039)	(.031)	(.057)	(.050)	(.118)
1973	36.852	.519	1.250	.739	3.020	2.364	17.452
	(.126)	(.025)	(.038)	(.030)	(.059)	(.054)	(.120)

[a] $e_{15}^O = 62.196$. Standard errors in parentheses.

TABLE 8.9
Expectation of Life at Age 15 in the Seven Labor Force Statuses, Nonwhite Females,
1969-1973 (1970 Nonwhite Female Life Table)[a]

	Not-in-labor force (1)	Sub-un-employ-ment (2)	Unem-ploy-ment (3)	Low hours (4)	Low income (5)	Mis-match (6)	Adequate (7)
1969	30.129	.830	1.803	1.513	3.168	2.238	17.276
	(.318)	(.082)	(.116)	(.115)	(.158)	(.137)	(.310)
1970	29.998	.739	1.958	1.716	3.039	2.394	17.113
	(.320)	(.076)	(.122)	(.123)	(.154)	(.144)	(.311)
1971	30.500	1.049	2.352	1.937	2.548	2.308	16.264
	(.312)	(.090)	(.130)	(.128)	(.142)	(.138)	(.301)
1972	30.376	.956	2.488	1.291	2.638	2.369	16.841
	(.321)	(.085)	(.135)	(.107)	(.146)	(.144)	(.310)
1973	31.603	.933	2.270	1.102	2.660	2.676	16.712
	(.328)	(.087)	(.132)	(.101)	(.149)	(.156)	(.318)

[a] $e_{15}^O = 56.957$. Standard errors in parentheses.

females, respectively. Comparisons among these tables are distorted by the dramatically different mortality experiences of the four race–sex subpopulations, but comparisons over time within any subpopulation show clearly the time-period variation in underemployment. In 1970, life tables for the sex–race-specific subpopulations were used for each time-period, so that the quantities are age-standardized regarding across-time comparisons within a race–sex group. (Mortality rates did not change appreciably in this time span for any race–sex group.)

For white males (Table 8.6), we see more clearly the impact of declining labor force participation, the increase in mismatch, the doubling of unemployment, and the moderate fluctuations in the other kinds of underemployment that occurred during this time span. A revealing statistic is the percentage of the total life expectation after age 15 that white males spend in adequate employment. We see that the 1969 rates imply that 63.3% [$=(34.726/54.896) \times 100$] of remaining life for 15-year-olds would be spent in adequate employment but that by 1973, this percentage had dropped to 58.6% [$=(32.167/54.896) \times 100$].

Tables 8.7, 8.8, and 8.9, pertaining to nonwhite males, white females, and nonwhite females, show the same trends discussed previously. We see in Table 8.7 the steady decline in labor force participation for nonwhite males, indicated by an increasing life expectation in the not-in-labor-force category. We also see that 55.0% of the life years lived by nonwhite males (given 1973 conditions) would be lived in adequate employment, which is slightly less than the corresponding figure for white males. Particularly important in the labor force experience of white females (Table 8.8) is the rise in labor force participation, which is not matched at all by any apparent trend in labor force participation for nonwhite females (Table 8.9). The other quantities show approximately the same trends in underemployment that we have discussed earlier. The simplicity of the present measures, in terms of the units of measurement and in terms of presenting the long-run implications of current rates of underemployment, make them preferable in certain respects to the more conventional rates and ratios.

It could be of interest to examine the long-run "productive potential" of the various sex–race subpopulations from the point of view of the modified life table. Life years spent outside the labor force, in the sub-unemployed status, or in the unemployed status contribute nothing to the *formal* economic product. Life years spent in the involuntary part-time status or in the low-income status result in economic products that are inferior owing to insufficient input (hours of work) or are inferior with respect to low-quality output (reflected by a low work wage). (We assume that wage rates reflect the economic value of the product produced, so that life years spent in low-income status mark the years a person spends in the production of inferior goods and services.) The expectation of mismatched life years, plus the expectation of "adequately employed" life years at, say, age 15, is therefore a measure of the eventual contribution of a cohort of persons aged 15 to the production of economically desirable goods over the life span, given current mortality and labor force conditions. Let T_{15}^6 denote the life years lived in the state of mismatch after age 15, and let T_{15}^7 denote the life years lived in the state of adequate employment after age 15. The quantity $(T_{15}^6 + T_{15}^7)/l_{15}$, the expectation of life in mismatch or adequate employment per survivor at age 15, when adjusted for the sex–race composition of the total population at age 15, denotes the "eventual productive value" of persons aged 15.

In Table 8.10, these statistics of "eventual productive value" are presented for 1969 (a boom economy) and for 1972 (a recession economy). We see that given the underemployment conditions in 1969, the implications for long-run "productive life years per person" or "productive value" are striking, with white males contributing 59.5% to the eventual economic product; white females, 27.6%; nonwhite males, 8.0%; and nonwhite females, 4.9%. Conditions in 1972 imply that the eventual economic product would be $(28.049/28.840) \times 100 = 97.3\%$ of that implied by 1969 conditions. There is then a dramatic difference in the long-run product implied by the 2 years. We also see, however, that white females would increase their share of economic product over the long run, principally as a result of the higher participation of white women and the lower participation of white men in 1972 relative to 1969. This conception of the "eventual productive value" of the cohort aged 15 is another extension of the modified life table in the analysis of current underemployment. There are, of course, many means by which the eventual productive years per person can be raised or lowered, and the modified life table enables us to examine their implications. Increasing labor force participation, decreasing underemployment, or declines in mortality are three mechanisms whereby the eventual product per person could be raised, for example, and the implications of each mechanism could be easily worked out in the modified life table.

Another method whereby the implications of current conditions can be examined is suggested by the following. Let us narrow the age interval under consideration to ages 20–65, the rationale being that this age group contributes the most to labor force activity in general. Since retirement patterns after age 65 differ somewhat among the race–sex groups, and since labor force participation differs considerably prior to age 20 for the race–sex groups, focusing exclusively upon this age interval will allow the examination of current underemployment rates apart from differential retirement and early labor force participation patterns. We therefore impose

TABLE 8.10
Eventual Productive Life Years of the Sex-Race Subpopulations Aged 15, for 1969 and 1972

	White males	Nonwhite males	White females	Nonwhite females
1969				
Expected years in mismatch after age 15	4.486	2.734	1.831	2.238
Expected years in adequate employment after age 15	34.726	29.052	17.247	17.276
Total productive life years	39.212	31.786	19.078	19.514
1972				
Expected years in mismatch after age 15	5.346	3.449	2.155	2.369
Expected years in adequate employment after age 15	32.165	26.416	17.196	16.841
Total productive life years	37.511	29.865	19.351	19.210
Percent of total population aged 15 (July 1, 1970)	43.68	7.30	41.77	7.25

Total product resulting from sex-race group	White males	Nonwhite males	White females	Nonwhite females	Total
1969					
Number	17.128	2.320	7.969	1.415	28.832
Percent	59.5	8.0	27.6	4.9	100.0
1972					
Number	16.583	2.180	8.083	1.393	28.041
Percent	58.4	7.8	28.8	5.0	100.0

the current conditions upon an hypothetical cohort aged 20 and examine their implications as if they were to reign for 45 years.

Tables 8.11 and 8.12 present an analysis of the implications of current mortality and underemployment rates for the age interval 20–65, for males and females, respectively. We have again assumed that 1970 mortality conditions prevail throughout, so that once more, the time comparisons

TABLE 8.11

Decomposition of Years of Life during Age Interval 20–65, for Male Survivors at Exact Age 20, 1969–1973

Year	Life years lost to mortality (1)	Not-in-labor force (2)	Economic underemployment (3)	Mismatch (4)	Adequate (5)	Total life years 20–65 per survivor at age 20 (6)
			White males			
1969	3.744	3.039	2.590	4.277	31.349	41.256
1970	3.744	3.054	3.076	4.368	30.758	41.256
1971	3.744	3.150	3.758	4.754	29.595	41.256
1972	3.744	3.215	3.753	5.136	29.151	41.256
1973	3.744	3.466	3.283	5.449	29.057	41.256
			Nonwhite males			
1969	7.299	3.901	4.194	2.684	26.922	37.701
1970	7.299	4.242	4.855	2.659	25.946	37.701
1971	7.299	4.364	5.871	3.127	24.340	37.701
1972	7.299	4.286	5.548	3.381	24.486	37.701
1973	7.299	4.662	4.329	3.449	25.261	37.701

TABLE 8.12

Decomposition of Years of Life during Age Interval 20–65, for Female Survivors at Exact Age 20, 1969–1973

Year	Life years lost to mortality (1)	Not-in-labor force (2)	Economic underemployment (3)	Mismatch (4)	Adequate (5)	Total life years 20–65 per survivor at age 20 (6)
			White females			
1969	1.923	22.210	4.203	1.646	15.018	43.077
1970	1.923	21.889	4.306	1.728	15.154	43.077
1972	1.923	21.729	4.584	1.985	14.780	43.077
1972	1.923	21.305	4.716	1.966	15.090	43.077
1973	1.923	21.002	4.644	2.207	15.223	43.077
			Nonwhite females			
1969	4.118	16.775	6.440	2.151	15.516	40.882
1970	4.118	16.659	6.589	2.276	15.516	40.882
1971	4.118	16.766	6.912	2.221	14.983	40.882
1972	4.118	17.108	6.350	2.298	15.126	40.882
1973	4.118	16.904	6.084	2.571	15.322	40.882

are mortality adjusted (i.e., age-standardized) within each sex–race group. We see that the average years lost by virtue of mortality (column 1 of Tables 8.11 and 8.12) are 3.7, 7.3, 1.9, and 4.1 for white males, nonwhite males, white females, and nonwhite females, respectively. The other quantities presented in those tables, life table indicators of underemployment, are "truer" to the across-time comparisons that we presented in Chapter 4 for the race–sex-specific subpopulations for this age interval. If indicators of underemployment based upon the expected life span during ages 20–65 were important to consider, then these indicators would be more advantageous than the usual crude rates, for the same reasons enumerated elsewhere in this section. Different conceptions of "equity" and of sex–race differentials in underemployment are clearly forced into consideration owing to the very different mortality experience of these sex–race groups.

8.3 THE LONG-RUN CONSEQUENCES OF SUSTAINED DECREASES IN UNDEREMPLOYMENT

The modified life table that takes into account labor force history is somewhat analogous to the cause-of-death life table. One application of the life table by cause of death is to examine the gain in overall life expectancy given a hypothetical reduction in the rates of mortality by one or more causes of death (Preston, 1976; Preston et al., 1972; Spiegelman, 1968; Keyfitz, 1977). Similarly, the modified life table here permits the examination of long-run implications of sustained reductions in the underemployment rates, demonstrating another useful application of the present technique.

In the time series considered here, the conditions of 1972 best represent the impact of a recession economy upon labor force participation and the risks of underemployment. Over 6% of the labor force were unemployed in March 1972, and the other underemployment rates were also at high levels. Some proposals have been suggested that aim at the long-term provision of public service employment, which would guarantee sustained 3 or 4% unemployment rates.[4] Presumably, those same proposals would also dramatically reduce the rate of sub-unemployment (i.e., the aggregate volume of "discouraged workers"), the rate of involuntary part-time un-

---

[4] We are referring to proposals similar to the so-called Humphrey-Hawkins bill, introduced to the U.S. Congress as the Full Employment and Balanced Growth Act of 1976, Amendment No. 1468, Ninety-fourth Congress, Second Session, March 16, 1976. Proposals such as these depend critically on a conception of "full employment ," but unfortunately, there is no agreement about the "full employment unemployment rate." (These questions were also

employment, and the rate of the low-income underemployment. We have argued previously that, indeed, these four forms of economic underemployment are at least *statistically* closely intertwined, so that proposals aimed at reducing unemployment would also presumably reduce the other forms as well.[5] Let us also assume that the rate of mismatch, not yet explicitly addressed by government, would also be reduced by these hypothetical policies.

We now examine the eventual implications of a *sustained* reduction of the forms of underemployment upon the life expectancy in the various states of underemployment for a hypothetical life-table cohort of persons. The important quantities to consider are the "average productive years" per person in the life table and various other expectations of life to be lived in the states of underemployment. We examine the implications of sustained 4% and sustained 3% unemployment rates given the following assumptions:

1. The labor force participation rates observed in 1972 remain unchanged throughout the relevant life history of the life-table cohort.
2. The overall reduction in unemployment from over 6% to 4% or to 3% takes place through a mechanism that reduces each of the age-specific rates by a fixed proportion. A 4% unemployment rate corresponds to a 27.67% reduction in 1972 observed unemployment rates, and a 3% unemployment rate corresponds to a 45.75% reduction in 1972 observed rates, and we have applied this proportionate reduction to the rates of unemployment at every age.
3. The age-specific rates of the other forms of underemployment are also reduced proportionately as much as unemployment is reduced.
4. The reduction schedule is *sustained,* not merely a transitory characteristic of one or a few years, so that it is meaningful to apply the life-table model to work out long-run implications.

The assumptions are very hypothetical, since presumably mismatch would not be much affected by the kinds of proposals currently being considered. Also, it is unreasonable to assume that labor force participation rates would remain unchanged under the sustained provision of conditions producing 4% or 3% unemployment. Labor force participation

---

taken up in Chapter 4.) For references to this subject, see Casselman (1955), Beveridge (1945), Hansen (1947), Lerner (1951), Viner (1950), Friedman (1968), and Humphrey (1973). The 3% and 4% unemployment figures are adopted from earlier discussions of full employment; presently, somewhat higher figures are being cited in the press as depicting full employment levels.

[5] See results presented in Chapter 5.

would surely rise over time in such an event, thereby contributing significantly to the pool of persons at very high risk of all the underemployment forms. It might even be argued that such decreases in unemployment would necessarily imply an *increase* in part-time work and an increase in the number receiving low wage income. With these qualifying reservations, however, it could still be important to consider the consequences of such assumptions within the life-table framework.

Table 8.13 presents the expectation of life at birth in the various labor force statuses implied by 1972 conditions and the corresponding life expectations that would be implied by reduction in underemployment producing 3% or 4% unemployment rates. It is of interest first to examine the expected number of life years to be lived in productive employment for newborn babies. This is the sum of the expectation of mismatched life years plus the expectation of adequately employed life years and is the quantity previously referred to as the "productive life years" or "eventual productive value" of an arbitrarily chosen member of the life-table cohort at birth. We see that the "total productive life years" per person at birth was 27.0 in 1972, but with a sustained reduction in underemployment rates corresponding to 4% unemployment rates throughout the life span of the life-table cohort, this figure would rise to 28.4, or a gain in 1.4 years per person. In proportionate terms, this corresponds to the dramatic increase in productive value *per person* of 5.5%. The reduction schedule corresponding to 3% unemployment rates throughout the life span of the

TABLE 8.13

Eventual "Productive Value" of a Life Table Cohort, Given Two Schedules of Reduction in Underemployment Rates and No Change in Labor Force Participation (1972 Total Population as Base)

	Expectation of life at birth	Not-in-labor force	Economic underemployment	Mismatch	Adequate	Total Productive value
Observed in 1972	70.855	38.572	5.317	3.503	23.463	26.966
4% unemployment	70.855	38.572	3.845	2.533	25.904	28.437
3% unemployment	70.855	38.572	2.885	1.900	27.498	29.398

[a]Percent increase in "productive value." Reduction schedule corresponding to 4% unemployment = $[(28.437/26.966) \times 100] = 5.5\%$. Reduction schedule corresponding to 3% unemployment = $[(29.368/26.966) \times 100] = 9.0\%$.

TABLE 8.14

Eventual "Productive Value" of a Life Table Cohort Aged 20, Given Two Schedules of Reduction in Underemployment Rates and No Change in Labor Force Participation (1972 Total Population as Base)[a]

	Average years lived in ages 20–65	Life years lost to mortality	Economic under-ployment	Mismatch	Adequate	Not-in-labor force
Observed in 1972	41.832	3.168	4.448	3.414	21.629	12.341
4% unem-ployment	41.832	3.168	3.217	2.469	23.804	12.341
3% unem-ployment	41.832	3.168	2.413	1.852	25.226	12.341

[a]Productive value during interval 20 to 65. Percent increase in "productive value": reduction schedule corresponding to 4% unemployment = 4.9%; reduction scheule corresponding to 3% unemployment = 8.1%.

life-table cohort corresponds to total productive life years per person of 29.4, which implies a 9.0% increase in productive value per person. Such a massive policy move would, in the long run, have tremendous implications for the total economic product of the life-table cohort (if each productive life year resulted in the same economic product as previously), but it would also involve tremendous outlays of public funds over the long run (if the jobs "created" by public policy themselves resulted in inferior economic product, or if the costs of the public works were not offset by the inertia of new economic products created).

Table 8.14 presents the implications of the above underemployment reductions and focuses upon total product gained in the 45-year time span from ages 20–65 for an arbitrary survivor at age 20. These results show the implications of the 4% or 3% unemployment rates (and the corresponding reductions in other 1972 underemployment rates), where it is assumed that the reductions pertained only to the ages 20–65. Corresponding to these more restrictive assumptions we see more modest gains in "total productive life years" per survivor at age 20, with the first reduction schedule increasing productive years 20–65 by 4.9% and the second reduction schedule increasing productive years 20–65 by 8.1%.

The long-run implications of policy proposals regarding the underemployment problem (namely unemployment) are easily derived by reference to the kind of modified life table of this chapter. Inasmuch as labor force policy proposals are now being geared to the long run, as opposed to the merely temporary Keynesian disturbances in the incidence of underemployment, the demographic approach set forth in this chapter might prove beneficial. It is a simple affair to modify the computer program used in all of the above computations to examine the eventual implications of any kind of age–race–sex-specific schedule of reductions in underemployment.[6] The relatively simple measure of "average productive life years" per person could be a meaningful summary index of use in policy discussion and could also be used to summarize various kinds of underemployment differentials that should be brought into the policy arena.

8.4 THE IMPLICATIONS OF A MERITOCRACY FOR LABOR FORCE HISTORY FOR THE RACE–SEX SUBPOPULATIONS

Another interesting application of the modified life-table approach to the analysis of underemployment is the examination of the long-run implications of a labor force composition based exclusively upon the principles of a meritocracy. Meritocracies have been discussed periodically by utopian writers at least since Plato, and the goal of achieving a meritocracy now dominates the mood of many social scientists, social engineers, and government officials in liberal democratic societies. Current thinking on the subject by policymakers and social theorists is, however, in disarray, principally because it is not clear how "merit" can be legitimately determined. One currently popular view, simplified somewhat for the present discussion, is that a meritocracy would necessarily ensure equal rewards for the sex–race groups and that for practical purposes, a meritocracy would be said to exist if the sex–race groups received equal rewards in the labor force. This concept of meritocracy suggests the approach of the present section.[7]

In the labor force context, it can reasonably be assumed that the merit of an individual should depend upon age. Merit clearly accumulates with

[6] Easterlin *et al.* (1978) present age-specific schedules of unemployment that they believe are consistent with low rates of inflation. The consequences of such a schedule for labor force life history could be easily examined, for example.

[7] Actually, there is no necessary relationship between the condition where the race–sex groups achieve an equitable distribution of labor market rewards and the strict meritocracy that would distribute labor market rewards according to "true" merit. Past inequities that translate into current difficulties in the attainment of merit might, for example, imply that even with a true meritocracy an equalization in race–sex differentials would be long in the offing. It is this dilemma that underlies the modern moral philosophy concerning inequality (compare Rawls, 1971; Coleman, 1974). The present conception of a meritocracy is to be regarded merely as an hypothetical one.

experience and training (i.e., with age), at least to a certain point in the life span of the individual. After that point, merit probably decreases with age owing to the deterioration of health, to the outmoded skills that an older individual possesses, etc. For each age, let us now suppose that the proportionate allocation of persons into the seven labor force statuses occurs through a mechanism approximate to a meritocracy. Since merit should not, in the standard argument, depend at all upon the race or sex of an individual, this would imply that the race–sex groups would achieve a kind of equity in the rates of labor force participation and in the rates of underemployment.[8] In the labor force context, it is approximately true that in a meritocracy, for each interval of age, the labor force status we have continually referred to as the "adequately utilized" status would be filled with persons of high merit. The other six labor force statuses, including economic inactivity and the five underemployment statuses considered in this study, would be filled with persons of low merit.

A meritocratic circumstance, even in the happiest of utopias, cannot of course fill up the desirable vacancies (those with high rewards or the adequately utilized labor force status) with all the persons who presumably would have qualified for these positions under the imperfect stratification system typifying premeritocratic society. Constraints upon the number of persons admitted to the high merit positions exist in all economies bounded by the finiteness of technology, resources, and the like. We assume here that the limitations themselves are also age-graded, that is, that the meritocracies can only provide a certain number of high merit positions to societal members of a given age. We assume further that this number is the same as that which characterized the premeritocratic society typified here by the United States in 1970. This latter assumption will appear unwarranted, since if persons were recruited into the desirable positions exclusively on the criterion of merit, then the product of those persons would be considerably greater than under the old regime, where some unproductive dolts were recruited into the desirable positions solely upon the basis of ascribed status. Since the economic product of persons in the high reward occupations would increase in a meritocratic condition, there would be need for fewer workers in the preferred statuses than formerly. Greater competition would ensue over the attainment of these statuses. In a true meritocracy, then, the size of the "adequately utilized" labor force status in any age interval would necessarily decrease.

We now put these assumptions into operation in the concrete case of the U.S. labor force in 1970 and examine the implications of the kind of

---

[8] We might assume, for example, that a sufficiently radical reorganization of society has occurred that ensures that the race–sex groups, on the average, possess the same merit.

meritocracy referred to in the preceding discussion. We assume that the age-specific underemployment *rates* and the age-specific *rates* of labor force participation were to reach an "equitable" distribution among the race–sex groups. Assuming also that the invisible hand of the economy is blind to the mode of recruitment—meritocratic or otherwise—into the desirable positions, we can also suppose that the change from status assignment based upon ascription (in part) to one based universally upon achievement (or merit) does not affect the amount and kind of employment that the meritocratic society is allowed to offer to its population of persons of working age. In the stationary population of the life table, we can assume that the proportions in the ith labor force status for the total population have reached an "equitable" distribution with respect to the sex–race groups but that also the number of total life-table years lived in the various states during any age interval are fixed by economic constraints.

Formally, we have the following argument, which rests upon some of the notation introduced in Appendix B. Let b_1, b_2, b_3, and b_4 refer to the proportions of total babies in the four sex–race groups in a stationary population, with $\Sigma_{j=1}^4 b_j = 1$. If each of the sex–race subpopulations is stationary (i.e., if the four subpopulations taken together are "jointly stationary"), then the total population is also stationary. If $l_0^j = 1$ represents the arbitrary radix value of the life table for the jth group, then the total life-table obtained by a weighting of the four sex–race-specific life tables has radix

$$l_0 = 1 = b_1 + b_2 + b_3 + b_4 \qquad (8.1)$$

The stationary age distribution $_5L_x$ in the total population, defined with reference to the arbitrary radix value $l_0 = 1$, is also a weighted sum of the stationary age distributions of the four subpopulations, where these are now redefined in terms of the radix value b_j appropriate for each subpopulation. We have

$$_5L_x = \sum_{j=1}^4 b_{j5}^j L_x \qquad (8.2)$$

where $_5^j L_x$ is the stationary population in $(x, x + 5)$ for the jth subpopulation obtained from the ordinary life table, and the b_j are defined as before. These formulas could be easily modified to take into account jointly *stable* population age distributions, but we will not go into those details here.

Now, let $_5^j P_{i,x}$ denote the *observed* rate of occurrence of the ith labor force status for the jth subpopulation, $i = 1, \ldots, 7; j = 1, \ldots, 4;$ in age interval $(x, x + 5)$. And let

$$\substack{i\\5}L^i_x = \substack{i\\5}P_{i,x}\substack{i\\5}L_x \tag{8.3}$$

denote the stationary population in the ith status, for the jth subpopulation. The total population in age interval $(x, x + 5)$ in the ith status is given by

$$_5L^i_x = \sum_{j=1}^{4} b_{j5}L^i_x \tag{8.4}$$

Our assumptions leave the quantity on the left-hand side of Equation 8.4 unchanged, since the total life years in the ith status that a society can provide is assumed fixed by technological-economic constraints. Assuming that survivorship also remains unchanged in a meritocracy, the $\substack{i\\5}L_x$ of (8.3) also remain unchanged. If rates of occurrence of the ith status are equal to each other for the race–sex groups (equal to, say, $_5P^*_{i,x}$), then the following argument shows how these equitable rates can be obtained.

Since

$$_5L^i_x = \sum_{j=1}^{4} b_{j5}P_{i,x}\substack{j\\5}L_x$$

by substituting (8.3) into (8.4), and since $_5L^i_x$ is to remain fixed, equitable rates that ensure this condition are defined by

$$\begin{aligned}_5L^i_x &= \sum_{j=1}^{4} b_{j5}P^*_i, x_5^j L_x \\ &= {}_5P^*_{i,x} \sum_{j=1}^{4} b_{j5}^j L_x\end{aligned} \tag{8.5}$$

The $_5P^*_{i,x}$ are thus determined by

$$_5P^*_{i,x} = \frac{_5L^i_x}{\displaystyle\sum_{j=1}^{4} b_{j5}^j L_x} \tag{8.6}$$

All the quantities on the right-hand side of (8.6) are *known* quantities, obtained from the race–sex life tables and current labor force data, except for the b_j. Some assumptions must be made in order to determine the b_j, since it is not clear what the sex–race distribution of newborn babies would be in jointly stationary populations. We have made assumptions about the magnitudes of the b_j that appear plausible, but for the argument here, alternative assumptions would not greatly affect our inferences.[9]

[9] As an expedient, we have taken the proportionate share of the race–sex subpopulations under 5 years of age as the set of weights to combine the sex–race life-table functions into one total life table. This approximation reproduces the total life table very closely. There are

TABLE 8.15

Decomposition of Life Expectation for the Sex–Race Subpopulations Assuming "Equity" in Labor Force Participation and Underemployment Rates

	Total life expecta- tion	Not-in- labor force	Economic underem- ployment	Mismatch	Adequate
		Expectation of life at birth[a]			
White	67.993	36.122	4.654	3.031	24.186
males		(26.512)	(3.910)	(4.468)	(33.103)
Nonwhite	61.319	32.822	4.245	2.725	21.527
males		(26.094)	(5.778)	(2.600)	(26.847)
White	75.606	41.460	4.929	3.233	25.984
females		(51.758)	(4.904)	(1.889)	(17.055)
Nonwhite	69.380	37.698	4.630	3.014	24.038
females		(43.407)	(7.179)	(2.307)	(16.487)
		Expectation of life at age 15[a]			
White	54.896	22.104	4.789	3.119	24.884
males		(12.218)	(4.021)	(4.597)	(34.058)
Nonwhite	49.214	19.332	4.451	2.858	22.573
males		(12.278)	(6.059)	(2.726)	(28.152)
White	62.196	27.315	5.035	3.303	26.543
females		(37.835)	(5.009)	(1.930)	(17.422)
Nonwhite	56.957	24.073	4.805	3.128	24.951
females		(29.998)	(7.452)	(2.394)	(17.113)

[a]Observed 1970 expectations in parentheses.

Once the $_5P^*_{i,x}$ are determined by (8.6), these equitable rates are entered into our modified life table to determine the various expectations of interest.

Table 8.15 presents the expectation of life to be lived per person in each of the statuses not-in-labor force, economic underemployment, mismatch, and adequate employment at age 0 and at age 15 for the four sex–race subpopulations. The quantities actually observed in 1970 are also reported for comparative purposes. The implications of the kind of meritocratic circumstance outlined previously are very striking indeed. The expected number of years of life to be lived outside the labor force would increase

difficulties in any procedure for weighting the sex–race life tables into one combined table; here we have only sought out a reasonable set of weights whereby the total life table would be consistent with the published life table for the total population. Other, more "natural" sets of weights (e.g., the race–sex distribution of babies born in 1970), although true to the meaning of the total life table, do *not* by our calculations do as well in reproducing the total life table from the sex–race-specific life tables as does our ad hoc method.

9.6 years for white males, which would be offset by increased labor participation by females. Nonwhite males would decrease their years in the labor force by 6.7 years, white females would increase participation by 10.3 years, and nonwhite females would increase participation by 5.7 years. Owing to longer length of life of white women, their expected number of years in adequate employment would exceed that of white males by 1.8 years. The number of years lived by white females in economic underemployment would be approximately the same as that implied by 1970 conditions. That is, in this sense, there would be no decrease in economic underemployment for white women as a whole.

Only differing mortality experience now accounts for the discrepancies among the race–sex groups with regard to these expectations, with the obvious implication that expectation in, say, the adequate employment status for the subpopulations is nearly proportional to their ability to withstand mortality. Other conceptions of meritocracy could conceivably produce a life cycle opportunity structure that produced equivalent life expectations in the labor force statuses for the race–sex groups or equivalent expectations in the labor force statuses in some interval of age (e.g., ages 20–65). As should now be apparent, these other conceptions of "equity" would produce very different conceptions of current underemployment differentials. By varying the technique used to produce Table 8.15, these other kinds of circumstances could also be examined.

A salient feature of the quantities in Table 8.15 is the strikingly small number of years spent in the adequately utilized labor force status regardless of the particular sex–race group. We see that only 35.6% of the average white male's life, 35.1% of the average nonwhite male's life, 34.4% of the average white female's life, and 34.6% of the average nonwhite female's life would be spent in adequate employment in the circumstances that we have envisioned. That is, under these explicitly defined assumptions of equity and the constraint on the total life years of adequate employment that an economy can provide, only about one-third of the life span would be spent in adequate employment by any sex–race group. Another point to consider is that the 1970 rates were used here as the base for comparison, and the underemployment conditions of that year were extremely favorable. If the long-run labor force situation were to be somewhat worse than 1970 conditions, a likely possibility given the present outlook, then the years actually spent in the status of adequate employment would correspondingly decrease. These are, then, *liberal* estimates of the average life years lived in adequate employment and *conservative* estimates of the average life years lived in underemployment.

The most questionable assumption in our calculations is, of course, the essentially economic-technological constraint on life years in the several labor force statuses that an economy can provide to its members. We have assumed that the rewards of the labor market are fixed, constituting something like a zero-sum game. Surely this assumption is not true in any strict sense, but critics would do well to see how dramatic a change in the labor market would have to be brought about to ensure everyone the degree of opportunity that white males now enjoy. Current thinking on this subject is similar, in our opinion, to the eighteenth-century projections of the utopians Condorcet and Godwin, who believed that the constraint of mortality itself would one day be conquered by science. The Malthusian retort to their megalomania is once again necessary. Even if we allowed *reasonable* increases in the provision of adequate employment—and there are limits imposed on the extent of increase even if we cannot now express them—the preceding figures would not be changed substantially. In the event of race–sex equity that we have considered here, the end result would surely be shared disillusionment for all parties in the work-oriented societies. A fuller analysis would take into account the variance of the above expectations, since in a meritocratic condition the variance of life years lived in the labor force might also be the same for the various sex–race groups. This timely topic is certainly worthy of further investigation.

Another interesting indicator of the condition of the meritocratic society is the "eventual productive value" of the various race–sex groups. This was previously defined as the expected years per person lived in the mismatched or the adequately employed statuses. Table 8.16 presents these quantities, pertaining to the "eventual productive value" per person at age 15. The proportions corresponding to the contribution of the sex–race groups to total eventual productive value are obtained from "revised" estimates of the resident population aged 15 on July 1, 1970 (U.S. Department of Commerce, 1975). We see that in this hypothetical case, white males and white females have come to share almost equally in the total product, with white males losing about 15.9% and white females gaining an apparent 15.4% over conditions prevalent in 1969. Some sociological theorists might wish to equate this "eventual productive value" to the socioeconomic power that the race–sex groups command. This demographic approach to the analysis of distribution of power in society would also be fruitful, but we will not pursue it further here.

In sum, the kind of equity in the labor force for which we have worked out the implications in this section would have dramatic impact upon the race–sex composition of the labor force and upon labor force history for each of the race–sex groups. Very dramatic changes in the relative position of the race–sex groups as regards expected life years in the various labor force statuses would ensue. The very small number of years lived in

TABLE 8.16
Eventual Productive Value of the Sex–Race Subpopulations Aged 15, Assuming
"Equity"in Labor Force Participation and Underemployment Rates (in Percentages)

	White male	Nonwhite male	White female	Nonwhite female
Percent of total population aged 15 (July 1, 1970)	43.68[a]	7.30[a]	41.77[a]	7.25[a]
Productive life years per person	28.884	25.431	29.846	28.079
Total product resulting from each subpopulation	12.617	1.856	12.467	2.036
Percent	43.5	6.4	43.0	7.0
Percent share of product in 1969	59.5	8.0	27.6	4.9

[a]These were the observed proportions in age 15 for the civilian July 1, 1970 population, based upon revised estimates of the Bureau of Census. Apparently, these figures are not consistent among themselves, for they show that males are still the dominant sex at age 15. Rather than adjust estimates to reflect the probable female dominance by age 15, we have used these estimates to arrive at our "Total product resulting from each subpopulation." These weights are quite arbitrary, and so these figures should only be interpreted as rough estimates, which are only valid in the life table (i.e., stationary population) context.

adequate employment per person given this contrived state of affairs is a telling indicator of actual labor force opportunity in the United States.

8.5 A FORMAL ACCOUNT OF "EVENTUAL PRODUCTIVE VALUE"

It is interesting to formalize the quantity we have previously referred to as the "eventual productive value" of a life-table cohort. Here, that index is given different meaning through continuous (as opposed to discrete) life-table functions, basic accounts of which occur in Chiang (1968) and in Keyfitz (1968). The following quantities are useful:

$l(x)$, the probability that a newborn child will survive to exact age x;

$$u(x) = \lim_{\Delta x \downarrow 0} \frac{l(x) - l(x + \Delta x)}{l(x)\,\Delta x} = \frac{-d\,\ln[l(x)]}{dx}$$

the instantaneous death rate, or force of mortality; ω, the upper age limit of life. The expectation of life at age x is now expressed as

$$\mathring{e}_x = \frac{\int_0^{\omega-x} tl(x + t)u(x + t)\, dt}{\int_0^{\omega-x} l(x + t)u(x + t)\, dt}.$$ (8.7)

The denominator in Equation 8.7 is interpreted as the number of persons of the life-table radix who die after age x, which is simply $l(x)$. Applying the definition of $u(x)$, (8.7) can be simplified further, and upon integration by parts, we obtain a familiar formula for life expectation at age x, $\mathring{e}_x = T(x)/l(x)$. If $l^p(x)$ is the probability that a newborn child will be in a productive labor force status at age x, then the index of productive value is

$$\mathring{e}_x^p = \frac{\int_0^{\omega-x} tl^p(x + t)u(x + t)\, dt}{\int_0^{\omega-x} l(x + t)u(x + t)\, dt}$$ (8.8)

which simplifies to $T^p(x)/l(x)$, in obvious notation. The quantity in (8.8) can be thought of as the average productive life years remaining *per person* alive at age x. Another way to view the index is suggested in the stationary population interpretation of the life table. In that interpretation, we see that $\mathring{e}_x^p$ is the ratio at any point in time of two quantities that remain unchanged through time if stationariness persists. The numerator is the first moment of $l^p(x)u(x)$, and the denominator is the population total over age x. The quantity $\mathring{e}_x^p$ is now seen to be the ratio of all persons productively employed aged x and over per person alive at age x. By some simplifications similar to those used to obtain $T^p(x)/l(x)$ from (8.8), we see that

$$\mathring{e}_x^p = \frac{\int_x^{\omega} l^p(t)\, dt}{l(x)}$$ (8.9)

The variance associated with $\mathring{e}_x^p$ is given by

$$\frac{\int_0^{\omega-x} t^2 l^p(x + t)u(x + t)\, dt}{l(x)} - (\mathring{e}_x^p)^2$$ (8.10)

An extension of the index of productive value to the general stable population, where the intrinsic growth rate r need not equal zero, is suggested by the following. Since in a stable population the age distribution is proportional to $e^{-rx}l(x)$, we can define our index of productive value in general as

$$\mathring{e}_x^p(r) = \frac{\int_x^\omega e^{-rt}l^p(t)\,dt}{e^{-rt}l(x)} \tag{8.11}$$

The interpretation of this index in the stable population with growth rate r is equivalent to that given to this index in the stationary population, that is, it is the number of productively employed persons aged x and over per person aged x. It would be interesting to compare $\mathring{e}_x^p$, $\mathring{e}_x^p(r)$, and the productive value observed in current populations, in order to determine the influence of r upon productive value (see related comments in Chapter 9). The possiblity of speaking of productive value at any point in time for observed populations, for stationary populations, and for stable populations therefore exists. The simplicity of this measure recommends it for demographic study of the labor force.

It is also interesting to note the connection of productive value with the theory of human capital accumulation (Becker, 1971). One means by which human capital is increased is on-the-job experience, and presumably the experience of a worker in the labor force statuses corresponding to *productive* statuses would have higher "rates of return on investment" than the unproductive or subproductive labor force statuses. If ρ is the annual rate of interest by which human capital compounds when utilized or "invested" in a productive labor force status, then in the t years a person spends in a productive status, his endowment of human capital increases from E_0 (his initial endowment) to E_t by the familiar formula

$$E_t = E_0 e^{\rho t}$$

If we can ignore the unproductive labor force statuses altogether as having negligible returns upon human capital endowment, then the total human capital accumulation in a life-table cohort after age x (disregarding accumulation which occurs outside the productive labor force statuses) is

$$E_\omega = \frac{\int_x^\omega e^{\rho t}l^p(t)\,dt E_x}{l(x)} \tag{8.12}$$

where E_x is the endowment at age x. It would be fruitful, in our view, to develop the demographic theory of human capital accumulation and the concept of productive value further.

8.6 CONCLUSION

This chapter has presented elementary extensions of the life table or stationary population model modified to take into account the long-run labor force history implied by currently observed mortality and labor force conditions. The labor force indicators derived from this modified life table are in certain respects preferable to the more usual rates and ratios in terms of the units of measurement (life years), in the consideration of mortality experience (and implicitly the age distribution) of the population, and in allowing us to examine the long-run implications of current conditions. With the modified life table, we were able to deduce in relatively simple terms the across-time and the sex–race differentials that we previously discussed in Chapters 2, 3, and 4. The life-table approach forces us to consider different kinds of underemployment differentials than those in the observed rates owing to the dramatically different survivorship of the respective race–sex groups.

We also presented an index of adequate employment, the "eventual productive life years" per person, or "productive value," which might prove useful in policy discussion. The long-run implications of sustained reductions in underemployment, such as are envisioned by proponents of the Humphrey–Hawkins bill in the U.S. Congress, were analyzed within the life-table framework. Similarly, the long-run implications of a kind of "equity" in the labor force were also worked out. Of special importance in all the results of this chapter were the proportions of the life span spent in adequate employment for the race–sex subpopulations. Even for white males, this proportion was surprisingly small, at around 49%, and under conditions of equity and reasonable assumptions about the ability of the economy to provide adequate employment to its population of working ages, we found that each of the race–sex groups would spend only about one-third of the life span in adequate employment. Although the methods used in this chapter are elementary, the characterization of underemployment that they provided was quite different from that which is obtained from analyses disregarding the role of survivorship.

9

some new directions for mathematical demography

To our knowledge, there has been little research on the labor force subject from the point of view of formal demographic models. For example, the text by Keyfitz (1968) contains only slightly more than a paragraph concerning labor force dynamics. Other texts by Pollard (1973), Bartlett (1960), Coale (1974), and Ludwig (1974), while containing models that can certainly be extended to the labor force context, contain little explicit consideration of labor force dynamics. Some of the "multiregional" demographic models suggested by Rogers (1971, 1975) would also be pertinent to the labor force subject, but again there is little explicit treatment of the labor force apart from that implied by his models for geographic mobility. This chapter presents a brief introduction to the labor force topic from a more formal point of view, taking as its point of entry the concept of labor force structure developed elsewhere in this work. The questions to be addressed pertain to the following topics:

1. The relationship between the intrinsic rate of growth and underemployment in a stable population
2. Measurement of "true" dependency on productive employment
3. The age distribution of employment opportunity

We believe that any formal mathematical treatment of labor force dynamics should begin with these topics. Our initial consideration of them, not all details of which are surveyed here, suggests that a high degree of empirical regularity in labor force structure exists that begs for further analytic appraisal.

9.1 THE RELATIONSHIP BETWEEN UNDEREMPLOYMENT AND THE INTRINSIC RATE OF GROWTH IN A STABLE POPULATION

If we are given the age-graded character of underemployment, and if we can assume that this age dependence is a persistent feature of the social organization of the labor force, then the crude rate of underemployment will depend on the rate of population growth in a clear manner. All other things being equal, populations with a high rate of growth would have high underemployment, since in a high-growth population, the bulk of the labor force would be concentrated in the younger ages, where the risk to underemployment is the greatest. In a stable population the crude rate of underemployment, assuming institutionalized rigidity in the age distribution of employment, would then depend only on the intrinsic rate of growth r and the survivorship probabilities. Since no convenient mathematical results presently appear suitable to express the dependence of crude underemployment rates upon the rate of growth, a simulation approach is followed here to demonstrate the form of that dependence. The basis of our inferences are the mortality conditions and the underemployment conditions of the U.S. male population of 1970. These conditions typify a very favorable labor force condition (with unemployment rates around 4%) and the favorable survivorship of an advanced population (with life expectation around 66 years).

The population K_x in age interval $(x, x + 1)$ in a stable population with growth rate r can be determined by applying certain numerical integration techniques to

$$K_x = \int_0^1 \exp[-r(x + t)]l(x + t) \, dt \qquad (9.1)$$

(See Keyfitz, 1968, pp. 259ff.) By applying observed age-specific labor force participation rates and age-specific rates of (economic) underemployment to the age distribution K_x that results, we can easily trace out the influence of the rate of growth r upon (a) the crude rate of labor force participation, (b) the crude rate of underemployment, and (c) dependency burdens. In connection with dependency burdens, we consider *total dependency on productive employment* defined as the number of economically inactive or economically underemployed persons per adequately employed person. This kind of dependency ratio is truer to the meaning of dependence than are the more usual age-dependency ratios, since inactive persons and underemployed persons regardless of their age are in some

TABLE 9.1

Dependence of Some Labor Force Characteristics upon the Intrinsic Rate of Growth (Male Populations with Mortality and Labor Force Conditions Like the United States in 1970)

Intrinsic rate of growth $r(\times 100)$	Percentage in the labor force[a]	Percentage of labor force underemployed	Total dependency[b]
−1.0	63.7	9.7	.738
− .8	63.4	9.8	.750
− .6	62.9	9.9	.765
− .4	62.4	10.0	.781
− .2	61.8	10.1	.800
+ .0	61.1	10.2	.821
+ .2	60.4	10.3	.844
+ .4	59.7	10.4	.870
+ .6	58.9	10.5	.898
+ .8	58.0	10.6	.999
+1.0	57.1	10.7	.962
+1.2	56.1	10.9	.962
+1.4	55.2	11.0	1.037
+1.6	54.1	11.1	1.078
+1.8	53.1	11.2	1.122
+2.0	52.0	11.4	1.169
+2.2	50.9	11.5	1.219
+2.4	49.8	11.6	1.272

[a]Includes the sub-unemployed with the usual labor force.

[b]Dependency ratio $= \dfrac{\text{all economically inactive plus underemployed}}{\text{all adequately employed}}$.

way dependent upon the adequately employed persons, either through direct support or indirect support through tax transfers and the like.[1]

Table 9.1 contains the simulated results for values of r from $-.010$ to $+.024$ in intervals of $.002$. The range of values of r is certainly unrealistic for developed populations like the United States, but values of r from say, $-.004$ to $+.014$, are certainly plausible for populations of this type. The patterns that are observed in Table 9.1 are certainly those that are ex-

[1] The age-dependency ratio typically used in economic demography and elsewhere is merely the persons younger than age 15 or older than age 65 per person in the interval 15–65. This assumes that (*a*) all persons under age 15 and all persons over age 65 are in a state of dependency and that (*b*) all persons 15–65 are productive. This ratio is described in many instances (compare United Nations, 1968, 1973), and has been used (with only slight modifications) in historical analysis (Durand, 1948, pp. 42–46; Durand, 1975). The pioneer work in economic demography by Coale and Hoover (1958) also made use of the customary index of dependency, and use of this index had much to do with their appraisal of the substantial economic benefits to be reaped by rapid fertility decline.

pected, but the form of the relationships and the numerical levels of those indexes of labor force characteristics are interesting in their own right. We see an almost exact linear relationship between r and the crude rate of underemployment in the labor force, with an increase in r of .001 producing about a .5% increase in the crude rate of underemployment. In the range of r appropriate for advanced populations, we see that the crude rate of underemployment could change by about 1% with reasonable changes in growth rates. The proportion of the total population in the labor force changes from .64 with $r = -.01$ to .50 with $r = +.024$, certainly a dramatic dependence of overall labor force participation upon the rate of growth. We see that the relationship between labor force participation and the intrinsic growth rate r is a mildly negative and curvilinear one. More interesting, in our view, are the dependency burdens implied by the various rates of growth. Total dependency—the ratio of all persons in a state of dependency to all persons in productive employment—exhibits a strong positive and *quadratic* relationship to r. We see that with an intrinsic growth rate of $-.010$, there would be .74 persons dependent on each adequately employed person, but that with an $r = +.024$, there would be 1.27 persons dependent on each adequately employed person. This total dependency ratio is, in our view, a very meaningful figure, since it is a truer measure of total dependence upon productive labor force activity than are age-dependency ratios alone.

These relationships are presented by way of illustration and, of course, depend critically upon the *ceteribus paribus* assumption. Economists can immediately shatter our simulation here with a plethora of reasons why all things cannot remain constant as r changes. Nevertheless, the form of the relationships brought out here is suggestive of the underlying strength of the rate of growth upon labor force structure. We might conclude that it is precisely these relationships to which an adaptive society orients itself when adjusting to the rate of growth of its population. Another deduction relates to the sensitivity of dependency to marked changes in age structure. Coale and Hoover (1958), in their landmark study of the positive economic effects of rapid fertility decline, assumed that dependency would decline in proportion to the decline in the percentage of the population under age 15. But since a great part of the new dependency ratio is composed of dependent persons in the age interval 15–65 (economically inactive and economically underemployed persons), it can be shown that rapid fertility decline—or other perturbations in the age structure—will *not* change the "true" dependency burden to as great an extent. Because this new dependency ratio is a summary of the dependency burdens across all age intervals, it is less responsive to transient shifts in age structure. It seems apparent that measures of dependency that take account of the underemployment burden, in ways similar to the measure suggested here, would improve economic and sociological use of dependency as either an independent or a dependent variable.

9.2 THE AGE DISTRIBUTION OF EMPLOYMENT OPPORTUNITY: THE CONSTANT AGE ELASTICITY OF UNDEREMPLOYMENT

We have often made reference to the age distribution of underemployment and to the age distribution of labor force participation as a structural characteristic of the socioeconomic organization of the American labor force. Age certainly appears as a master indicator of socioeconomic position, since underemployment risks so clearly depend on the age of the person. In this section, a very compelling model will be developed to account for the age distribution of employment opportunity for males, and we will find that this model will account for the age pattern of underemployment over most of the age span of labor force activity for a male labor force with very favorable economic conditions (e.g., 1970 conditions) and for a male labor force with very unfavorable economic conditions (e.g., 1972 conditions). This model is mathematically tractable, so that its functional form could very well come to play a role in the formal mathematical theory of the labor force.

Employment opportunity at any age might be indicated by two characteristics: the proportion of the age group participating in the labor force and the proportion of the labor force that is underemployed. (We here use the "economic" underemployment category, obtained by collapsing all the forms of underemployment but mismatch into one class.) In fact, labor force participation rates and proportions of the labor force underemployed are moderately correlated (Pearson correlation = .63 for ages 15–69 in 1970), implying that either might plausibly be used as an indicator of employment opportunity. Since the labor force at any given age is presumed to contain all persons optimizing their capacity to seek out adequate employment, the proportion of the labor force underemployed at a given age is perhaps a truer indicator of employment opportunity than are labor force participation rates alone. The reason for preferring the proportion of the labor force underemployed to the labor force participation rate is that the latter quantity is dependent upon the number of persons who are not optimizing their capacity to seek out adequate employment (since persons outside the labor force are not currently seeking work) and upon a certain number of persons who under no circumstances would seek out work (the "stayers" in economic inactivity). We therefore use the proportion of the labor force (actually the modified labor force spoken of in earlier chapters) that is economically underemployed as a rough indicator of employment opportunity.

The age distribution of underemployment was discussed earlier in Chapters 2 and 4. Underemployment is very high at the younger ages, declines steadily until the mid-30s, is quite low in the middle ages, and rises again in the older ages. With economic recession, the rates of under-employment rise the most in the young ages, but they also rise somewhat in the higher ages. After age 70, underemployment does not follow the pattern implied by the curve for the earlier ages, perhaps as a result of the peculiarities of labor force activity after retirement age. In the model that is developed in this section, we will ignore ages 70+ and will therefore only model employment opportunity for ages 15–69. Some other compli-cations arise for the very young ages (15–19) and for the older ages (65–69), and these will also be discussed.

We consider a model for the age distribution of underemployment (say, the age distribution of employment "inopportunity") in which the propor-tion p_x underemployed at age x is related to age by

$$p_x = A \, \exp(BZ) X^\gamma X^{\delta Z} \exp(u) \tag{9.2}$$

where $Z = 0$ for ages 15–34 and $Z = 1$ for ages 35+, X is age in single years, and $\exp(u)$ is a multiplicative disturbance term. For age interval 15–34 we see that Equation 9.2 reduces to

$$p_x = AX^\gamma$$

apart from the disturbance term, with a similar expression for p_x for age range 35+. The case where γ is negative will generate a convex curve sloping downward appropriate for ages 15–34, and the case where $\gamma + \delta$ is positive will generate a convex curve sloping upward appropriate for ages 35–69. Econometricians use a model like (9.2) in statistical demand analy-sis because it corresponds to the assumption that the *elasticity* between the dependent variable (p_x in this context) and the independent variable (X, or age in this context) is *constant* for the range of the independent variable. Model 9.2 assumes constant age elasticity in age interval 15–34 and con-stant age elasticity in age interval 35–69. That is, since the elasticity between p_x and X is defined as

$$\frac{X}{p_x} \frac{(dp_x)}{(dX)} = \frac{d[\ln(p_x)]}{d[\ln(X)]} \tag{9.3}$$

we find that the age elasticity of underemployment is γ for ages 15–34 and $\gamma + \delta$ for ages 35–69 by substituting (9.2) in (9.3). This model, assuming constant age elasticity of underemployment (in the relevant age span), is attractive because, by taking logarithms, it can be estimated easily by linear regression and because of its substantive interpretation in the labor force context. We may, following the approach of the econometricians, treat the model as a representation of the age-specific *demand* for labor, or we may take it as a representation of the age-graded structure of employment opportunity, or we may treat it in other ways (see Johnston, 1972, pp. 51–52). We can, for example, regard age as a variable reflecting the "price" of labor and p_x as the proportionate quantity demanded at that price. The two elasticity parameters γ and δ summarize the age variability in underemployment. We will now see that this model can explain the data very well indeed.

Table 9.2 presents the results of applying model 9.2 to predict the proportion p_x of the labor force underemployed at age x for data by single years of age. Some complications arise for ages 15–19 and for ages 65–69, probably owing to the peculiarities of labor force activity as persons prepare for careers or approach retirement, so separate regressions were run for ages 15–69 (Part A of Table 9.2), ages 15–64 (Part B of Table 9.2), and

TABLE 9.2
Regression Results: A Model for the Age Distribution of Underemployment
(1970 Male Data)

A. Model for Ages 15–69		
Parameter estimate	Ages 15–34	Ages 35–69
ln(constant)	6.027	−7.417
Elasticity	−2.534	1.232
		Overall F = 80.81 on 3 and 51 degrees of freedom
		Multiple R^2 = .826
		Standard error of estimate = .240
B. Model for Ages 15–64		
Parameter estimate	Ages 15–34	Ages 35–64
ln(constant)	6.027	−5.860
Elasticity	−2.534	.821
		Overall F = 95.14 on 3 and 46 degrees of freedom
		Multiple R^2 = .861
		Standard error of estimate = .219
C. Model for Ages 20–64		
Parameter estimate	Ages 20–34	Ages 35–64
ln(constant)	9.042	−5.860
Elasticity	−3.444	.821
		Overall F = 94.46 on 3 and 41 degrees of freedom
		Multiple R^2 = .874
		Standard error of estimate = .158

ages 20–64 (Part C of Table 9.2). We see that for the 1970 data, this simple model does very well indeed, with multiple R^2 ranging from .82 to .87 and the F statistics ranging from 80.81 to 95.14. Depending upon the age range considered, this model therefore accounts for 82–87% of the age variation in underemployment [i.e., in $\log(p_x)$]. The magnitude of each of the estimated coefficients is at least 10 times its standard error, so we have found a most compelling model indeed of the age structure of underemployment (or the age-specific demand for labor). Inspection of the pattern of residuals does reveal systematic trends in the deviation of predictions from the observed p_x's, but the simplicity of this model perhaps recommends it over other models that might be proposed.

Table 9.3 presents the corresponding results for 1972—a recession year with underemployment conditions very different from 1970. We see once again that the model 9.2 does very well, with its F statistics ranging from 72.10 to 117.65. It accounts for 81–90% of the age variation in underemployment for this recession year. The assumption of constant age elastic-

TABLE 9.3
**Regression Results: A Model for the Age Distribution of Underemployment
(1972 Male Data)**

	A. Model for ages 15–69	
Parameter estimate	Ages 15–34	Ages 35–69
In(constant)	5.996	−7.160
Elasticity	−2.456	1.203
		Overall F = 72.60 on 3 and 51 degrees of freedom
		Multiple R^2 = .810
		Standard error of estimate = .258
	B. Model for ages 15–64	
Parameter estimate	Ages 15–34	Ages 35–64
In(constant)	5.996	−5.156
Elasticity	−2.456	.673
		Overall F = 89.12 on 3 and 46 degrees of freedom
		Multiple R^2 = .853
		Standard error of estimate = .233
	C. Model for Ages 20–64	
Parameter estimate	Ages 20–34	Ages 35–64
In(constant)	9.654	−5.156
Elasticity	−3.559	.673
		Overall F = 117.65 on 3 and 41 degrees of freedom
		Multiple R^2 = .896
		Standard error of estimate = .151

TABLE 9.4
Regression Results: A Model for the Age Distribution of Underemployment
(Combined 1970 and 1972 Data, Males Aged 15–64)

	Ages 15–34	Ages 35–64
1970		
ln(constant)	5.929	−5.590
1972		
ln(constant)	6.094	−5.426
Elasticity	−2.495	.747
		Overall F = 143.75
		Multiple R^2 = .858
		Standard error of predicted $\ln(p_x)$ = .223

ity of underemployment (in the relevant age spans) certainly appears plausible, although we have not yet examined the influence of recession upon the estimated parameters. By considering ages 25–59, thereby ignoring the labor force ages where employment opportunity is less well predicted by our model, we can actually obtain multiple R^2 coefficients of about 95%. This functional form for the age distribution of employment opportunity therefore appears adequate and demonstrates that the age structure of underemployment can be captured by elementary statistical models. Inasmuch as the cross sections here can be regarded as pertaining to the real life history of successive cohorts, a very simple model of the life-cycle progression through age-graded employment opportunity structure has been obtained.

The heterogeneity of the parameters in Tables 9.2 and 9.3 was also considered. Rather than presenting all the details of that analysis of covariance, we note that (a) the elasticities are *constant* over time for 1970 and 1972 (since the t ratios testing the heterogeneity in the elasticities were all of magnitude less than 1), and (b) only a *single* multiplicative factor is necessary to reflect the change in the location parameters A and $\exp(BZ)$. The estimated parameters from this regression are presented in Table 9.4. With a multiple R^2 of 86% for ages 15–64, we see that a most compelling model of the *changes* in age-specific opportunity structure over time has been obtained. The proportion economically underemployed at age x can be predicted very well by the equations:

1970

$$\ln(\hat{p}_x) = 5.929 - 2.495(\ln X), \qquad X \text{ in interval } 15\text{–}34$$
$$\ln(\hat{p}_x) = -5.590 + .747(\ln X), \qquad X \text{ in interval } 35\text{–}64$$

1972

$$\ln(\hat{p}_x) = 6.094 - 2.495(\ln X), \qquad X \text{ in interval } 15\text{--}34$$
$$\ln(\hat{p}_x) = -5.426 + .747(\ln X), \qquad X \text{ in interval } 35\text{--}64$$

The striking feature is, of course, that the elasticities remained unchanged during 1970–1972 and that only the constant terms require a simple modification to reflect changing economic opportunity. Our hypothesis is that the age elasticities would remain unchanged over time, reflecting structural organization of the labor force about age, but that the location factors would change with economic fluctuation. If this hypothesis were correct, then a very simple model of the age dynamic of employment opportunity would ensue. The mathematical tractability of this model also lends itself to a formal account of such labor force concepts as "productive value," as we defined it in Chapter 8. We will not go into those details here.

Various other models could certainly be applied, and surely different estimation techniques could be used even for the model just considered. Ordinary least-squares does not adequately deal with the inherently heteroscedastic disturbances in model 9.2, and so a weighted least-squares procedure would improve the efficiency of the estimates. Another approach would be to model the *odds* of being underemployed at each age, estimating parameters by maximum likelihood methods for logit analysis. Still another approach would exploit the close similarity of the age-specific risks to underemployment to an age curve of survivorship, perhaps resulting in a Gompertz–Makeham-type model (see Keyfitz, 1968). We leave these analytic questions to others, having demonstrated the striking degree of empirical regularity evidenced in the age–underemployment relationship. In our view, mathematical demographers interested in the labor force topic would do well to begin with an analytic appraisal of this regularity.

10

conclusion

Our study has been a demographic analysis of labor force structure, where the dimensions of that structure have been inferred from measures of the several forms of underemployment. The population of working ages was partitioned into seven different statuses, several of which were categories new (or relatively new) to labor force statistics. These categories were (a) those not in labor force, (b) the sub-unemployed, (c) the unemployed, (d) the involuntary part-time unemployed, (e) the underemployed by low work-related income, (f) the mismatched (i.e., those whose skill attainment measured by completed years education was considerably greater than that of their peers in the same occupation), and (g) the adequately employed. Given these indicators of labor force structure, for the most part modifications or direct extensions of previous work by Hauser and Sullivan, cross-sectional differentials and time-period change in the age–race–sex components of the American labor force were examined. Statistical techniques suitable for this kind of "social indicator" analysis were proposed, adopted, or modified for the study. Inasmuch as social indicator models of the future will be geared to the parameterization of time-period change on the basis of repeated cross-sectional measurement, the methods presented in our work could come to play a role in the social indicator branches of sociology and demography. The perspectives on time-period change and cross-sectional differentials in the American labor force are also substantial contributions to the theory of the labor force. We first summarize methodological aspects of our work and then suggest some theoretical contributions that stem from the approach we have taken to the analysis of labor force structure.

10.1 METHODS

The main methodological emphasis of our study has been to develop an approach by which the several forms of underemployment could be measured from existing labor force surveys such as the Current Population Survey (CPS) of the United States. Following guidelines set forth by Hauser, the new measures of the low-income and the mismatch forms of underemployment were applied to five time-period observations from the March CPS for years 1969–1973. These measures were congruent with accepted definitions of labor force concepts and could therefore enjoy widespread application in the collection of labor force statistics in general. The potential of these new labor force indicators is considerable. Particularly important is the Hauser-Sullivan measure of the low-income form of underemployment. That new labor force measure was found to uncover age and sex differentials in labor force structure that were not being adequately measured by other, more common labor force indicators. In addition, it was found that the 10% of the labor force located in the low-income status (determined on the basis of *previous year's* income) had current rates of unemployment and part-time unemployment six to eight times greater than the 90% of the labor force not in this status. This new low-income measure of underemployment is thus a good indicator of labor force marginality, since it can predict the risk to unemployment and part-time unemployment very well. We found that the rate of mismatch increased for the age group 20–34 by about 1% per year, rising steadily despite countervailing tendencies in the other forms of underemployment. We believe that we have convincingly demonstrated the *potential* of the new measures for inferring a labor force structure that has been obscured in the past by exclusive use of indicators of the time dimension of underemployment. The new measures could suggest new labor force policy priorities and policy alternatives; they could also release the present socioeconomic theory of the labor force from its preoccupation with the time spent in employment.

The configuration of the labor force that resulted from application of the Hauser-Sullivan approach was a very complicated one. First, it was complicated by the sheer number of labor force statuses (seven in all) subject to simultaneous consideration. Second, it was complicated by the potential ambiguity arising from multiple underemployment, such as the joint occurrence of unemployment and mismatch. These, in turn, implied that comparisons across time and/or across demographic strata were also complicated. In part, these difficulties led to our consideration of the several different methodological tools of this study. These methods were considered because of the ease with which they can be applied to repeated cross-sectional surveys such as the CPS. By way of summary, these methods were as follows.

Application of standard results on the collapsing of cross-tables led, in Chapter 3, to the analysis of the additional "statistical information" in the newly proposed measures of invisible underemployment. Gauging the across-time information in the new measures was one such application. We found that the mismatch form added somewhat to our characterization of time-period change in the labor force. We also found that the low-income measure added a tremendous amount of statistical information about sex and age differentials in labor force experience.

Hierarchical log-linear models expressing the partial heterogeneity among a set of contingency tables are well suited to the social indicator perspective. These methods were used in Chapter 4 to examine the time-period heterogeneity of the labor force, demonstrating that changing demographic composition with time is a critical factor in overall time-period heterogeneity of the labor force. Almost one-half of the total time-period heterogeneity of the labor force could not be explained without taking into account changing demographic composition and/or the changing relationship of the demographic variables with underemployment. These models also showed that the statistical information contained in only a few marginal tables is sufficient to characterize across-time changes in underemployment. A fairly simple representation of the demographic structure-time dynamic of the labor force resulted from application of these methods.

Direct standardization or adjustment of rates, long a central part of demographic method, was used to examine the effect of changing age composition upon the crude indicators of underemployment. We found in Chapter 4 that even in the span of 5 years, changes in age composition could not be ignored; changing age distribution of the labor force had no small effect upon the extent to which crude rates of underemployment unambiguously measure structural (as opposed to frictional) changes in labor force structure. We found that, for the time span considered here, underemployment increased by .11–.28% per year as a result of changing age composition of the labor force alone. A new method for adjustment of rates, based upon the multiplicative model, was also developed and successfully applied (see Appendix H).

Latent structure methods developed by Goodman were applied in Chapter 5 to the cross-classification of the labor force by type of underemployment, treating the *manifest* relationships observed in that cross-classification as the result of an *indirect* observation of latent labor force classes differing from each other in terms of degree of marginality. Changing patterns of *multiple* underemployment were summarized in parameters of these models. A general computer program for latent structure analysis for polytomous (not necessarily dichotomous) variables was developed (Appendix C). Models developed through Goodman's modified latent structure approach lent themselves to interpretation from several different points of view (e.g., from a kind of scaling point of view). Some new kinds of latent structures were entertained in order to explain the changing association among the forms of underemployment with the progress of time.

The diagonals parameter model of Goodman was also shown to be potentially advantageous to the social indicator perspective. Cohort differentiation in the labor force that could not be attributed to aging or time-period effects was documented. There was ambiguity in estimating the actual "cohort effects," but we are confident that additional work from the point of view set forth in Chapter 6 will be fruitful in resolving some of that ambiguity. A computer program for cohort analysis using multiplicative models and the modified multiple regression approach was developed (Appendix G), and a method for "purging" time-period variation in demographic rates of the extraneous cohort disturbance was proposed (Appendix F). The cohort models for qualitative data used in Chapter 6 could become important to the sociological study of social change, since cohort differentiation indicates one kind of social change that has been central to sociological theory since Mannheim.

Forecasting social events based upon the time-trend information in a series of contingency tables is a problem partly resolved by the methods proposed in Chapter 7. The log-linear forecast of qualitative variables seems to be a desirable manner in which to proceed. It would not be difficult to utilize time-trend information as we have done with the simple models proposed in this chapter in the forecasting of labor force characteristics and of other kinds of social (i.e., qualitative) variables. Forecasting qualitative events and time-trending proportions in various social statuses are important objectives of social indicator methodology.

The life-table or stationary population approach of Chapter 8 also presents a means whereby the labor force information obtained at a given point in time can be abstracted away from the transitory exigencies of the moment. The long-run implications of current conditions, new demographic indexes of underemployment and labor force productivity, and policy uses of the life table modified to take into account underemployment history quickly derive from this approach. It is our belief that this approach, involving strictly demographic conceptions of the manner in which the race–sex groups interact and compete for desirable labor force statuses, will lead, when pursued to its extreme, to a *demographic* theory of labor force structure, incorporating fertility and mortality dynamics. It is clear that age dependency alone, or changes therein over time, by no means exhausts the capability of the demographic perspective to the study of the labor force.

It is not to be surmised that the *theoretical* contributions suggested by our work are themselves of slight significance, even though the organization of the study appears on the face to minimize matters of theoretical importance. Theoretical developments based upon the modeling of empirical relationships will closely follow the social indicator perspective that has been the lodestone of our study. Although we feel that there are several significant theoretical implications in our study, we choose here only four of those topics that are illustrative of the theoretical scope of the work. These topics are (*a*) time-period heterogeneity in labor force structure and the theory of frictional underemployment, (*b*) latent class structure and labor market (labor force) dualism, (*c*) cohort differentiation with respect to labor force status and the tempo of cohort-induced social change, and (*d*) interaction of the race–sex groups in a constrained labor market. Although our study provides no definitive resolution of these critical theoretical issues, some elementary contributions to our understanding of them were suggested.

10.2 TIME-PERIOD HETEROGENEITY IN THE LABOR FORCE AND THE THEORY OF FRICTIONAL UNDEREMPLOYMENT

The total rate of unemployment is composed of a *structural* part (that part indicating slack demand for labor, or "true" unemployment) and a *frictional* part (that part indicating the normal unemployment characterizing a dynamic labor force). The other forms of underemployment may also be presumed to have structural and frictional parts. Labor force theory would be enhanced if a method for ascertaining the mix of these two unobservable parts could be determined. Our study sheds at least some light upon the *changes* in the mix between the two types that occur with time, although we were not able to estimate the mix itself. Sociological and economic thinking about this mix is properly understood as the theory of frictional underemployment.

A labor force composed of demographic parts such as age–race–sex groups (represented by the symbol D) can change over time (T) in three distinct ways relevant to our understanding of underemployment (U). The general incidence of underemployment can vary and would be signified by a $T-U$ interaction. The demographic composition of the work force can change and would be signified by a $D-T$ interaction. Finally, the relationship of the demographic parts to underemployment itself can change with time and is reflected in the magnitude of the $D-T-U$ interaction. It is well known that the several demographic parts to the labor force have very different risks to underemployment, and it may reasonably be assumed that they also have very different *intrinsic* levels of risk to frictional underemployment. With the progress of time, the relative share of the labor force secured by each of the demographic parts changes as a result of changing labor force participation patterns and other factors. The changing level of frictional underemployment in the labor force can be at least partly monitored by examining the size of the $D-T$ interaction, reflecting time-period change in demographic composition. If demographic composition changes to a great extent, then we can properly infer that the mix between frictional and structural underemployment has also undergone great change, since the demographic parts themselves have very different intrinsic levels of frictional underemployment. Using a conservative approach to estimate the extent of changing demographic composition (i.e., the size of the $D-T$ interaction), we calculated the proportional distribution of total time-period heterogeneity reported in Chapter 4.

In a time span involving dramatic changes in underemployment (i.e., great changes in $T-U$), we found that 46–50% of the *total* time-period heterogeneity of the labor force cannot be taken into account without considering changes in demographic parameters of the labor force. Changes in demographic parameters were just as important as were parameters governing the changing prevalence of underemployment. We found that 22–26% of this "total effect" of time-period was due to changing demographic composition alone. The unobservable mix between structural and frictional underemployment therefore must have changed appreciably in this time span. Our conclusion is that *the level of frictional underemployment increased substantially,* since most of the changes in demographic composition produced a labor force of intrinsically higher risk to underemployment. The most important demographic change was with respect to age distribution; as a result of changing age composition of the population of working ages and of changing labor force participation patterns by age, the labor force steadily increased its intrinsic risk to underemployment. The labor force became more and more concentrated in the youthful ages, where the risk to underemployment (and to frictional underemployment) is the greatest. Other demographic changes (namely increasing participation of white women and decreasing participation of men) also resulted in a labor force with intrinsically higher risk to underemployment.

Focusing only upon changing age distribution within the labor force, for the age range 20–64, we showed in Chapter 4 that underemployment increased by the following average annual amounts during 1969–1973 as a result of changing age distribution alone:

Total labor force	White males	Nonwhite males	White females	Nonwhite females
.15%	.17–.20%	.11–.15%	.21–.28%	.25%

The proper inference from the above estimates is that in even a short span of time (e.g., 5 years), the changing age composition of the labor force affects the crude indicators of underemployment (thought to reflect the structural condition of the labor market) in ways that cannot be ignored. Considering only age distribution changes (and only changes within the age range 20–64) indicates that frictional underemployment has increased by a significant amount.

Although the approach used to infer the changes in the mix between the unobservables of structural and frictional underemployment is not a novel one, we believe that our study forcefully documents a marked increase in frictional underemployment. As a result of demographic factors alone, there is sufficient reason to question the extent to which the crude rates of underemployment reflect structural conditions of most interest to labor force theory and labor force policy.

10.3 LATENT CLASS STRUCTURE AND LABOR MARKET (LABOR FORCE) DUALISM

One classical theory of the operation of the labor market and of the structure of the labor force, tracing back to Malthus, Marx, and others, concerns the differential *risks* to underemployment characterizing different *labor force classes*. The theory of the dual labor market (or dual labor force) postulates the existence of *two* latent labor force classes and distinguishes between the two classes in terms of the degree of marginality characterizing each class. Letting the four main dichotomous underemployment measures of our study be considered as indicators of the *indirectly* observable condition of labor force marginality in the two classes, we used the cross-classification of the labor force by type of underemployment to infer latent class structure to the labor force. The cross-classification of the labor force by type of underemployment was analyzed at length in Chapter 5. This twelvefold table denoted the manifest underemployment structure but only indirectly measured the latent condition of marginality. The observed data confounded the underemployment risks of the two latent classes, implying that we could not characterize the latent classes by elementary means alone.

One model that could conceivably explain the mainfest structure is the hypothesis of independence among the indicators. This model would be interpreted as an hypothesis of no latent class structure in the labor force. With a χ^2 of 2233.05, we found that this model of the labor force was not tenable and that it was therefore not plausible to assume that the labor force was an homogeneous aggregate, uniformly exposed to the risks of underemployment. A latent class structure to the labor force may be presumed to exist.

A second model of the labor force exploited the special meaning attaching to the low-income measure of the study—that it was based upon the labor force experience of the *entire past year*. The income measure was treated in this second model as an exact indicator of latent labor force marginality. We found a χ^2 of 36.75 for this model, showing that low income is indeed a critical factor to explaining intrinsic marginality.

A third model, an unrestricted two-class latent structure, was also fit to the data, yielding a χ^2 of 5.50. Evidently, it is not necessary to consider models more complicated than two-class models to explain the manifest structure of underemployment. Our data therefore support the theory of labor force dualism.

A model that further characterized the latent labor force classes was developed, based upon the assumption that any *multiple underemployment* denotes a condition of marginality. Persons experiencing two or more kinds of underemployment were assumed to be marginal workers. A model prohibiting multiple underemployment in the latent nonmarginal class was tested and had a χ^2 of 1.01. In many respects, this latter model was preferable to the several other models proposed to explain the manifest structure of underemployment. It fit the data well for all the time-periods of the study. It allowed observed underemployment to be partitioned according to the marginal class and to the nonmarginal class, analogous to the partitioning of underemployment into structural and frictional parts. The characterization of latent labor force classes afforded by some of the models is summarized in Table 10.1 for the 1970 data.

Many other models that would be isomorphic to various theoretical conceptions about labor force class structure were also tested, but none were found as statistically and substantively compelling as the modified two-class model previously presented. That model says that a full one-quarter of the American labor force is in a marginal condition within the labor market. Across-time comparisons of parameters of this model were also illuminating, showing that a rise in the overall unemployment rate of 1% produced an increase in unemployment risk for the marginal class of

TABLE 10.1

	Model			
	No latent class structure	Low income as exact indicator of marginality	Unrestricted two-class latent structure	Modified two-class model
Likelihood-ratio χ^2	2233.05	36.75	5.50	1.01
df	7	4	3	3
Proportion of labor force in marginal class (%)	0.0	9.4	20.2	25.2
Risk to underemployment for marginal class (%)				
Unemployment	0.0	17.4	23.6	17.5
Low hours	0.0	8.9	12.3	8.8
Low income	0.0	100.0	34.0	37.5
Mismatch	0.0	9.1	8.0	9.1
Risk to underemployment for the non-marginal class (%)				
Unemployment	4.8	3.5	.0	0.5
Low hours	2.6	2.0	.2	0.5
Low income	9.4	0.0	3.2	0.0
Mismatch	10.6	10.8	11.2	11.1

about 3%. The size of the two classes remained fairly constant over time, and the risks to underemployment for the nonmarginal class remained very stable. Latent class membership can be predicted very well on the basis of observed responses to the underemployment indicators. These are elementary contributions to the theory of labor force dualism, showing the utility of the latent class technique and the new labor force indicators for that classical theory.

10.4 COHORT DIFFERENTIATION WITH RESPECT TO LABOR FORCE STATUS AND THE TEMPO OF COHORT-INDUCED SOCIAL CHANGE

The forms of underemployment divide the population of working ages into distinct statuses, and the distribution of persons throughout these statuses should depend upon age, time-period, and cohort. Three mutually exclusive and exhaustive statuses of special interest are obtained by collapsing certain of the underemployment forms together. A first labor force status is the not-in-labor-force category and is characterized by negligible or *nil productivity* (since persons outside the labor force are imagined to contribute nothing to the formal economic product). A second labor force status is that denoting *subproductivity* by virtue of time spent in employment or wage income derived from work. Sub-unemployed persons (our proxy for "discouraged workers" thought to be marginally attached to the labor market and labor force), the unemployed, the part-time unemployed, and the underemployed by low income are all members of this second status. A third status is that of *productive* employment and includes both the mismatched and the adequately employed. Goodman's diagonals parameter model was applied separately to each of the race–sex groups aged 20–34 to examine the dependence of this trichotomous variable denoting labor force productivity upon age, time-period, and cohort. The multiplicative models for cohort analysis used in our Chapter 6 suggest contributions to our theoretical understanding of time-period change and of social change in the labor force.

Assuming that the two oldest cohorts should not differ from each other in terms of "intrinsic" distribution throughout the labor force statuses, identified cohort parameters were calculated for each of the sex–race groups. We presented identified effects of cohort category upon labor force participation and upon subproductivity for labor force members. According to these parameter estimates, we inferred the "intrinsic" cohort patterns of distribution throughout the three labor force statuses mentioned earlier. These estimated cohort effects contradicted the popular understanding of cohort tendencies, most notably with regard to white males and females. The cohort patterns that we estimated provide much fodder from which to enrich sociological theory of changing labor force characteristics (namely the changing labor force participation of women and men in this era).

10.5 INTERACTION OF THE RACE–SEX GROUPS IN A CONSTRAINED LABOR MARKET

Assuming that labor force status is independent of survivorship, it is possible to work out the expectation of life to be lived per person in the several labor force statuses. The mortality and labor force conditions of 1970, if allowed to reign indefinitely, produced the expectations in the labor force statuses presented in Chapter 8. These life expectations showed how, with survivorship of the various race–sex groups taken into account, the labor force statuses have been allocated among the race–sex groups. For the 1970 data, we saw, for example, that 49% of the white male life span is spent in adequate employment and that the corresponding figure is 44% for nonwhite males, 22% for white females, and 24% for nonwhite females. These indexes summarize the implications of survivorship, of the age-graded social structure about which the labor force is organized, and of the technological-economic conditions producing employment opportunity. Differing years of life lived in the various labor force statuses for the race–sex groups, differing *proportions* of the life span lived in the various states, and differing *age-specific* risks to the several labor force statuses all denote "interaction of the race–sex groups" in the labor market and labor force.

In a total population in which the race–sex groups were *jointly* stationary, so that the age distribution of any subpopulation would be determined from the relevant survivorship (or "life years") column $_5L_x$ of the life table, the age distribution of the total population would be

$$_5L_x = P_{wm} \, _5L_x^{wm} + P_{nwm} \, _5L_x^{nwm} + P_{wf} \, _5L_x^{wf} + P_{nwf} \, _5L_x^{nwf}$$

The P's in the above equation represent the proportion of total babies born in the given race–sex group, and the $_5L_x$'s denote survivorship obtained from ordinary life tables for the race–sex groups, in obvious notation. Assuming (a) that the age-graded character of the labor market persisted (so that the economy continued to discriminate among workers according to age), and (b) that the total life years at any age that the economy (society) allocates into each labor force status is also fixed by technological–economic constraints, we asked what would happen if the race–sex groups were in "perfect competition," as would be the case in a meritocratic labor force. What would the kind of sex–race interaction implied by a meritocracy produce in terms of life expectations in the labor force statuses given these assumptions? The implications are dramatic, even with the favorable 1970 labor force conditions imposed. The race–sex groups, in the event of equitable age-specific rates of underemployment and labor force participation, would come to have dramatically different labor force life expectations. In the event of "equity" in race–sex labor force chances, each group would come to have *only about one-third* of their life expectancy in the status of adequate employment. The declines for white males relative to current conditions would be very dramatic. In certain respects, the increases for other groups (e.g., white females) would not be dramatic. In the kind of equitable "interaction" among the race–sex groups that we have conceived, there would be the same average number of years lived in underemployment for white women as was the case in the nonmeritocratic labor force in 1970. The superior survivorship of women over men, producing numerical dominance of women in labor force ages, accounts for these circumstances.

We can also assume changes in the technological-economic conditions and examine their implications for life expectations in the labor force statuses. Assuming the same survivorship and age risks to underemployment as were found with 1972 conditions, we asked what would be the long-run consequences of sustained decreases in underemployment, such as are envisioned by proponents of the Humphrey-Hawkins bill. The survivorship and labor force conditions of 1972 (a recession economy with unemployment in excess of 6%) implied that each person would spend, on average, 27.0 years in productive labor force activity. With a sustained provision of conditions producing 4% unemployment this figure would rise to 28.4, or a gain of productive life years *per person* of 5.5%. A sustained provision of labor force conditions producing 3% unemployment would raise this figure to 29.4, or a 9.0% increase in productive life years per person. These calculations aggregate the race–sex groups and so do not directly address the interaction of them in a constrained labor market. Consideration of this would, however, be straightforward.

Other calculations allocated total productive life years in the total population into parts due to each of the sex-race groups. This distribution was observed over time, showing how the "interaction" of the race–sex groups in the labor market changed with time. The stationary population approach to the analysis of labor force structure appears to be a fertile area from which one could develop a demographic theory of the labor force. Jointly stationary and jointly stable populations with different fertility, survivorship, and labor force chances can be considered from this perspective. Constraints of age, survivorship, available "life years" of productive employment, and the mode of race–sex interaction would all be taken into account in such a theory.

10.6 CONCLUSION

Although our work has been organized around methods for the measurement of underemployment, we feel that substantial theoretical groundwork has also been laid. It would be difficult indeed for us to imagine topics in the labor force area more critical to sociodemographic theory than the four topics considered in the preceding sections. These theoretical issues have been kept in mind throughout the methodological development, even if at times we appeared to be sidetracked away from them. We look forward to the further development of these theories with much excitement about their importance to sociology and social policy and with much confidence that the methods proposed will be sufficient for their further elaboration.

operational procedures for applying the labor utilization framework to the March Current Population Survey

This appendix details the operational procedures used in this work to measure the forms of underemployment. Definitions are made explicit, problems of comparability are mentioned, some alternative strategies are suggested, and the substantive meaning of the new measures is discussed. The material here will be of interest to researchers concerned with measuring underemployment from the Current Population Survey and will hopefully facilitate the constructive modification of our operational procedures. The strategies followed here are virtually identical to those used by Sullivan (1978) in her analysis of census data; readers are directed to her study for a fuller exposition of the labor utilization framework and a comparison of it with other approaches (also see Sullivan and Hauser, 1978). It is hoped that with but few revisions, the procedures presented here can be used by other researchers engaged in the analysis of labor market and labor force characteristics.

The labor utilization framework was initially conceived as a response to deficiencies in the unemployment rate. A critique of the use of the unemployment rate in developing societies was forcibly developed by Myrdal (1968) and Turnham (1971), among others. That the unemployment rate has also met with severe criticism in the United States is evidenced by the several special committees that have been formed to study its logical makeup and conceptual difficulties. Among these are (*a*) a 1954 conference held under the auspices of the National Bureau of Economic Research (NBER, 1957), (*b*) an extensive reassessment of unemployment concepts stemming from the Gordon Committee of 1962 (President's Committee to Appraise Employment and Unemployment Statistics, 1962), and (*c*) another committee commissioned by President James Carter, proceedings of which will be available in 1979 (see Sullivan and Hauser, 1978). The International Labour Organization (1976) summarized many of these deficiencies but concluded with a suggestion to measure forms of *under*employment—in addition to unemployment—whether the context be that of a more developed or a less developed society. The ILO pointed to the need to measure "invisible" underemployment and singled out the forms of low income, underutilization of skill, and low productivity. Recognizing the extreme difficulty in developing productivity measures on a per-worker basis from standard labor force surveys, Hauser (1974) focused on measures of the low-income and skill "mismatch" forms, choosing to postpone the measurement of the productivity dimension of invisible underemployment until a radically different type of labor force survey could be developed. Many others have proposed frameworks for the measurement of underemployment, and the reader might wish to compare Hauser's approach and our procedures for operationalizing it with them. Of the several frameworks that we have reviewed in the course of this work, the approaches summarized in Vietorisz *et al.* (1975), Gilroy (1975), and Levitan and Taggart (1974) perhaps stand out as plausible alternatives, but the labor utilization framework—or some close relative to it—would provide at least some work force information that these approaches exclude.

Our data are from the March Current Population Survey ("Annual Demographic File") as commercially marketed by DUALABS of Arlington, Virginia. The data are arranged according to hierarchical record types: the raw data contain family records as the first record type, and for each family record, there is one person record for every nonmilitary person over 14 who is a member of that family.[1] Special computer software is necessary to utilize the information on *both* family and person records. Such programs as CENTS-AID, CENTS-AID Version 2, SOS (SPSS Override System), TPL, and others will process hierarchical files, the first two at least with admirable efficiency. (CENTS-AID was used in our data retrieval, but comparisons of it with SOS and TPL were not made.)

To facilitate comparison of our verbal description with actual data codes found in the CPS, we have indicated the data fields within each type of record (family or person) necessary to the determination of the labor utilization variable. An "F" refers to family records, while a "P" refers to

---

[1] There are also records for military persons and for persons under age 14, but these can be ignored in a study of the civilian labor force.

person records. For example "F128,P124" refers to information occurring in the one hundred and twenty-eighth field of family records and in the one hundred and twenty-fourth field of person records. All definitions are "standard" definitions used in the CPS, and so detailed reference to the official source of the definitions is not necessary (see U.S. Department of Commerce, 1963, 1978; Bancroft, 1958; Morton, 1969; Levitan and Taggart, 1974).

A.1 NOT IN LABOR FORCE

Economic inactivity is said to characterize those persons out of work and not looking for work in the reference week immediately prior to the survey (4, 5, 6, or 7 in P152). This variable is an adjustment of the "major activity" variable (P151), reflecting the usual modifications for full-time students, housewives, and some others who spend only a small amount of time at work. Those not in the labor force include "students, housewives, retired workers, seasonal workers enumerated in an 'off' season who are not looking for work, inmates of institutions, or persons who cannot work because of long-term physical or mental illness or disability."

Included in the not-in-labor-force category are the class of persons denoted as "discouraged workers," that is, those persons out of work and not seeking work because they consider job seeking a futile activity.[2] These persons are, in most cases, a "ready reserve" labor supply, since with an increase in demand they would presumably begin seeking work and so are not as disassociated from the labor market as the labor force concept makes them appear. Considerable fluctuation in their numbers occurs with economic growth or recession. Consideration of discouraged workers could alter demographic comparisons based upon unemployment rates or upon labor force participation rates and would accordingly distort perceptions of labor market change over time.

Willard Wirtz, secretary of labor under President Lyndon B. Johnson, considered discouraged workers in his indexes of underemployment, and this was to some extent responsible for his findings of 45% underemployment (or "subemployment") in urban ghettoes.[3] The discouraged worker presents problems not only in the comparison of rates but also in attempts

[2] On the determination of "discouraged workers" and the importance of the concept of discouraged workers, see Flaim (1972).

[3] See W. Willard Wirtz, "A report on employment and unemployment in urban slums and ghettoes: Memorandum for the president," December 23, 1966. In U.S. Congress, Senate Subcommittee on Employment, Manpower and Poverty, *Comprehensive manpower reform,* Ninety-second Congress, Second Session, Part 5. Washington, D.C.: Government Printing Office, 1972.

to model the working life of the individual (e.g., as in tables of working life), since it is unclear how to calculate base populations "exposed to the risk of employment," given the borderline status of these marginal labor force participants.

Note also that the not-in-labor-force category does *not* include persons such as *new entrants* and *reentrants* to the labor force, whose labor force "participation" is nearly as tenuous as that of the discouraged worker. Sullivan, using 1970 census data, was able to isolate entrants and reentrants for special analysis; however, we have been unable to locate them for a similar analysis with the March CPS data.

A.2 SUB-UNEMPLOYED

Ideally, for the reasons mentioned above, we would like to isolate discouraged workers for the first category of underemployment, following that approach used by Wirtz and subsequently used in the "sub-employment" index or in Levitan and Taggart's (1973) Index of Earnings Inadequacy. However, questions aimed at determining the volume of discouraged workers (e.g., "What is the reason for not looking for work in the past month?") are not part of the March series of the CPS.[4] But a proxy for them can nevertheless be obtained. If a person not in the labor force during the reference period of the survey (4, 5, 6, or 7 in P152) was a *part-year worker* whose reason for part-year work was that he or she was "looking" for full-year work (1 in P146), then our claim is that the given individual resembles the discouraged worker. Also, if a person is not in the labor force, did not work last year, and reported the main reason for not working last year as "unable to find work" (4 in P149), then the person again resembles the discouraged worker. No other questions in the March CPS, to our knowledge, allow a clearer identification of discouraged workers. Because our method of locating these members of the marginal labor force is a crude one, we prefer to designate the category thus obtained as the "sub-unemployed." Because of the confusion over the tenuous work force status of these types of persons, we presented in Chapter 2 various ratios and rates reflecting different base populations.

The labor force consists of those persons working, persons with jobs but

---

[4] Levitan and Taggart (1974), using the March CPS for years 1968–1972, did attempt to measure "discouraged workers," but a question, or series of questions, suited for this task is not actually a part of the March CPS. Levitan and Taggart must have used approximate criteria similar to the ones we have used; inspection of their tables indicate that our approach provides slightly larger aggregate estimates of the number of discouraged workers than their approach.

not at work, or persons looking for work (1, 2, or 3 in P152). All of the subsequent definitions pertain to members of the standard labor force.

A.3 UNEMPLOYED

Unemployed persons "are those civilians who, during the survey week, had no employment but were available for work and (*a*) had engaged in any specific job-seeking activity within the last four weeks" (3 in P152) or (*b*) were with a job but not at work and were "waiting to be called back to a job from which they had been laid off. . . or . . . were waiting to report to a new wage or salary job within 30 days" (2 in P152 and 5, 6, or 7 in P159).

All persons aged 14 and over who were at work (1 in P152) or were "with a job but not at work" but were temporarily absent because of illness, vacation, bad weather, labor dispute, or other (noneconomic or personal) reasons (2 in P152 and 1, 2, 3, 4 or 8 in P159) are the employed. With the 1970 census and in several Bureau of Labor Statistics publications prior to that time, the formal working age on which unemployment statistics are based was raised from 14 to 16 years. We maintained the 14-year minimum in some of our work; distortions in crude rates by reason of the inclusion of ages 14 and 15 can be expected to be minimal. These formally employed persons, with some modifications, are subject to the subsequent sorts.

A.4 UNDEREMPLOYED BY LOW HOURS

This category is equivalent to the "part-time unemployed" or the "part-time for economic reasons" category already in wide use. The Census Bureau and the Bureau of Labor Statistics use 35 hours as the minimum full-time workweek. Any person working 34 hours or less is subject to the sort for "underemployment by hours," with the following qualifications.

Only employed persons who were "at work" during the reference week are classified by hours of work (1 in P152). Employed persons not at work during the reference week (2 in P152 and 1, 2, 3, 4, or 8 in P159) are assumed to be adequately utilized by hours of work. Although this is certainly not the optimal strategy for determining involuntary part-time unemployment, this expedient is necessary because no questions are asked of employed persons not at work regarding their hours of work in the week last worked. To the extent to which employed persons not at work (by virtue of personal reasons, etc.) are in fact working less than the full workweek, the category underemployed by hours can be expected to provide a *conservative* estimate of the real extent of part-time unemployment. The number of workers not working but counted as employed is moderate and so could affect our estimates here by perhaps as much as .2%. The wish to conform to a definite time referent, useful in computing rates and gauging trends over time, is responsible for the CPS format regarding these persons. We have accordingly determined the part-time unemployed (i.e., the part-time employed for economic reasons) following this format. Part-time workers are defined as those working less than 35 hours during the survey week (1–34 in P153–154). Economic reasons for working less than 35 hours include "slack work, material shortages, repairs to plant or equipment, start or termination of job during the week, and inability to find full-time work" (1, 2, 3, 4, 5, or 6 in P157–158).

A caveat is necessary concerning the extent to which short hours "for economic reasons" is a measure of diminished demand for labor. The reason for part-time work of "material shortage" is not necessarily a reflection of the demand for labor but is instead a measure of the extent to which the material factors of production are in short supply. The reasons listed as "repairs to plant or equipment" and "start or termination of a job during the week" are also not necessarily measures of the extent of slack demand for labor. These reasons are perhaps gauges of *frictional* part-time employment. Only the reasons "slack work" and "inability to find full-time work" are true measures of the extent to which the economy is unable to provide a full workweek to those who demand such work. We can probably surmise, however, that the variation in the underemployed-by-hours category over time will result principally from reasons reflecting the variable demand for labor. In dealing with the underemployed-by-hours category, then, we encounter a difficulty in interpreting our operationalization of Hauser's LUF as a measure of slack demand for labor. Future applications of this framework could take these criticisms into account; our wish to conform to the standard definitions insofar as possible has resulted in this deficiency.

Note that with our modifications thus far, the category of unemployment is equivalent to the standard definition of unemployment, and the category of underemployed by hours is equivalent to the BLS's category of "part-time for economic reasons." These two categories are thus *jointly* compatible with the similar BLS categories that have been used for many years.

A.5 UNDEREMPLOYMENT BY LOW INCOME

With the underemployed-by-low-income category, we make a minor departure from the approach of Sullivan. The comparability of our results with Sullivan's will thus be smallest when considering this form. The difference pertains to the determination of proper income thresholds; this critical issue is far from resolved by Sullivan's or our own approach, even if it is agreed that the poverty thresholds of the Social Security Administration should be somehow used as the basis for this determination. The problem of defining underutilization by low income is critically dependent upon the distinction between family versus individual and primary versus secondary earners. All approaches thus far fall short of the desideratum because of the extreme difficulty in determining the influence of the decision processes within households with two or more earners that concern the allocation of employment potential to the labor market. The degree of involuntariness of underemployment by income (as well as by other criteria) is a necessary datum to unambiguous classification of workers within the same household but unfortunately cannot be ascertained in the usual labor force survey. Conceivably, employment producing a low wage rate is much more "severe" for heads of households or for primary earners than it is for nonheads or secondary earners.[5]

Persons previously classified are not subject to our income sort. In addition, *voluntary* part-time workers are not subject to the income sort because they are assumed to earn low wages in proportion to their voluntarily shortened hours. Full-time students (i.e., persons whose major activity was "school") were excluded from the income sort for reasons similar to those given by Sullivan (1978). Therefore, with the exception of voluntary part-time workers, full-time students, and persons previously classified, the universe to which the income sort applies are full-time workers (1 in P152 and P152–154 greater than 34). This universe also contains those persons "with a job but not at work" (2 in P152 and 1, 2, 3, 4, or 8 in P159).

The universe on which Sullivan's income sort applied also omitted "new entrants" and "reentrants" to the labor force. New entrants are "persons who never worked at a full-time job lasting two weeks or longer." Reentrants are "persons who previously worked at a full-time job lasting two weeks or longer but who were out of the labor force prior to beginning to look for work." Entrants and reentrants to the labor force may be either employed or unemployed. The CPS data only provide information on entrants and reentrants *who are unemployed* and, further, only on those unemployed persons who are looking for work (P168). These unemployed entrants and reentrants are, of course, already

---

[5] Levitan and Taggart (1974), in the construction of their Index of Earnings Inadequacy, have chosen to apply poverty thresholds only to household heads. On the other hand, we have made a determination of the low-income form for persons who are not household heads, although the set of criteria used for this procedure is much different from that applied to household heads.

classified as unemployed. Therefore, in our use of CPS data, entrants and reentrants who are working cannot be deleted from the universe to which our income sort applies, which is different from Sullivan's analysis of census data. Entrants and reentrants who are unemployed are already classified in category (*a*) above, the unemployed. Entrants and reentrants who are employed (i.e., those who recently entered the labor force and found work) may have little or no work-related income for the *preceding* year, complicating the determination of the low-income form for them.

With the universe selected according to this procedure, it was necessary to select income thresholds that could serve to define underemployment by low income. The determination of income thresholds for each worker within a household is based upon the poverty thresholds derived by the Social Security Administration and used in the CPS. No other set of income levels, to our knowledge, has been developed with the underlying criterion of minimum subsistence in mind.[6] (Many other informal measures of "poverty" are, of course, used, but these are largely based upon ad hoc conceptions of poverty. Clearly, one could adjust poverty thresholds and find as much poverty as desired.) The Social Security Administration's index gives a figure for *total* family income that is a minimum annual expenditure necessary to ensure at least subsistence levels of household welfare. These thresholds are based upon age and sex of household head, size of family, and farm/nonfarm residence of the family. Since the income data on the CPS are based upon the *preceding* year, a departure from the desired time-reference comparability is encountered here. The preceding categories, of course, did have the desired time comparability with the usual unemployment statistics.

Briefly, the income sort, given the universe above, consists of the following steps.

1. *Work-related income* was calculated for each worker. This is the sum of (*a*) wage or salary income, (*b*) nonfarm self-employment income, and (*c*) farm self-employment income (P67–72, P73–78, P79–84). Work-related income excludes unearned income such as Social Security, dividends, interest, rental income, welfare, and unemployment compensation. The assumption is that work-related income for the preceding year can be used as a proxy for income for the current year. This assumption implies that the income category of the LUF will not be particularly sensitive to

---

[6] Some critics have claimed that this approach confuses concepts of "poverty" with concepts of low-income underemployment by virtue of its implicit use of the poverty thresholds. Such a charge is not justified, however, since poverty or need is not the same thing as low-income underemployment: we have merely used the poverty thresholds for families and individuals as benchmark figures. Other cutoffs could conceivably be used.

short-term fluctuations in the demand for labor. (However, as we indicated in Chapter 5, this measure of the low-income form has certain advantages, e.g., as an indicator of marginality that can be used partially to explain the occurrence of the other forms.)

2. Annual work-related income is converted to an *equivalent weekly wage,* using the "weeks worked last year" variable (P131).

3. Poverty thresholds for every worker in the household were determined. For the chief income recipient (not necessarily the head of house), the cutoff point was assumed to be the threshold for the family as a whole. These cutoffs vary with age and sex of household head, size of family, and farm/nonfarm residence.

4. For secondary earners, we used the poverty threshold for a primary individual with the same age, sex, and residence characteristics. Sullivan applied the poverty thresholds for a single urban (i.e., nonfarm) male under 65 years of age uniformly to *all* secondary male workers, and she applied the poverty threshold for a single urban (i.e., nonfarm) female under 65 years of age uniformly to *all* secondary female earners. We *included* the age and residence detail, in addition to sex detail, for the secondary workers so that the criteria for partitioning secondary workers be made similar to that used for primary earners. This constitutes a slight modification of Sullivan's approach.

5. For members of subfamilies (4 in F27–29 or 4 in P27–28), an alternative strategy had to be employed altogether, since poverty status is not determined in the CPS for subfamilies. The reason for this curious omission is that subfamilies are considered to be dependent upon some primary family, the poverty status for which has already been determined, assuming that the subfamily is dependent upon its primary family. Rather than adjusting income levels for primary families containing subfamilies and then treating both as separate families on which the original criteria for determining thresholds would be used, we chose to treat workers in subfamilies as if they were primary individuals. We are merely assuming that workers in subfamilies, by virtue of their formal dependence on a primary family, should be regarded in the same way we regard secondary workers in general.

For members of subfamilies, and for all secondary workers, the weekly income thresholds used in our research are given in Table A.1. Subfamily members and secondary workers are classified as underemployed by income if their weekly wage income was below the corresponding figure in the table. Note that the thresholds for the year preceding the year of the relevant CPS were applied to determine poverty status for that year, since all income data in a given survey pertain to the previous year.

TABLE A.1

Weekly Income Thresholds Yielding Poverty Cuts for Primary Individuals, Workers in Sub-families, and All Secondary Workers

| | Nonfarm | | Nonfarm | |
	Male	Female	Male	Female
1972				
14–65	45	42	38	35
65+	40	40	34	33
1971				
14–65	44	40	37	34
65+	39	39	33	33
1970				
14–65	42	39	36	33
65+	38	37	32	32
1969				
14–65	40	37	34	31
65+	35	35	30	30
1968				
14–65	33	30	28	26
65+	30	29	25	25

Source: Calculated from U.S. Department of Commerce, *Characteristics of the Low-Income Population: 1973* (Washington, D.C.: U.S. Government Printing Office, 1975), Tables A-1, A-3, pp. 159–162. We assumed a 48-week work-year.

A.6 UNDEREMPLOYED BY MISMATCH

All persons not included in the above categories are subject to the mismatch sort, including voluntary part-time workers. The mismatch category is the most difficult to interpret, owing partly to the artificial means by which "overeducation" is inferred. We applied directly the cutoff points for completed years education for educationally homogeneous occupational strata used by Sullivan. For years 1969–1970, the CPS used the 1960 census occupational classification. For these years, Sullivan's adjustments for the 1960 census were utilized. For years beyond 1970, we used her education cutoffs for the 1970 census occupational classification. For the details of her procedures, including the adjustments for occupational strata dominated by females (whose educational attainment is typically higher than that of males for some occupational groups), the reader is referred directly to her work (1978). Completed years education is obtained from P57–58 and P59. *Current* occupation, necessary for determining mismatch in relation to current economic conditions, is obtained from a detailed recode of P172–174, the three-digit occupational codes developed by the Census Bureau.

The rationale used in the mismatch classification is essentially the following. Workers are denoted as mismatched if their own completed years education is more than one standard deviation above the mean completed years education for their occupational group. Such an operational strategy is clearly open to charges of being arbitrary and somewhat artificial, and for this reason, absolute levels of mismatch are extremely difficult to interpret by themselves. However, we have directly applied the educational cutoffs determined for 1970 uniformly to all years of the study so that across-time change in mismatch levels can be inferred. Changes in real mismatch, owing to diminished or increased demand for skilled labor, are approximately measured by our time-series measures of mismatch. The principal deficiency of our approach is that the shape (including the skew) of educational distributions within occupational strata might change over time in ways unrelated to the extent of true mismatch. Educational requirements for entry to an occupation might increase, perhaps reflected in a higher mean education, giving the impression that younger workers are mismatched relative to older workers. Or, with technological innovation, the educational requirements of the specific occupations within an occupational strata might change over time, resulting in both a change in location and a change in scale, again overstating the extent of mismatch. Other factors can also conceivably distort our mismatch measure. These criticisms are mitigated somewhat in this study by the fact that only a short time span (5 years) is considered, and the changing shape of the educational distribution in the short run is probably mainly the result of real change in mismatch. In determining mismatch trends over the long run, perhaps some type of annual adjustment would have to be devised.

Although the mismatch category is perhaps the least satisfactory measure of underemployment in this study, we are not aware of a more rational means to determine it than Hauser's original suggestion. But the benefits obtained from this approach seem to far outweigh the disadvantage of ignoring mismatch altogether. Indeed, the cross-sectional differentials and across-time change in mismatch that we have documented, all of which are consistent with our prior understanding of the mismatch problem, add to the face validity of this approach.[7]

[7] We refer the reader to Freeman (1976) or to the U.S. Department of Labor (1978). In the latter study, for example, it was predicted that roughly 25% of the college graduates in 1976–1985 will have to settle for jobs that have not traditionally required college diplomas. These figures are consistent with our time-series comparisons of mismatch, where we found an increase in mismatch 1969–1973 of about 1% per year. If this trend continues, then such a forecast is not unrealistic at all.

A.7 ADEQUATELY UTILIZED

Adequately utilized workers are merely the residual category left over after the above sorts have occurred. No attempt was made in our work to separate this category into full- and part-time adequately utilized, as was done by Sullivan.

In sum, the inclusion of the sub-unemployed category is an attempt to identify discouraged workers but does not affect the composition of the other categories. The unemployed category is identical to official definitions. Also, the underemployed-by-hours category is formally equivalent to the "part-time for economic reasons" category of the BLS. The underemployed-by-low-income category is somewhat different from Sullivan's, although the poverty thresholds are used similarly in both her and our own approach. The mismatch category is identical to hers and is difficult to interpret generally because of the confounding of education distribution changes and the extent of real mismatch. Because of the changes we made, the proportions observed in the categories will be slightly different from those observed by Sullivan, although the differences are, in the aggregate, very slight.

Other minor modifications of the above approach were attempted for the 1970 CPS, but considerations of space preclude discussion of these results here. Further refinements of these measures would require both different strategies of dealing with existing CPS questions concerning labor force status and related matters and some additional information that is not now part of the CPS. As an apology for this tiresome appendix, we point out that different strategies could have affected the proportions observed in the basic underemployment categories by as much as 2%. A method of determining unemployment that results in a 2% difference from another method is cause for serious alarm. Surely, the methods for determining the other forms of underemployment are to be viewed with as much caution as unemployment statistics generally. The tedium that we have detailed in this appendix is necessary for these reasons.

APPENDIX B

the life table modified to take into account labor force status

The standard life table can be easily modified to provide a demographic summary of the labor force status variable, as labor force status has been conceived in our work. Since these statuses exhibit a marked dependence on age, the life-table approach to summarizing their incidence appears to have a rich potential. The approach presented here appears to have general significance in the demographic analysis of age-graded social statuses, however, and is by no means confined to the labor force subject. The modified life table to which we refer begins with a set of age-specific rates of occurrence of the particular social statuses and the functions of a life table governing the survivorship of the population (or populations) in question. Since survivorship did not change appreciably for any of the race–sex groups in our study over the interval 1969–1973, the necessary (abridged) life-table functions were obtained from published 1970 life tables (U.S. Department of Health, Education, and Welfare, 1974).

We assume here that the life-table functions are nonstochastic, and therefore all inferences to be made from the modified life table are conditional on the life-table values actually "observed" and published for the race–sex groups. The underemployment rates, however, are subject to sampling error, since they have been estimated from the Current Population Survey. The sampling theory for a life table estimated from sample data is discussed by Chiang (1968) and Keyfitz (1968), and it would not be difficult to extend their results here to take account of sampling variability in both estimated death rates and underemployment rates. The important life-table functions are l_x, the number of survivors at exact age x given an arbitrary radix value l_0; $_5L_x$, the number of person years lived in the interval $(x, x + 5)$, or the "stationary population" in the same interval; T_x, the number of person years lived after exact age x; and $\mathring{e}_x = T_x/l_x$, the average number of years lived after age x per survivor at age x.

Let $_5n_{i,x}$ denote the number of persons in the ith status in age interval $(x, x + 5)$ observed in the sample, where

$$\sum_{i=1}^{I} {_5n_{i,x}} = {_5n_x}$$

is the total number of persons in the sample in interval of age $(x, x + 5)$. There are I mutually exclusive and exhaustive statuses in all; in our application in the present work, $I = 7$. That is, we considered the seven statuses corresponding to (a) not in the labor force (actually, the *modified* labor force spoken of in Chapter 2 was used as a criterion in measuring this status); (b) sub-unemployment; (c) unemployment; (d) involunatry part-time employment; (e) underemployment by low work-related income; (f) mismatch; and (g) adequate employment or utilization. Now let $_5\hat{p}_{i,x}$ denote the observed proportion in the ith status in the interval $(x, x + 5)$; that is, $_5\hat{p}_{i,x} = ({_5n_{i,x}})/({_5n_x})$. The $_5\hat{p}_{i,x}$ are based on the $_5n_{i,x}$, which derive from a cross section in time (e.g., the survey week in March used in the CPS). We apply the $_5\hat{p}_{i,x}$ to the life table as if they were *annual rates;* that is, the assumption is made that the cross-sectional rates obtained from the survey are representative of the annual experience. Although this assumption is not met in any strict sense, it appears plausible for the kind of inferences drawn in our Chapter 9.

Clearly we have

$$\sum_{i=1}^{I} {_5\hat{p}_{i,x}} = 1 \tag{B.1}$$

so that labor force status for age interval $(x, x + 5)$ can be regarded as a multinomial random variable. The variance of the $_5\hat{p}_{i,x}$ can be approximated by

$$\text{Var}({_5\hat{p}_{i,x}}) = ({_5\hat{p}_{i,x}})(1 - {_5\hat{p}_{i,x}})/{_5n_x} \tag{B.2}$$

when $_5n_x$ is large. [There were roughly a dozen $_5\hat{p}_{i,x}$ that were zero for the nonwhite samples. As an expedient we have assigned the value $({_5n_x})^{-1}$ to $_5\hat{p}_{i,x}$ for these cases, reestimating the variance by (B.2)].

The rates of occurrence of the ith status at exact age x are denoted as $\hat{p}_{i,x}$. We set $\hat{p}_{1,15} = 1$ in our calculations to express the fact that at age 15 virtually everyone is outside the labor force. Accordingly, we set $\hat{p}_{i,15} = 0$ for $i = 2, \ldots , 7$. The remainder of the $\hat{p}_{i,x}$ for $x = 20,25, \ldots$, were obtained by linear interpolation of the $_5\hat{p}_{i,x}$:

$$\hat{p}_{i,x} = (_5\hat{p}_{i,x-5} + _5\hat{p}_{i,x})/2 \tag{B.3}$$

Equation B.3 assumes linear change in the rates over the age interval $(x - 5, x + 5)$, and is therefore crude for some ages. Other kinds of interpolation formulas could have been used (e.g., for ages 15–25, where changes in underemployment rates are only roughly linear), but they were not in the interests of simplicity. The variance of the $\hat{p}_{i,x}$ may be approximated by

$$\mathrm{Var}(\hat{p}_{i,x}) = [\mathrm{Var}(_5\hat{p}_{i,x-5}) + \mathrm{Var}(_5\hat{p}_{i,x})]/4 \tag{B.4}$$

Equation B.4 assumes that the sample of persons obtained for age interval $(x - 5, x)$ is collected in a way that guarantees zero covariance with the sample of persons obtained for age interval $(x, x + 5)$. This assumption would be satisfied, for example, with simple random sampling, with stratified random sampling with age as the stratifying criterion, and in some other sampling schemes.

The number of survivors at exact age x who are in the ith labor force status is estimated as

$$\hat{l}_x^i = (\hat{p}_{i,x})l_x \tag{B.5}$$

with approximate sampling variance of

$$\mathrm{Var}(\hat{l}_x^i) = \mathrm{Var}(\hat{p}_{i,x})(l_x)^2 \tag{B.6}$$

The life years lived in a given status during $(x, x + 5)$ is estimated by

$$_5\hat{L}_x^i = (_5\hat{p}_{i,x})_5L_x \tag{B.7}$$

Since in (B.7) the quantity $_5L_x$ can be interpreted as the product of a constant and the probability of surviving to be counted in the age interval $(x, x + 5)$ (compare Keyfitz, 1968), an assumption implicitly made here is that survivorship is stochastically independent of labor force status. A host of social epidemiological studies indicate that this assumption is false (compare Kitagawa and Hauser, 1973, and references cited there), but this assumption would be very difficult to amend, since survivorship depends on labor force status in largely unknown, and certainly nonquantifiable, ways. The sampling variance associated with $_5\hat{L}_x^i$, assuming $_5L_x$ fixed or conditionally given, is approximated by

$$\mathrm{Var}(_5\hat{L}_x^i) = \mathrm{Var}(_5\hat{p}_{i,x})(_5L_x)^2 \tag{B.8}$$

Similarly, $\hat{T}_x^i$, the number of person years lived in the ith labor force status after age x per randomly chosen survivor at age x, is given as

$$\hat{T}_x^i = \sum_{x'=x}^{\omega} {}_5\hat{L}_{x'}^i \tag{B.9}$$

where ω is taken here as the open-ended interval 70+. Under the assumptions thus far made, we have

$$\text{Var}(\hat{T}_x^i) = \sum_{x'=x}^{\omega} \text{Var}({}_5\hat{L}_{x'}^i) \tag{B.10}$$

The estimate of the average number of years lived in the ith status per survivor at age x is now given as

$$\mathring{e}_x^i = \hat{T}_x^i/l_x \tag{B.11}$$

with approximate sampling variance of

$$\text{Var}(\mathring{e}_x^i) = \text{Var}(\hat{T}_x^i)(l_x)^{-2} \tag{B.12}$$

(Note that $\mathring{e}_x^i$ is a sample estimate, but for ease of expression we have not used the customary circumflex in the notation.)

Since the ${}_5\hat{p}_{i,x}$ are multinomial proportions, under the sampling assumptions thus far made the quantities considered above will be normally distributed with large samples by repeated application of the central limit theorem. By virtue of the fact that the ${}_5\hat{p}_{i,x}$ are maximum likelihood estimates (except for the cases where the ${}_5\hat{p}_{i,x}$ were modified owing to certain sampling counts of zero), the quantities considered here are all efficiently estimated. Standard errors of the above quantities could be used to set up confidence intervals about the population parameters of interest or to test certain hypotheses concerning those parameters.

The life expectation at age x, $\mathring{e}_x$, is easily decomposed into parts lived in each of the statuses by the formula

$$\mathring{e}_x = \sum_{i=1}^{I} \mathring{e}_x^i \tag{B.13}$$

The average number of years lived in any age interval (x, x^*) (e.g., ages 20–25) per randomly chosen survivor at exact age x is given as

$$(T_x - T_{x^*})/l_x \tag{B.14}$$

which can also be decomposed into parts lived in the ith status according to

$$(\hat{T}_x^i - \hat{T}_{x^*}^i)/l_x \tag{B.15}$$

Other quantities associated with the modified life table follow from straightforward manipulation of the above quantities, so we do not provide further details here. When estimating the above quantities, round-off error can become important in some of the formulas, and this round off can cumulate if care is not taken. To circumvent these difficulties, we based our calculations upon life-table functions expressed so that the radix $l_0 = 1.0$, and we then performed the necessary manipulations using double precision arithmetic.

It is customary in accounts of life-table methodology applied to analyze working life (taking into account, *e.g.*, labor force participation rates) to consider another set of functions pertaining to the "expectation of working life" *per economically active survivor,* instead of per survivor as we have done here. Those functions are supposed to permit analysis of economic activity by considering increments to the labor force owing to labor force entry and decrements from the labor force by retirement (as well as by death). The assumptions for such tables of working life are very tenuous when applied to cross-sectional data, especially for women who typically have multiple entries to and exits from the labor force over the life cycle. These kinds of working life tables were not constructed in this study, since across-time comparisons of table functions would not have been meaningful. We could not have used the time series of this study, for example, to analyze changing patterns of retirement because of the fluctuation in numbers of discouraged workers and labor force participants that is known to occur with oscillation in labor market conditions. When the objective is to summarize the incidence of the various labor force statuses over the short run, the tables of working life given by Garfinkle and others would be inappropriate (compare Garfinkle, 1957; Denton and Ostry, 1969; United Nations, 1968).

a general computer program for unrestricted or restricted maximum likelihood latent structure analysis

The computer program MLLSA (Maximum Likelihood Latent Structure Analysis) used in all the latent structure analysis of this work is available on request from the writer. This program is a considerable revision of a program used by Goodman (1974a, 1974b) in his fundamental work on the latent structure method. The present program handles polytomous (not necessarily dichotomous) observed variables, allows the estimation of some additional kinds of latent structures that arise in the case of polytomous data, computes some measures that allow assessment of model adequacy (e.g., the λ measure of association between the latent variable and the observed variables), and provides clearly labeled output. Many options are available. For a complete discussion of the use of the program, the reader is referred to a manual prepared by the author (Clogg, 1977) and to Goodman's papers on the subject.

Other computer programs now exist for the analysis of latent structure models, and these could also be used. These include Haberman's program based on a Newton–Raphson algorithm (see Haberman, 1974b, 1976, 1977); related programs based on Fisher's method of scoring (see Haberman, 1976, 1977; Dayton and Macready, 1976a,b); Carroll's canonical decomposition algorithm (Carroll, 1975; Green, Carmone, and Wachspress, 1976); Formann's algorithm based on a logit-type transformation of model parameters and a certain gradient method (Formann, 1978), and others. Goodman's (1974a) method based on iterative proportional scaling of parameter estimates is the one used in our program MLLSA. It avoids matrix inversion, and appears to be more flexible and more general than the other programs with which we are familiar. This program guarantees permissible parameter estimates (unlike the older LASY computer program based on a determinantal method, and unlike some of the older maximum likelihood methods). We believe that MLLSA, or programs very similar to it, will enable latent structure methods to enjoy the serious empirical application that they so richly deserve.

Approximately 30 researchers have thus far used MLLSA, and their feedback to the author has been very encouraging. Convergence to a solution can, in some cases, be slow, but in applications thus far, the program has proved reasonably cost efficient. For comments on the convergence properties of the algorithm used in MLLSA, the reader is referred to Haberman (1976) and Goodman (1978).

APPENDIX D

the quality of single-year age data by sex in the March Current Population Survey, 1969-1973

This appendix considers the quality of single-year age data by sex in the March Current Population Survey. Accurate age data are mandatory in the routine application of many demographic techniques. Moreover, any social indicator approach assumes quality age data in order to analyze the implications of cohort succession regarding any dependent variable under study. In this book, age data accurate apart from sampling error were assumed in several of the chapters. Accurate single-year age data were particularly critical in our discussion of cohort effects for the population aged 20–34 in Chapter 6. We will present an approximate statistical method for assessing the quality of single-year age data based on a sample survey (e.g., the Current Population Survey). This method is related to other, more usual methods reported by Shryock and Siegel (1973). It is based upon a minimum number of assumptions, and the required numerical work is relatively straightforward.

Revised estimates of the civilian population by sex (and by race) in single years of age are given in Current Population Reports, Series P-25, No. 614 (U.S. Department of Commerce, 1975). Those estimates are based upon revising the 1970 census population counts by single years of age for net undercount and then "inflating" or "deflating" age-specific categories according to birth and death records from the National Center for Health Statistics and from estimates of net immigration. Their method "preserves the actual pattern of population change by age rather than by cohort,'' and users interested in changes over time in *cohorts* could be misled by using their estimates.

We assume herein that the age distribution in the 5-year age categories obtained from the CPS for the civilian population is accurate, and we examine the consistency of the observed distribution in single years of age with the pattern observed in the 5-year categories. That is, our inference about the quality of the single-year data is *conditional* upon the age distribution in 5-year categories. The method used to establish the correct pattern of age distribution in single years of age is based upon Greville's method of "osculatory" interpolation. That method is summarized in several sources, so we merely note here that Greville's method is based upon the successive fitting of polynomial curves with the condition that the tangents to the obtained age-frequency curve are consistent for successive 5-year age groups (see Shryock and Siegel, 1973; Keyfitz, 1968, Chapter 10). For example, the tangent to the curve at age 25 is the same for the curve approaching age 25 from the left as for the curve approaching age 25 from the right. The curve is thus fit to the observed 5-year age distribution with conditions on the left and right *derivatives* of the interpolated curve. Interpolated values for single years of age are easily derived once the smooth graduated curve is obtained. Other methods, such as those associated with Sprague and Beers, would presumably give nearly the same results.

The observed age distribution may be laid out in a kind of 3 × 5 cross-table as in Table D.1. The graduated values obtained by Greville's "osculatory" interpolation method are also presented in that table, showing that, apart from round-off error, the "marginal totals" for the 5-year categories of the original distribution have been preserved.[1] The observed distribution can be expected to differ from the graduated distribution by virtue of sampling error and by virtue of real irregularities in single-year age data that the graduation technique does not take into account. Assuming that the real irregularities in single-year age data are nil, we can assess the statistical significance of the departures of the observed from the expected frequencies by means of the common χ^2 statistic. Real irregularity in single-year age data for ages $(x, x + 5)$ at time t could be due to irregular fertility patterns during time $(t - x - 5, t - x)$, to irregular mortality patterns experienced by the several single-year cohorts, to distortions resulting from net immigration, to military service patterns that are not smoothly distributed by age (the data under consideration here pertain to the *civilian* population), or to some combination of the above factors. To

---

[1] The numerical results of this appendix were obtained from a modified version of a computer program found in Keyfitz and Fleiger (1971).

TABLE D.1
An Example of Greville's Method of Osculatory Interpolation for the Male Population
Aged 15–29, 1969 March Current Population Survey

		Single years of age					
		$i + 0$	$i + 1$	$i + 2$	$i + 3$	$i + 4$	Total
		A. Observed table					
Age in	$i = 15$	1637	1500	1484	1331	1113	7065
5-year	$i = 20$	944	902	973	781	886	4486
intervals	$i = 25$	977	1032	819	885	831	4544
		B. Graduated table					
		1680	1560	1420	1273	1133	7066
		1011	917	860	842	856	4486
		890	924	936	918	875	4543

C. The fit between observed and expected age distribution

	Goodness-of-fit χ^2	Index of dissimilarity
Ages 15–19	9.29	1.73%
Ages 20–24	25.00	3.19%
Ages 25–29	39.15	4.28%
Total	73.44	—

our knowledge, for the age patterns under detailed scrutiny here (ages 20–34), it is reasonable to assume that single-year age data should be regularly distributed within respective 5-year categories. The χ^2 for each 5-year age category (i.e., for each row of Table D.1) will have degrees of freedom less than 4, because in addition to fitting the row marginal, we have imposed other kinds of constraints upon the expected frequencies. Measures that assess the closeness of the "fit" apart from sample size are the usual index of dissimilarity and the Φ^2 coefficient (X^2/n). We see that the observed frequencies for ages 15–19 are quite possibly in line with the graduated frequencies ($X^2 = 9.29$), but that ages 20–29 are not by statistical criteria in accord with the graduated frequencies. In addition, then, to the CPS *undercount* of persons ages 20–29 that is known to occur, the single-year data for this age interval are not, by our judgment, internally consistent. The pattern of percentage distributions does not seem to indicate that digit preference on the part of the respondents could, however, account for this discrepancy. We nevertheless have some evidence of real inaccuracy of single-year age data for these years. This conclusion is only an approximate one, however, since we have not taken into account the complex sampling design of the CPS, nor have we been able to determine the exact number of degrees of freedom associated with the χ^2 statistics. An examination of the *cohort* pattern in these data observed over time could also be illuminating. One approach that would take into account the cohort pattern would be to apply the above method to age intervals i, $i + 5, i + 10, \ldots$, at time t, to age intervals $i + 1, i + 6, i + 11, \ldots$, at time $t + 1$, etc., thereby examining the relative merits of successive sample surveys in achieving the necessary degree of accuracy in single-year age data. We will not pursue those details here.

The complete results obtained by application of the above method are too bulky to present here but are available from the writer. We applied the above method to male and female samples obtained from the CPS for all years 1969–1973. We found that, in general, there is evidence of inaccuracy of single-year age data for ages 20–29 and 65–69, although the magnitude of the inaccuracy varies for males and females. Males seem to be recorded less accurately than females in the age range 20–29, and females seem to be recorded less accurately than males in ages 65–69. A summary of these results for ages 20–29 appears in Table D.2, where the differentials in recording age for the sexes is brought out. These apparent sex differences lead us to suspect that peculiar fertility experience cannot *by itself* explain the age peculiarities noted here. Part of the irregularity may, however, be due to the peculiar fertility patterns of American women during 1940–1946.

TABLE D.2
Summary of the Discrepancies between Observed and Interpolated Age Distribution, for Ages 20-29[a]

	1969	1970	1971	1972	1973
Ages 20–24					
Male	25.00	64.35	61.92	15.40	8.26
	(3.19)	(5.43)	(5.24)	(2.07)	(1.55)
Female	38.16	32.90	27.06	26.79	8.05
	(3.53)	(3.10)	(2.96)	(2.97)	(1.77)
Ages 25–29					
Male	39.15	5.35	18.65	24.99	35.24
	(4.28)	(1.47)	(2.74)	(3.50)	(4.17)
Female	12.36	5.62	11.19	14.59	27.40
	(2.13)	(1.35)	(2.23)	(2.09)	(3.49)

[a]The first number in each cell is the χ^2 statistic, and the second number enclosed in parentheses is the index of dissimilarity.

The total χ^2 for all ages ranged from 75 (1972 males) to 174 (1969 females), whereas the total index of dissimilarity ranged from 1.5 to 2.1%. These results, especially for ages 20–29, force us to reconsider some of the results of this work that were based upon single-year age data (e.g., Chapter 6). Since much of the across-time variation in aggregate underemployment results from underemployment variation in this critical age group, it would be indeed important to take these discrepancies into account.

Many of the methods developed for "correcting" age data in census enumerations, in addition to the one used here, could apparently be modified for the usual sample surveys upon which virtually all of our labor force information is based. Although this appendix by no means constitutes a complete analysis of the accuracy of single-year age data, the results here are suggestive of the irregularities in the age data used throughout the work.

normed effects in log-linear models for dichotomous data

In this appendix, we present a normed measure appropriate for each of the effects (interactions) in hierarchical models for dichotomous data. We also point to possible extensions of this measure to the case when some or all of the variables are polytomous (not necessarily dichotomous). This normed index was used in the latent class context of Chapter 5 and was used implicitly in some of the other chapters. It is analogous to Yule's Q for the 2×2 table and is, in fact, equivalent to it when applied to the two-factor interaction in the hierarchical model for the 2×2 table. This measure might be useful in some situations because it has a range $[-1, +1]$, whereas the multiplicative effects have a range $[0, \infty]$ and the log-multiplicative effects have a range $(-\infty, \infty)$.

In the notation of Goodman, the saturated hierarchical multiplicative model for the 2×2 table can be written as

$$f_{ij} = \theta \tau_i^A \tau_j^B \tau_{ij}^{AB}, \qquad i, j = 1, 2 \tag{E.1}$$

The superscript A refers to the row variable with $i = 1, 2$ classes, and the superscript B refers to the column variable with $j = 1, 2$ classes. Equation E.1 expresses the expected frequencies in the table (equal to the observed frequencies f_{ij} in the saturated model with $0\,df$) in terms of a main effect θ, a row effect τ_i^A, a column effect τ_j^B, and a two-factor interaction τ_{ij}^{AB} between the row and column variables A and B (Goodman, 1972b). The τ_{ij}^{AB} parameters are usually of most interest because they measure the "interaction," "association," or "dependence" between the dichotomous variables A and B. Since

$$\prod_i \tau_{ij}^{AB} = \prod_j \tau_{ij}^{AB} = \prod_{i,j} \tau_{ij}^{AB} = 1,$$

there is only one nonredundant parameter $\tau^{AB} = \tau_{11}^{AB}$, and all other τ_{ij}^{AB} parameters may be obtained from it. The parameter τ^{AB} is defined in terms of the observed frequencies as

$$\tau^{AB} = \tau_{11}^{AB} = \left(\frac{f_{11} f_{22}}{f_{12} f_{21}}\right)^{1/4} \tag{E.2}$$

that is, it is the fourth root of the odds ratio for the 2×2 table. Since τ^{AB} has range $[0, \infty]$, it is desirable to define a normed measure with range $[-1, +1]$, as has been suggested in the general context of measures of association for qualitative attributes (Goodman and Kruskal, 1954, 1959; Lancaster, 1969).

A natural measure is Yule's Q, defined for the 2×2 table as

$$Q^{AB} = \frac{f_{11} f_{22} - f_{12} f_{21}}{f_{11} f_{22} + f_{12} f_{21}}$$

$$= \frac{(f_{11} f_{22} / f_{12} f_{21}) - 1}{(f_{11} f_{22} / f_{12} f_{21}) + 1} \tag{E.3}$$

This measure has a long history (Yule, 1912) and may be rewritten in terms of the multiplicative effect τ^{AB} as

$$Q^{AB} = \frac{(\tau^{AB})^4 - 1}{(\tau^{AB})^4 + 1} \tag{E.4}$$

(See Equation E.2.) We see that Yule's Q for the 2×2 table may be obtained by raising τ^{AB} to the fourth power and then proceeding as in Equation E.4.

For the parameters τ_i^A, there is really only one nonredundant parameter, since $\prod_i \tau_i^A = 1$, and we can denote this parameter as $\tau^A = \tau_1^A$. The parameter τ^A is defined as

$$\tau^A = \tau_1^A = \left(\frac{f_{11} f_{12}}{f_{21} f_{22}}\right)^{1/4} \tag{E.5}$$

which, by analogy to (E.3), may be transformed into a normed measure

$$Q^A = \frac{f_{11} f_{12} - f_{21} f_{22}}{f_{11} f_{12} + f_{21} f_{22}}$$

$$= \frac{(\tau^A)^4 - 1}{(\tau^A)^4 + 1} \tag{E.6}$$

The measure in (E.6) suggests that we first convert τ^A into a quantity of the same geometric scale as the common odds ratio (i.e., raise it to the fourth power), and then compute Q^A as we computer Yule's Q (i.e., Q^{AB} in Equation E.4). This implies that comparisons of Q^A with Q^{AB} will be valid, since the respective quantities are functions of numbers of the same geometric scale. It would not be appropriate to raise τ^A and τ^{AB} to *different* powers, because then the measures obtained by proceeding as in Equations E.4 or E.6 (where the formulas are modified accordingly) would not be functions of numbers of the same scale. A quantity Q^B based upon τ_1^B can also be computed, and this quantity is of the same kind as Q^A.

Consideration of the three-way table composed of three dichotomous variables A, B, and C suggests the proper extension of these Q measures to m-way tables composed of m dichotomous variables. The saturated hierarchical log-linear model for the $2 \times 2 \times 2$ table may be written in multiplicative form as

$$f_{ijk} = \theta \tau_i^A \tau_j^B \tau_k^C \tau_{ij}^{AB} \tau_{ik}^{AC} \tau_{jk}^{BC} \tau_{ijk}^{ABC}, \qquad i, j, k = 1,2 \qquad (E.7)$$

The parameter τ_{ij}^{AB} denotes the two-factor interaction between variables A and B, and because of multiplicative constraints, we need consider only one of these, say $\tau^{AB} = \tau_{11}^{AB}$. This parameter is defined as

$$\tau^{AB} = \tau_{11}^{AB} = \left\{ \left(\frac{f_{111} f_{221}}{f_{121} f_{211}} \right) \left(\frac{f_{112} f_{222}}{f_{122} f_{212}} \right) \right\}^{1/8} \qquad (E.8)$$

Equation E.8 shows that τ^{AB} is the eighth root of the product of the odds ratio corresponding to variables A and B when $C = 1$ and the odds ratio corresponding to variables A and B when $C = 2$. Raising τ^{AB} to the fourth power produces

$$(\tau^{AB})^4 = \left[\left(\frac{f_{111} f_{221}}{f_{121} f_{211}} \right) \left(\frac{f_{112} f_{222}}{f_{122} f_{212}} \right) \right]^{1/2} \qquad (E.9)$$

which is a quantity directly comparable in scale to the odds ratio, that is, it is a geometric mean to two odds ratios. A normed measure comparable to Yule's Q for the two-factor A–B interaction in the three-way table is thus seen to be

$$Q^{AB} = \frac{(\tau^{AB})^4 - 1}{(\tau^{AB})^4 + 1} \qquad (E.10)$$

and this quantity is comparable to Q^{AB} presented earlier for the two-way table (see Equation E.4). Normed measures for the τ_{ik}^{AC} and the τ_{jk}^{BC} parameters are directly analogous to the above Q^{AB} measure for the τ_{ij}^{AB} parameters.

The parameters denoting the three-way interaction among variables A,

B, and C are the τ_{ijk}^{ABC}, i, j, k = 1, 2. Because of multiplicative constraints we need only consider one such parameter $\tau^{ABC} = \tau_{111}^{ABC}$, and this parameter is defined as

$$\tau^{ABC} = \tau_{111}^{ABC} = \left[\left(\frac{f_{111}f_{221}}{f_{121}f_{211}} \right) \left(\frac{f_{122}f_{212}}{f_{112}f_{222}} \right) \right]^{1/8} \qquad (E.11)$$

We see from (E.11) that τ^{ABC} is the eighth root of the product of the odds ratio between variables A and B when $C = 1$ and the inverse of the odds ratio between variables A and B when $C = 2$. The form of τ^{ABC} is thus the same as for τ^{AB}, so that when we raise τ^{ABC} to the fourth power, this quantity will be comparable to $(\tau^{AB})^4$, implying that a normed measure Q^{ABC} comparable to Q^{AB} is provided by

$$Q^{ABC} = \frac{(\tau^{ABC})^4 - 1}{(\tau^{ABC})^4 + 1} \qquad (E.12)$$

Similar arguments show that for the parameters of the kind τ_i^A, τ_j^B, τ_k^C, we can produce the proper normed measure by raising them to the fourth power and then proceed as before to obtain measures of the kind Q^A, Q^B, Q^{AB}, Q^C, and these would also be comparable to Q^{AB}, Q^{AC}, Q^{BC}, and Q^{ABC}. For both the two- and three-way table, we see then that the number 4 is the power that should be used to convert the τ parameters into a quantity of the same form as the odds ratio and that this quantity should be used in formulas like (E.4), (E.6), (E.10), and (E.12) to produce the proper normed effect analogous to Yule's Q.

For the m-way cross-table of dichotomous variables, $m \geq 2$, we may show inductively that for any τ parameter in the multiplicative model we can define an appropriate Q measure according to the formula

$$Q = \frac{(\tau)^4 - 1}{(\tau)^4 + 1}$$

and these Q measures would allow the researcher to assess the comparative importance of interactions of any order (one-factor, two-factor, three-factor, etc.), since they are all functions of numbers of the same form as the odds ratio. Davis proposed different normed effects than the above, letting the power used to transform the τ parameter vary according to the order of the interaction (Davis, 1972). His methods can be misleading when attempting to make comparisons among interactions of different orders, since we have shown that the power to be used is always 4 and does not depend at all upon the order of the interaction involved.

An example in which the two methods (i.e., the method of Davis and our method) produce very different results is not difficult to find. In a five-way table composed of dichotomous variables that was analyzed earlier by Goodman (1970), we find $\tau^{AB} = 1.152$ and $\tau^{ABC} = .873$. The additive parameters (i.e., the log-τ parameters) are $\lambda^{AB} = .141$ and $\lambda^{ABC} = -.136$. From these facts we know that the A–B interaction (i.e., τ^{AB}) is stronger than the A–B–C interaction (i.e., τ^{ABC}). Using the appropriate power four to transform the tau parameters into a quantity like the odds ratio and then producing the appropriate normed effects presented earlier, we find $Q^{AB} = .276$ and $Q^{ABC} = -.265$, which also shows the A–B interaction to be the stronger, since the distance of these Q statistics from zero (the value reflecting zero interaction) is the greater for Q^{AB}. By following Davis's procedure, raising τ^{AB} to the fourth power and τ^{ABC} to the eighth power, we find a normed measure for the A–B interaction of .276 (identical with our Q^{AB}) but a measure for the A–B–C interaction of $-.443$. This approach therefore produces a misleading impression, since it would indicate that the A–B–C interactions were much *stronger* than the A–B interaction, and we showed above that this was definitely not the case.

The above result for the m-way cross-table composed of m dichotomous variables derives from what is at first sight a more general result for the m-way table with m polytomous (not necessarily dichotomous) variables. For a cross-classification of m variables $A_1, A_2, \ldots, A_m$ with dimensions $I_1, I_2, \ldots, I_m$, respectively, denote S as the set of d elements ($1 \leq d \leq m$), which appear in the superscript of a given τ parameter. That is, τ^S is a parameter reflecting a d-way interaction of the variables contained in S. We find that the proper power necessary to transform the τ^S parameter into a quantity of the same multiplicative scale as the odds ratio is given as

$$K_S = 2^{2-d} \prod_{\substack{i \ni \\ A_i \in S}} [I_i/(I_i - 1)] \qquad (E.13)$$

With a 2^m cross-table, we see that $K_S = (2^{2-d})(2^d) = 4$, which does not depend on d or m. The proof of Equation E.13 is rather complicated but is available from the writer.

To understand the meaning of the quantity K_S defined in (E.13), we make the following observations. The common odds ratio for the 2×2 table is $(f_{11}/f_{12})(f_{22}/f_{21})$, or is the product of two odds. By letting $o_1 = f_{11}/f_{12}$, the odds that variable $B = 1$ when $A = 1$, and by letting $o_2 = f_{22}/f_{21}$, the odds that variable $B = 2$ when $A = 2$, we see that the odds ratio for the 2×2 table is simply $o_1 o_2$. For any effect in a multiplicative model, we see that the τ parameter can be written in a form

$$\tau^S = (o_1 o_2 \ldots o_I)^{1/p} \qquad (E.14)$$

where p is the dimension (i.e., the number of cells) in the table, and I is the number of ratios of frequencies (not necessarily all distinct from each other) used to define an interaction. The quantity K_S in (E.13) transforms the τ parameters into a quantity of the same geometric scale as $o_1 o_2$, that is, $(\tau^S)^{K_S}$ is of the same scale as $o_1 o_2$. If τ^S were the pth root of the product of four odds $o_1 o_2 o_3 o_4$, then $(\tau^S)^{K_S} = (o_1 o_2 o_3 o_4)^{1/2}$, and we see that K_S is the power which transforms τ^S into a quantity of the same geometric scale as the common odds ratio $o_1 o_2$. If $\tau^{S'}$ were the pth root of the product of three odds $o_1 o_2 o_3$, then $(\tau^{S'})^{K_{S'}} = (o_1 o_2 o_3)^{2/3}$, and we see that $K_{S'}$ is the power that transforms $\tau^{S'}$ into a quantity of the same geometric scale as the common odds ratio. This might suggest that we define our normed effects in general as

$$Q^S = \frac{(\tau^S)^{K_s} - 1}{(\tau^S)^{K_s} + 1} \tag{E.15}$$

and these measures would *apparently* be directly comparable in form to the measures presented earlier for the dichotomous case. For two different multiplicative parameters τ^S and $\tau^{S'}$, Q^S and $Q^{S'}$ would *apparently* be comparable to each other in the sense indicated above. Actually, however, using these powers K_S of (E.13) can be misleading.

Suppose that $\tau^S = \tau^{S'}$ for some $S \neq S'$. Then, in a general table composed of polytomous (not necessarily dichotomous) variables, K_S need not equal $K_{S'}$, implying that $(\tau^S)^{K_S}$ need not equal $(\tau^{S'})^{K_{S'}}$, which further implies that even though $\tau^S = \tau^{S'}$ the corresponding Q^S and $Q^{S'}$ measures suggested by (E.15) could be *different*, whereas in this case, we would probably desire normed measures of the S and the S' interactions that are *identical*. Therefore, there is some ambiguity in the choice of scale factors appropriate for the τ effects in general.

One approach that would allow comparison of normed effects obtained from completely different cross-tables is the following. If a cross-table has two dichotomous variables A_1, A_2, then for a two-factor interaction between those variables (i.e., an A_1–A_2 interaction) the power $K_{(A1, A2)}$ given by (E.13) is $2^{2-2} \times 4 = 4$, regardless of the dimensions of any of the other variables comprising the cross-table. This suggests that

$$Q^{A_1 A_2} = \frac{(\tau^{A_1 A_2})^4 - 1}{(\tau^{A_1 A_2})^4 + 1}$$

will also be analogous to Yule's Q, and comparable to any Q measure obtained in the case where all variables are dichotomous. Therefore, $Q^{A_1 A_2}$ is an unambiguous choice for a normed measure of the association between A_1 and A_2 when both A_1 and A_2 are dichotomous. It is not difficult to see, using Equation E.13, that when the power 4 is used in a formula like Equation E.14, the normed effect corresponding to any d-way interaction composed of d dichotomies will correspond to that same normed measure for the corresponding d-way interaction in the case where *all* variables are dichotomous. Thus, for interactions among dichotomies,

$$Q^S = \frac{(\tau^S)^4 - 1}{(\tau^S)^4 + 1} \tag{E.16}$$

is a normed measure that always involves the power 4, implying (*a*) that the original ordering among τ parameters will be preserved in the Q measures and (*b*) that in the case of interactions among dichotomies, the Q measures will be directly comparable to Yule's Q for the 2×2 table. These results, then, provide a rationale for always using the power 4 for interactions among dichotomous variables and then proceeding as in (E.16) to produce the proper normed measure.

The large sample variances of these Q statistics may also be developed. Since the large sample variance of the $\log-\tau$ (i.e., the λ) parameters is of the form $\Sigma a_i^2/f_i$, by application of the delta-method we find that

$$SE(\tau) = \tau(\Sigma a_i^2/f_i)^{1/2} \tag{E.17}$$

By repeated application of the delta-method to find the standard error of Q, a function of τ, we find that

$$SE(Q) = \tfrac{1}{2}(1 - Q)^2 \times 4\tau^{4-1} \times SE(\tau) \tag{E.18}$$

which in view of (E.17) can be simplified to

$$SE(Q) = 2(1 - Q)^2\tau^4(\Sigma a_i^2/f_i)^{1/2} \tag{E.19}$$

Other normed measures different from the Yule's Q analogue presented here could clearly be suggested. One such measure is

$$\alpha = (2/\pi) \arctan[\log(\tau)^4] \tag{E.20}$$

(see Fienberg and Gilbert, 1970). Upon plotting α and Q for a range of values $(\tau)^4$, we find that for τ^4 in the range of 1 to approximately 4.5, the two are virtually identical, but for the range from approximately 4.5 to infinity, we find that $Q > \alpha$, and the rate of change in α is smaller than that in Q relative to changes in τ^4. Similar comments apply to these quantities for τ^4 in the approximate range (1/4.5, 1) and (0, 1/4.5). Thus for at least part of the domain of α and Q, the two measures are very similar, although for part of the domain Q produces an impression of larger association than does α.

This provides the justification for the normed effects used in the dichotomous case in Chapter 5 and suggests that the technique can be extended to other more general contexts. Hopefully, these Q measures will prove useful to other researchers. It is interesting to note that these Q measures are related to some of the normed metrics recently discussed by Altham (1970a,b).

purging cross-classified data of diagonal effects, with application to demographic rates depending on age, time-period, and cohort

Goodman (1972c, 1975b) considered a "diagonals parameter" model for cross-classified data that is well suited for the demographic analysis of rates, when the rates can be viewed as depending on age, time-period, and cohort. These models were applied in Chapter 6 to examine the dependence of a trichotomous labor force status variable on age, time-period, and cohort category. In that chapter we also presented certain time-period rates that were purged of the influence of the cohort variable. This appendix provides the justification for that technique and will hopefully present the method in a general manner so that it can be critically evaluated and applied in other substantive contexts. The problem of inferring the extent of influence of the cohort variable on observed time-period (or age) variation in some dependent variable (e.g., fertility) is an old one in demography. The statistical method advocated here appears to have advantages over other methods, in part because it is based on the multiplicative model for cross-classified data.

In an $I \times J$ cross-table with row variable A with $i = 1, \ldots, I$ categories and with column variable T with $j = 1, \ldots, J$ categories, denote the population proportion in the (i, j) cell by π_{ij}. This $I \times J$ cross-table possesses $I + J - 1$ diagonals, which we accordingly index by $k = 1, \ldots, I + J - 1$, proceeding from the upper right to the lower left diagonals. For purposes of later discussion, we note that A (the row variable) might refer to age category and that T (the column variable) might refer to time-period category.

A model that expresses the π_{ij} in terms of an "effect" of row i and an "effect" of column j is the model where A is independent of T. In this case the π_{ij} can be written as

$$\pi_{ij} = \alpha_i \beta_j \tag{F.1}$$

for $i = 1, \ldots, I$ and $j = 1, \ldots, J$. The marginal proportions $\pi_{i+} = \Sigma_j \pi_{ij}$ and $\pi_{+j} = \Sigma_i \pi_{ij}$ are easily seen to be

$$\pi_{i+} = \alpha_i (\Sigma_j \beta_j)$$

and

$$\pi_{+j} = (\Sigma_i \alpha_i) \beta_i$$

showing that the row and column marginals are proportional to the α_i and the β_j, respectively. If the α_i and β_j were known quantities, then the row and column marginals could be determined from them. We can, for example, rescale the α_i by taking $\tilde{\alpha}_i = \alpha_i/(\Sigma_i \alpha_i)$, and these rescaled quantities would be identical to π_{i+}. Similarly, we could also rescale the β_j by taking $\tilde{\beta}_j = \beta_j/(\Sigma_j)$, and these rescaled quantities would be identical to π_{+j}. It is also easy to see that if the marginals π_{i+}, π_{+j} were known, then the α_i and β_j could be determined from them.

A model that expresses the π_{ij} in terms of an "effect" of row i, an "effect" of column j, and an "effect" of diagonal k (with $k = i - j + J$) is Goodman's (1972c) diagonals parameter model:

$$\pi_{ij} = \alpha_i \beta_j \delta_k \tag{F.2}$$

With this model the marginal proportions are

$$\pi_{i+} = \alpha_i (\Sigma_j \beta_j \delta_k)$$

and

$$\pi_{+j} = \beta_j (\Sigma_i \alpha_i \delta_k)$$

We see that with the diagonals parameter model the row marginals π_{i+} are *not* proportional to the α_i (because $\delta_k = \delta_{i-j+J}$ depends on the ith row category), and we see that the column marginals π_{+j} are *not* proportional to the β_j (because $\delta_k = \delta_{i-j+J}$ likewise depends on the jth column category). Except in the special case where $\delta_1 = \cdots = \delta_{I+J-1}$, the row and column marginals depend on the diagonal parameters δ_k, and are not directly proportional to the α_i or the β_j.

For the diagonals parameter model of (F.2), we can purge the π_{ij} of the diagonal effects by taking the simple transformation

$$\pi_{ij}^* = \pi_{ij}/\delta_{i-j+J} \tag{F.3}$$

We can see that $\pi_{ij}^* = \alpha_i\beta_j$, and by previous arguments the purged marginals π_{i+}^*, π_{+j}^* will be proportional to the α_i and the β_j, respectively. The π_{ij}^* are purged of the diagonal effects, in the sense that the δ_k have been ignored in calculating the π_{ij}^*. In order that the π_{ij}^* sum to unity, we can rescale them by taking $\tilde{\pi}_{ij}^* = \pi_{ij}^*/(\Sigma_{i,j}\pi_{ij}^*)$, and the $\tilde{\pi}_{ij}^*$ can be interpreted as the expected proportions in the cells of the $I \times J$ table conditional on ignoring the diagonal effects.

In (F.2) and (F.3), we have assumed that the model parameters were in fact known. Given these known parameters, it is possible to transform them into a different set of parameters that would also generate the π_{ij}. But it would be incorrect to use a set of parameter values other than the ones in (F.2) to define purged proportions. To demonstrate this problem and to show incidentally the identification problem that arises when trying to estimate from sample data the model parameters (compare Mason *et al.*, 1973), consider the following. By letting

$$\delta_* = (\delta_{k'}/\delta_{k''})^{(k''-k')-1} \tag{F.4}$$

for $k'' > k'$, and defining a new set of parameters

$$\tilde{\delta}_k = (\delta_k/\delta_{k''})\delta_*^{k-k'} \tag{F.5}$$

$$\tilde{\alpha}_i = \alpha_i\delta_{k''}\delta_*^{k''-i} \tag{F.6}$$

and

$$\tilde{\beta}_j = \beta_j\delta_*^{j-J} \tag{F.7}$$

we see that

$$\tilde{\alpha}_i\tilde{\beta}_j\tilde{\delta}_k = \alpha_i\beta_j\delta_k\delta_*^{k''-i+j-J+k-k''}$$
$$= \alpha_i\beta_j\delta_k$$
$$= \pi_{ij} \tag{F.8}$$

since $k = i - j + J$. Moreover, we see from (F.5) that $\tilde{\delta}_{k'} = \tilde{\delta}_{k''} = 1$, regardless of the values assumed by the true parameters in (F.2). These transformed parameters cannot be used to define population proportions purged of diagonal effects because the $\tilde{\alpha}_i$ depend on $\delta_*^{k''-i}$ and the $\tilde{\beta}_j$ depend on δ_*^{j-J}, and δ_* depends in turn on the two diagonal parameters $\delta_{k'}$ and $\delta_{k''}$. Except in the case where $\delta_{k'} = \delta_{k''} = 1$, the transformed parameters given by Equations (F.5–F.7) would produce an erroneous impression if used to purge the π_{ij} of the diagonal effects.

In the event that the α_i, β_j, δ_k are not known, we can estimate them from sample data if we are given knowledge about the relationship between two diagonal parameters. Without this information (or similar information regarding the relationship between any two of the parameters in the diagonals parameter model), the model parameters are unidentifiable, and hence the purged marginal proportions would likewise be unidentifiable. We cannot determine the identifying restrictions on the basis of inspection of the data, but instead we require strictly a priori knowledge about the magnitudes of at least two of the δ_k. If we knew that $\delta_{k'} = \delta_{k''} = 1$, then this would perforce identify the parameters in (F.2). Sample estimates a_i, b_j, d_k of the α_i, β_j, δ_k could then be uniquely determined (setting $d_{k'} = d_{k''} = 1$), and purged expected frequencies $F_{ij}^* = a_i b_j$ could be used to calculate the purged marginals.

As an example, consider Table F.1, a 4×4 cross-table exhibiting row, column, and diagonal effects. In this table the frequencies are determined exactly by

$$f_{ij} = a_i b_j d_k$$

The computer program described in Appendix G (and used in our Chapter 6), generated the a_i, b_j, and d_k that appear in Table F.2. (For illustrative purposes, we have assumed that $d_6 = d_7 = 1$ in order to identify the parameters, but the truth of this assumption cannot be verified by inspection of the data.) Finally, in Table F.3 the purged frequencies are provided, by taking $f_{ij}^* = a_i b_j$ and rescaling appropriately. Except for a scale factor, these purged frequencies differ from the observed frequencies only by an effect specific to the particular diagonal. The observed row marginals, when taken as proportions, were .333, .278, .222, and .167, but the purged row marginals were .533, .267, .133, and .067, showing that the differences among the purged marginals are much more dramatic than the differences among the observed marginals. This is a consequence of the fact that the estimates of α_i for the diagonals parameter model (i.e., the a_i) were much more variable than were estimates of α_i under the independence model.

TABLE F.1
Mock 4 × 4 Table with Row, Column, and Diagonal Effects

		Column				
Row	1	2	3	4	Total
1	4	10	18	28	60
2	3	8	15	24	50
3	2	6	12	20	40
4	1	4	9	16	30
Total	10	28	54	88	180

TABLE F.2
Parameter Estimates for Diagonals Parameter Model
Applied to Mock 4 × 4 Table[a]

Row parameters a_i	Column parameters b_j	Diagonal parameters d_k
1 255.69	.03127	.10951
2 127.91	.12507	.18764
3 63.97	.37515	.31265
4 31.98	1.0[b]	.50017
5 —	—	.75006
6 —	—	1.0[c]
7 —	—	1.0[c]

[a]Table F.1 is fit perfectly with the diagonals parameters model, so the χ^2 statistics turn out to be 0.0. There are four *df* for this model applied to the 4 × 4 table.

[b]The parameter b_4 was set equal to 1.0, in order to identify the parameters.

[c]The parameters d_6 and d_7 were set equal to 1.0, assuming that the sixth and seventh diagonals have equivalent effects.

Similar comments can also be applied to the column marginals and the purged column marginals. The diagonal effects distorted the observed marginals, in the sense that row and column marginals could not have been used to deduce the true row and column effects.

To see the relevance of the above exposition for demographic contexts, we now introduce a third variable, D, regarded as a dependent variable. The table of interest now is the $A \times T \times D$ three-way table, where the rows, columns, and relevant diagonals now refer explicitly to the age, time-period, and cohort variables. This is precisely the situation ad-

TABLE F.3
Frequencies Purged of Diagonal Effects

Row	Column 1	2	3	4	Total
1	1.96	7.84	23.51	62.69	96.00
2	.98	3.92	11.76	31.35	48.01
3	.49	1.96	5.88	15.67	24.00
4	.24	.98	2.94	7.84	12.00
Total	3.67	14.70	44.09	117.55	180.01[a]

[a]Total does not equal 180 because of rounding error.

dressed at length in Chapter 6, and when l (for $l = 1, \ldots, L$) is used to index the categories of D, we have a model similar to the diagonals parameter model,

$$\pi_{ijl} = \tau_{ij}^{AT}\tau_{il}^{AD}\tau_{jl}^{TD}\tau_{kl}^{CD} \tag{F.9}$$

In (F.9), the τ^{AT}, τ^{AD}, τ^{TD}, τ^{CD} refer to interactions between age and time-period, age and D, time-period and D, and cohort and D, respectively. It can be shown that the time-specific rates of occurrence of the categories of D,

$$r_{\cdot(j)l} = \pi_{+jl}/\pi_{+j+} \tag{F.10}$$

depend on the cohort–D interactions τ_{kl}^{CP} (since $k = i - j + J$) and are, in this sense, confounded with the cohort effect. In this situation, we can purge the π_{ijl} of the cohort–D interaction by taking

$$\pi_{ijl}^{*} = \pi_{ijl}/\tau_{kl}^{CD} \tag{F.11}$$

[Compare (F.11) with (F.3).] The π_{ijl}^{*} can be rescaled to ensure, for example, that the marginal totals π_{+j+}, which might be fixed by sampling design, are preserved. Adjusted or "translated" time-specific rates $r^{*}._{\cdot(j)l}$ can be obtained from the π_{ijl}^{*}, and a comparison of the $r._{\cdot(j)l}$ with the $r^{*}._{\cdot(j)l}$ would show the influence of the cohort variable on the rates. The $r^{*}._{\cdot(j)l}$ are "translated" into the $r._{\cdot(j)l}$ by the cohort variable, showing how the model of (F.9) relates directly to the "translation" problem in demography seminally discussed by Ryder (1964).

To develop an example that is simpler to grasp than the substantive applications discussed in Chapter 6, we consider a $4 \times 4 \times 2$ table derived by taking f_{ij1} equal to the entries in Table F.1 and by taking $f_{ij2} = 30 - f_{ij1}$. As with the diagonals parameter model discussed earlier, the parameters of (F.9) are unidentifiable unless certain restrictions are imposed. As an expedient here, we have set $\tau_{6l}^{CP} = \tau_{7l}^{CP}$ to identify the parameters, and with other usual constraints imposed, the parameters were then estimated from the data. The results are presented in Table F.4.

As will be apparent from inspection of the entries in Table F.4, the restrictions used here to identify model parameters are somewhat different from the ones used by Pullum (1977) or Fienberg and Mason (1978) in their consideration of the cohort model (F.9) for a discrete dependent variable. First, the cohort parameters for the sixth and seventh cohorts (i.e., τ_{6l}^{CP}, τ_{7l}^{CP}) were restricted to equal the observed cohort effect for the seventh cohort, treating the observations for the seventh cohort as a simple 2×1 table with entries f_{411}, f_{412}. This type of restriction allows, we believe, a more direct comparison of cohort parameters, since with this restriction the cohort parameters are implicitly compared with a directly observed

TABLE F.4
Parameter Estimates for Full Cohort Model Applied to Mock 4 × 4 × 2 Table

Age parameters τ_{il}^{AD}		Time period parameters τ_{jl}^{TD}		Cohort parameters τ_{kl}^{CD}	
$l = 1$	$l = 2$	$l = 1$	$l = 2$	$l = 1$	$l = 2$
1	11.523	.087	.235	4.260	.178	5.631
2	8.862	.113	.490	2.040	.119	8.406
3	6.260	.160	.916	1.091	.124	8.069
4	4.260	.235	1.828[a]	.547[a]	.140	7.131
5	—	—	—	—	.165	6.078
6	—	—	—	—	.186[b]	5.385[b]
7	—	—	—	—	.186[b]	5.385[b]

[a] The parameter τ_{41}^{TD} was calculated by taking the geometric mean of $(F_{141}/F_{142})^{1/2}, \ldots,$ $(F_{441}/F_{442})^{1/2}$, where F_{ijk} denotes the expected frequency in the (i,j,k) cell under the model. The parameter $\tau_{42}^{TD} = (\tau_{41}^{TD})^{-1}$.

[b] The cohort parameter $\tau_{71}^{CD} (= \tau_{61}^{CD})$ was calculated by taking $(F_{411}/F_{412})^{1/2}$ and the parameter $\tau_{72}^{CD} = \tau_{62}^{CD} = (\tau_{71}^{CD})^{-1}$.

interaction. Similarly, the time-period parameters for the fourth time-period (i.e., τ_{4l}^{TP}) were restricted to equal the actual time-period effect for the fourth time-period, and this expedient similarly allows a more direct comparison among the time-period parameters than might be the case with other types of restrictions imposed. As both Pullum (1977) and Fienberg and Mason (1978) note, however, the type of restriction used will not affect interpretation of patterns of effects, since, for example, the *pattern* of ratios $\tau_{k1}^{CP}/\tau_{k2}^{CP}$, for $k = 1, \ldots, I + J - 1$, is unchanged regardless of the way these restrictions are imposed. As was the case with the diagonals parameter model, however, the restriction that the sixth and seventh cohort effects were identical is a critical one and cannot be justified at all from inspection of the data.

In Table F.5 the observed and the purged time-period rates are compared. These were obtained by using formulas analogous to (F.10) and (F.11), with expected frequencies or purged expected frequencies substituted appropriately for the π_{ijl} or the π_{ijl}^*. Owing to the marked differences among cohort parameters (compare Table F.4), the purged rates are very different from the observed rates.

The application of this technique in Chapter 6 was wholly analogous to that presented in Tables F.4 and F.5 for a mock 4 × 4 × 2 table. The most critical assumption with this approach is ostensibly the a priori assumption that serves to identify the parameters of the cohort model. We provided reasonable justification for our identifying restrictions in the sub-

TABLE F.5
Observed Time-period Rates and Time-period Rates Purged of the Cohort Effect for the 4 × 4 × 2 Table

Time-period category, j	Observed rates[a]	Differences[b]	Purged rates	Differences[b]
1	.083	—	.770	—
2	.233	−.150	.932	−.283
3	.450	−.217	.978	−.046
4	.733	−.283	.993	−.015

[a]The rates are the rate of occurrence of the first class of D.
[b]Differences of successive rates.

stantive context of Chapter 6. However, in the absence of strong prior knowledge about the magnitude of various model parameters, it would be prudent to experiment with alternative restrictions that appear plausible, thereby obtaining some sense of the consequences of the different assumptions. We cannot agree with Glenn (1976), who argued in part that because of the identification problem arising with models such as these, cohort analysts are engaged in a "futile quest." There is always the danger of incorrectly specifying a model for the problem at hand, whether by virtue of omitting relevant variables, misspecifying the functional form, or erring when imposing identifying restrictions. But to abandon the effort altogether would require major retreat from the objectives of empirical social science.

APPENDIX G

a computer program for cohort analysis using multiplicative models and the modified multiple regression approach

A computer program available on request from the author can be used to consider eight different models that naturally arise in the cohort analysis of a discrete dependent variable (Goodman, 1975b). The goodness-of-fit χ^2 statistic, the χ^2 statistic based on the likelihood-ratio criterion, and the index of dissimilarity between observed and expected frequencies are provided for any model. Parameter estimates for the full model involving age, time-period, and cohort effects on the dependent variable are calculated by the program. To estimate identified parameters for the full model, the user must specify two *adjacent* cohorts that have equivalent effects, although the program could be easily modified to deal with other types of identifying or overidentifying restrictions. The user may also insert contrast vectors (orthogonal polynomials, Helmert contrasts, deviation contrasts, etc.) to examine various combinations of the age, time-period, and cohort parameters over the categories of the dependent variable. Purged frequencies and purged marginal frequencies, as discussed in Appendix F, can also be output. The program will analyze a rectangular two-way table, when it is of interest to consider various hypotheses about the row, column, or diagonal effects, merely by setting the number of "categories" of the dependent variable equal to 1 in the program input cards.

The algorithm used to obtain estimated expected frequencies is the second of the three algorithms presented in Goodman's fundamental *Berkeley Symposium* paper (Goodman, 1972c, pp. 665–666). For the rectangular table with no explicit dependent variable, the rescaling of parameters

255

in the algorithm is analogous to that presented by Goodman. For the case where a polytomous dependent variable is considered, the rescaling was somewhat different. It would be very tedious to describe the algebraic justification for this rescaling here. However, the suitability of the rescaling can be verified by comparing the expected frequencies obtained from this program with the expected frequencies that would be obtained by fitting the equivalent model using the ECTA program of Goodman and Fay (where the cross-table subject to analysis would be "unfolded" into an incomplete *four*-dimensional array).

Alternative computer programs for cohort analysis using multiplicative models are also available. Pullum (1977) describes the use of one such program that is similar to the present one. Fienberg and Mason (1978) also consider various cohort models in their comprehensive study and use the Newton–Raphson algorithm for estimation. The MULTIQUAL program of Bock and Yates (1973) can be used for all of their models (as well as for the models considered in this book). The choice among the various programs would have to be dictated in part by matters of convenience. We believe that the program discussed here will be found convenient and yet versatile enough to handle most problems in cohort analysis that arise in sociodemographic research. It would not be difficult to modify the program to deal with various cohort models arising from Goodman's (1972c) "triangles parameter" model, as was considered at length by Fienberg and Mason.

a computer program for adjustment of rates using multiplicative models

In this appendix, we briefly describe a new method for the adjustment of rates that is based on the multiplicative model. The approach is fully described in Clogg (1978) and should be compared to and contrasted with the methods described by Kitagawa (1955, 1964) and extended by Das Gupta (1978). A computer program general enough to deal with a variety of demographic situations is available on request from the author.

Let C refer to the composition variable with classes $i = 1, \ldots, I$. Of course, C could itself be composed of two or more composition variables. (For example, in Chapter 4 the joint variable age–race–sex group was taken as a single composition variable for some of the analysis.) Let G refer to the group variable, with classes $j = 1, \ldots, J$ (i.e., there are J groups in all to be considered). Finally, let D refer to the dependent variable of interest, with classes $k = 1, \ldots, K$. The data for this situation can be laid out in a three-way $I \times J \times K$ cross-classification of C, G, and D, with observed frequencies f_{ijk}, for $i = 1, \ldots, I; j = 1, \ldots, J;$ $k = 1, \ldots, K$. The "crude" or overall group rates will be denoted as $r_{\cdot(j)k}$ and are given by the relationship

$$r_{\cdot(j)k} = \frac{1}{f_{+j+}} \sum_{i} \left(\frac{f_{ijk}}{f_{ij+}} \right) f_{ij+}. \tag{H.1}$$

In (H.1), the "+" refers to a summation over the particular subscript, for example, $f_{+j+} = \Sigma_{i,k} f_{ijk}$. Since the quantity (f_{+jk}/f_{ij+}) is merely the rate of occurrence of the kth level of D in the ith class of C for the jth group, and since $(f_{ij+}/f_{+j+}) = c_{ij}$ is a "composition weight" for class i of C in the jth group, (H.1) can be rewritten as

$$r_{\cdot(j)k} = \Sigma_i (r_{i(j)k})c_{ij} \tag{H.2}$$

where $r_{i(j)k} = (f_{ijk}/f_{ij+})$. Since the c_{ij} depend on the group level j, an adjustment or "standardization" procedure begins by determining some hypothetical set of composition weights (say, c_i^*, for $i = 1, \ldots, I$) to apply to all groups. Once these weights are determined, standardized rates $r_{\cdot(j)k}^s$ are given by

$$r_{\cdot(j)k}^s = \Sigma_i (r_{i(j)k})c_i^* \tag{H.3}$$

for each group $j = 1, \ldots, J$. In (H.3) the composition marginal is in some sense "controlled" or "held constant," since the same weights c_i^* are applied to each group in order to obtain the standardized rates.

The customary methods summarized in the preceding paragraph can be criticized in the following way.

1. There is no explicit model for the data which underlies the observed rates, that is, no model linking the f_{ijk} to well-defined model parameters.

2. Adjusted rates are *conditional* on the set of weights (namely c_i^*, $i = 1, \ldots, I$) chosen for the analysis, and comparisons of adjusted rates depend—sometimes critically—on the set of weights chosen. That is, the adjusted rates are not uniquely defined, since the c_i^* are arbitrary.

3. The customary methods can be cumbersome when applied to analyze the rates on the D variable for more than two groups.

A method that remedies each of these deficiencies is the following.

The frequencies in the $I \times J \times K$ cross-classification of interest here can be expressed in terms of parameters of a multiplicative model in the following way:

$$f_{ijk} = \theta\tau_i^C\tau_j^G\tau_k^D\tau_{ij}^{CG}\tau_{ik}^{CD}\tau_{jk}^{GD}\tau_{ijk}^{CD} \tag{H.4}$$

Each of the model parameters has a well-defined meaning, and this meaning is fully discussed by Goodman (1970, 1972, 1973) and others. In the context of the $C \times G \times D$ cross-table that often arises in demographic situations, the two-factor interactions τ^{CG}, τ^{CD}, τ^{GD} and the three-factor interactions τ^{CGD} are of most interest. The parameters τ^{CD}, τ^{GD} denote the interactions of the composition and group variable with D, respectively, and in the multiplicative model framework, they contain all the information about the effects of C on D and the effects of G on D. The parameters τ_{ij}^{CG} explicitly measure the interaction between the composition and group variables; that is, they measure the extent to which the composition varies from group to group under the multiplicative model. Using (H.4) in (H.1), it is possible to show how the group rates $r_{.(j)k}$ are affected by the τ^{CG} and also how the group rates are affected by the other multiplicatively defined interactions. When the τ_{ij}^{CG} are not identically equal to unity (for $i = 1$, . . . , I; $j = 1$, . . . , J), composition–group interaction will affect the group rates, and in these situations an adjustment of rates is needed.

When the τ_{ij}^{CG} are not all identically 1, we suggest purging the f_{ijk}^* of the C–G interaction in the following way: merely transform the f_{ijk} to purged frequencies f_{ijk}^* by taking

$$f_{ijk}^* = f_{ijk}/\tau_{ij}^{CG} \tag{H.5}$$

When (H.5) is used to purge the data, the transformed frequencies may be written as

$$f_{ijk}^* = \theta\tau_i^C\tau_j^G\tau_k^D\tau_{ik}^{CD}\tau_{jk}^{GD}\tau_{ijk}^{CGD} \tag{H.6}$$

where the parameters on the right-hand side are the same parameters as appeared in (H.4). Rates calculated from the f_{ijk}^* will not depend on the τ^{CG}, but they do, of course, depend on all of the other relevant interaction parameters in the multiplicative model. The rates obtained from the f_{ijk}^* (say, the $r_{.(j)k}^*$) may be interpreted as follows: $r_{.(j)k}^*$ is the expected rate of occurrence of the kth class of D for the jth group when the C–G interaction estimated from the full $I \times J \times K$ table is removed from the data. Note that the τ^{CG} are unambiguously determined, given the use of standard contrasts used to define interactions in the multiplicative model, and that therefore the adjusted rates $r_{.(j)k}^*$ also uniquely defined (unlike the case with the more customary methods). Note, in addition, that (H.5) can be used for the comparison of rates among J groups (for $J \geq 2$), whereas the more usual approaches can be ambiguous when more than two groups are considered. And we note further that this method is based upon a multiplicative model for the f_{ijk} that has certain theoretical advantages over other models, and the adjusted rates were obtained in a logically consistent way from manipulating the parameters of this model. For a related but different approach to adjustment of rates using multiplicative models, the reader is referred to Teachman (1977).

In some situations the existence of three-factor interaction can distort an interpretation of both the crude rates and the adjusted rates, whether adjusted rates are obtained from this or the more usual methods (Kitagawa, 1966). When three-factor interaction exists, as measured by the τ^{CGD} parameters of (H.4), we recommend purging the f_{ijk} of both the C–G and the C–G–D interactions:

$$f_{ijk}^{**} = f_{ijk}^*/(\tau_{ij}^{CG}\tau_{ijk}^{CGD}) \tag{H.6}$$

It is not difficult to see that the f_{ijk}^{**} in (H.6) can be expressed as

$$f_{ijk}^{**} = \theta \tau_i^C \tau_j^G \tau_k^D \tau_{ik}^{CD} \tau_{jk}^{GD} \tag{H.7}$$

and rates obtained from the f_{ijk}^{**} will be free of the influence of C–G and C–G–D interactions, as they are determined under the multiplicative model.

It is possible to define rates for a variety of possible situations, using certain modifications of the preceding approach. For example, if one particular group were to be singled out as a standard for comparison, and all other groups were to be compared to it, then the τ_{ij}^{CG} could be suitably transformed to accommodate to this objective. The approach for performing such a modification relates to the subject of effects coding using "deviation contrasts" (see Bock, 1975, or Ott, 1977) instead of using the standard formulas to calculate then τ^{CG} as was simplicitly assumed in (H.4). It is also straightforward, though tedious, to calculate the sampling variance of adjusted rates obtained by this method. We do not pursue these details further in this book. Because of the central role of adjustment-of-rates methods in demographic analysis (compare Wunsch and Termote, 1978), this new method deserves of further scrutiny.

references

Altham, P. M. E. The measurement of association of rows and columns for an R × C contingency table. *Journal of the Royal Statistical Society,* Series B 32, 1970, 63–73.

Altham, P. M. E. The measurement of association in a contingency table: Three extensions of the cross-ratios and metrics methods. *Journal of the Royal Statistical Society,* Series B 32, 1970, 395–407.

Averitt, R. T. *The dual economy.* New York: Norton, 1973.

Bancroft, G. *The American labor force.* New York: Wiley, 1958.

Bartlett, M. S. *Stochastic population models.* London: Methuen, 1960.

Becker, G. *Human capital.* Chicago: University of Chicago Press, 1971.

Beveridge, W. H. *Full employment in a free society.* New York: W. W. Norton, 1945.

Bishop, Y. M. M., Fienberg, S. E., Holland, P. W. *Discrete multivariate analysis: Theory and practice.* Cambridge, Mass.: MIT Press, 1975.

Blau, P. M., & Duncan, O. D. *The American occupational structure.* New York: Wiley, 1967.

Bluestone, B. Low wages and the working poor. *Poverty and Human Resources* March–April, 1968. (Abstract)

Bluestone, B., Murphy, W. M., & Stevenson, M. *Low wages and the working poor.* Ann Arbor, Mich.: Institute of Labor and Industrial Relations, 1973.

Bock, R. D. *Multivariate statistical methods in behavioral research.* New York: McGraw-Hill, 1975.

Bock, R. D. & Yates, G. *MULTIQUAL: Log-linear analysis of nominal or ordinal data by the method of maximum likelihood.* Chicago: National Educational Resources, 1973.

Bonacich, E. A theory of ethnic antagonism: The split labor market. *American Sociological Review,* 1972, *37,* 547–559.

Bonacich, E. Advanced capitalism and black/white relations in the United States: A split labor market interpretation. *American Sociological Review,* 1976, *41,* 34–51.

Bowen, W. A., & Finegan, T. A. *The economics of labor force participation.* Princeton, N.J.: Princton University Press, 1969.

Box, G. E. P., & Jenkins, G. M. *Time series analysis, forecasting and control*. San Francisco: Holden-Day, 1970.

Bureau of Labor Statistics. *Work experience of the population 1973*. Washington, D.C.: U.S. Government Printing Office, 1975.

Cain, G. The challenge of segmented labor market theories to orthodox theory: A survey. *Journal of Economic Literature*, 1976, *14*, 1215–1257.

Carroll, J. Application of CANDECOMP to solving for parameters of Lazarsfeld's latent class model. Paper presented to the meeting of the Society for Multivariate Experimental Psychology, Gleneden Beach, Oregon, 1975.

Casselman, P. H. *Economics of employment and unemployment*. Washington, D.C.: Public Affairs Press, 1955.

Chiang, C. L. *Introduction to stochastic processes in biostatistics*. New York: Wiley, 1968.

Clogg, C. C. Unrestricted and restricted maximum likelihood latent structure analysis: A manual for users. University Park, Penn.: Population Issues Research Office, Working Paper 1977-09, 1977.

Clogg, C. C. Adjustment of rates using multiplicative models. *Demography*, 1978, *15*, 523–540.

Clogg, C. C. Interpolating, extrapolating, and forecasting qualitative attributes with loglinear models. Unpublished manuscript, 1979. (a)

Clogg, C. C. Characterizing the class organization of labor market opportunity: A modified latent structure approach. *Sociological Methods and Research*. Forthcoming, 1979. (b)

Coale, A. J. *The growth and structure of human populations: A mathematical investigation*. Princeton, N.J.: Princeton University Press, 1974.

Coale, A. J., & Hoover, E. M. *Population growth and economic development in low-income countries*. Princeton, N.J.: Princeton University Press, 1958.

Coleman, J. S. Inequality, sociology, and moral philosophy. *American Journal of Sociology*, 1974, *80*, 739–764.

Cortese, C. F., Falk, R. F., & Cohen, J. K. Further considerations on the methodological analysis of segregation indexes. *American Sociological Review*, 1976, *41*, 630–637.

Cox, D. R. *The analysis of binary data*. London: Methuen, 1970.

Das Gupta, P. A general method of decomposing a difference between two rates into several components. *Demography*, 1978, *15*, 99–112.

Davis, J. A. The Goodman log-linear system for assessing effects in multivariate contingency tables. Chicago: National Opinion Research Center, 1972. (Lithographed.)

Dayton, C. M., & Macready, G. B. *Computer programs for probabilistic models. (Tech. Rep.)*. College Park: University of Marlyland, Department of Measurement and Statistics, 1976. (a)

Dayton, C. M., & Macready, G. B. A probabilistic model for validation of behavioral hierarchies. *Psychometrika*, 1976, *41*, 189–204. (b)

Denton, F. T., & Ostry, S. *Working life tables for Canadian males*. Ottawa: Dominion Bureau of Statistics, 1969.

Doeringer, P. B., & Piore, M. J. *Internal labor markets and manpower analysis*. Lexington, Mass.: Heath-Lexington Books, 1971.

Duncan, O. D. *Toward a social report*. Washington, D.C.: U.S. Government Printing Office, 1969.

Duncan, O. D. Partitioning polytomous variables in contingency tables. *Social Science Research*, 1975, *4*, 167–182.

Durand, J. D. *The labor force in the United States, 1890–1960*. New York: Gordon and Breach Science Publishers, 1948.

Durand, J. D. *The labor force in economic development: A comparison of international census data, 1946–1966.* Princeton, N.J.: Princeton University Press, 1975.

Farkas, G. Cohort, age, and period effects upon the employment of white females: Evidence for 1957–1968. *Demography,* 1977, *14,* 33–42.

Feller, W. *An introduction to probability theory and its applications* (3rd ed.). New York: Wiley, 1968.

Fielding, A. Latent structure models. In C. A. O'Muircheartaigh & C. Payne (Eds.), *The analysis of survey data (Vol. I). Exploring data structures.* New York: Wiley, 1977.

Fienberg, S. E. & Gilbert, J. P. The geometry of a two by two contingency table. *Journal of the American Statistical Association,* 1970, *65,* 694–701.

Fienberg, S. E., & Mason, W. M. Identification and estimation of age-period-cohort models in the analysis of discrete archival data. In Karl F. Schuessler (Ed.), *Sociological methodology 1979.* San Francisco: Jossey-Bass, 1978.

Flaim, P. O. Discouraged workers and changes in unemployment. *Monthly Labor Review,* March 1972, *95,* 8–16.

Fleiss, J. L. *Statistical methods for rates and proportions.* New York: Wiley, 1973.

Formann, A. K. A note on parameter estimation for Lazarsfeld's latent class analysis. *Psychometrika,* 1978, *43,* 123–126.

Freeman, R. *The overeducated American.* Cambridge, Mass.: Harvard University Press, 1976.

Friedman, M. The role of monetary policy. *American Economic Review,* 1968, *58,* 1–17.

Garfinkle, S. *Work-life expectancy and training needs of women.* Washington, D.C.: U.S. Government Printing Office, 1957.

Glenn, N. Cohort analysts' futile quest: Statistical attempts to separate age, time-period and cohort effects. *American Sociological Review,* 1976, *41,* 900–904.

Gilroy, C. L. Supplemental measures of labor force underutilization. *Monthly Labor Review,* September 1975, *98,* 13–25.

Goodman, L. A. The analysis of cross-classified data: Independence, quasi-independence, and interactions in contingency tables with or without missing entries. *Journal of the American Statistical Association,* 1968, *63,* 1091–1131.

Goodman, L. A. An elementary approach to the population projection matrix, to the population reproductive value, and to related topics in the mathematical theory of population growth. *Demography,* 1968, *5,* 382–409. (b)

Goodman, L. A. The multivariate analysis of qualitative data: Interactions among multiple classifications. *Journal of the American Statistical Association,* 1970, *65,* 225–256.

Goodman, L. A. The analysis of multidimensional contingency tables: Stepwise procedures and direct estimation methods for building models for multiple classifications. *Technometrics,* 1971, *13,* 33–61. (a)

Goodman, L. A. Partitioning of chi-square, analysis of marginal contingency tables, and estimation of expected frequencies in multidimensional contingency tables. *Journal of the American Statistical Association,* 1971, *66,* 339–344. (b)

Goodman, L. A. A general model for the analysis of surveys. *American Journal of Sociology,* 1972, *77,* 1035–1086. (a)

Goodman, A modified multiple regression approach to the analysis of dichotomous variables. *American Sociological Review,* 1972, *37,* 28–46. (b)

Goodman, L. A. Some multiplicative models for the analysis of cross-classified data. *Proceedings of the Sixth Berkeley Symposium on Mathematical Statistics and Probability.* Berkeley: University of California Press, 1972. (c)

Goodman, L. A. Causal analysis of data from panel studies and other kinds of surveys. *American Journal of Sociology,* 1973, *78,* 1135–1191. (a)

Goodman, L. A. Guided and unguided methods for the selection of models for a set of T multidimensional contingency tables. *Journal of the American Statistical Association,* 1973, *68,* 165–175. (b)

Goodman, L. A. The analysis of systems of qualitative variables when some of the variables are unobservable. Part 1—a modified latent structure approach. *American Journal of Sociology,* 1974, *79,* 1179–1259. (a)

Goodman, L. A. Exploratory latent structure analysis using both identifiable and unidentifiable models. *Biometrika,* 1974, *61,* 215–231. (b)

Goodman, L. A. The analysis of systems of qualitative variables when some of the variables are unobservable. Part 2—the use of modified latent distance models. University of Chicago, 1974 (Mimeographed.) (c)

Goodman, L. A. A new model for scaling response patterns: An application of the quasi-independence concept. *Journal of the American Statistical Association,* 1975, *70,* 755–768. (a)

Goodman, L. A. A note on cohort analysis using multiplicative models and the modified multiple regression approach. University of Chicago, 1975. (Mimeographed.) (b)

Goodman, L. A. The relationship between the modified and the usual multiple regression approaches to the analysis of dichotomous variables." In D. Heise, (Ed.), *Sociological Methodology 1976.* San Francisco: Jossey-Bass, 1975.

Goodman, L. A. The analysis of qualitative variables using more parsimonious quasi-independence models, scaling models, and latent structures that fit the observed data. University of Chicago, 1976. (Mimeographed.) (a)

Goodman, L. A. How not to analyze nonrecursive systems pertaining to qualitative variables. University of Chicago, 1976. (Mimeographed.) (b)

Goodman, L. A. *A note on the estimation of parameters in latent structure analysis.* (Tech. Rep. 59), Chicago: University of Chicago, Department of Statistics, 1978.

Goodman, L. A., & Kruskal, W. H. Measures of association for cross-classifications. *Journal of the American Statistical Association,* 1954, *49,* 225–256.

Goodman, L. A. & Kruskal, W. H. Measures of association for cross-classifications, II. Further discussion and references. *Journal of the American Statistical Association,* 1959, *54,* 123–163.

Gordon, D. M. *Economic theories of poverty and underemployment.* Lexington, Mass.: Heath-Lexington Books, 1972.

Green, P. E., Carmone, F. J., & Wachspress, D. P. Consumer segmentation via latent class analysis. *Journal of Consumer Research,* 1976, *3,* 170–174.

Greville, T. N. E. (ed.). *Population dynamics.* New York: Academic Press, 1972.

Guttman, L. The basis for scalogram analysis. In S. A. Stouffer *et al.* (Eds.), *Measurement and prediction: Studies in social psychology in World War II* (Vol. IV). Princeton, N.J.: Princeton University Press, 1950.

Haberman, S. J. *The analysis of frequency data.* Chicago: University of Chicago Press, 1974. (a)

Haberman, S. J. Log-linear models for frequency tables derived by indirect observation: Maximum likelihood equations. *Annals of Statistics,* 1974, *2,* 911–922. (b)

Haberman, S. J. Log-linear models for frequency tables with ordered classifications. *Biometrics,* 1974, *30,* 589–600. (c)

Haberman, S. J. Product models for frequency tables involving indirect observation. *Annals of Statistics,* 1974, *5,* 1124–1147. (d)

Haberman, S. J. Iterative scaling procedures for log-linear models for frequency tables derived by indirect observation. *Proceedings of the American Statistical Association*

Annual Meeting, Statistical Computing Section. Washington, D.C.: American Statistical Association, 1976.

Hansen, A. H. *Economic policy and full employment.* New York: McGraw-Hill, 1947.

Hauser, P. M. The labour force and gainful workers—concept, measurement, and comparability. *American Journal of Sociology,* 1949, *54,* 338–355.

Hauser, P. M. The measurement of labour utilization. *Malayan Economic Review,* 1974, *19,* 1–17.

Hauser, P. M. The measurement of labour utilization—more empirical results. *Malayan Economic Review,* 1977, *22,* 10–25.

Hauser, P. M., & Sullivan, T. A. The measurement of underemployment in the United States. University of Chicago, 1975. (Mimeographed.)

Hocking, R. R. The analysis and selection of variables in linear regression. *Biometrics,* 1976, *32,* 1–49.

Hughes, E. C. *Men and their work.* New York: Free Press, 1958.

Humphrey, T. H. Changing views of the Phillips curve. *Monthly Review of the Federal Reserve Bank of Richmond,* July 1973, pp. 2–13.

International Labour Office. *International recommendations on labour statistics.* Geneva: International Labour Office, 1976.

Johnston, J. *Econometric methods* (2nd ed.). New York: McGraw-Hill, 1972.

Karlin, S. *A first course in stochastic processes.* New York: Academic Press, 1969.

Keyfitz, N. *Introduction to the mathematics of population.* Reading, Mass.: Addison-Wesley, 1968.

Keyfitz, N. Mathematical demography: A bibliographic essay. *Population Index,* 1976, *42,* 9–38.

Keyfitz, N. *Applied mathematical demography.* New York: Wiley, 1977.

Keyfitz, N. & Flieger, W. *Population: Facts and methods of demography.* San Francisco: W. H. Freeman, 1971.

Kitagawa, E. M. Components of a difference between two rates. *Journal of the American Statistical Association,* 1955, *50,* 1168–1194.

Kitagawa, E. M. Standardized comparisons in population research. *Demography,* 1964, *1,* 296–315.

Kitagawa, E. M., & Hauser, P. M. *Differential mortality in the United States.* Cambridge, Mass.: Harvard University Press, 1973.

Lancaster, H. O. *The chi-squared distribution.* New York: Wiley, 1969.

Land, K., & Spilerman, S. (Eds.). *Social indicator models.* New York: Russel Sage Foundation, 1975.

Lazarsfeld, P. F., & Henry, N. W. *Latent structure analysis.* Boston: Houghton-Mifflin, 1968.

Lerner, A. P. *Economics of full employment.* New York: McGraw-Hill, 1951.

Lerner, H. *Is full employment possible?* New York: New Century, 1962.

Levitan, S. A., & Taggart, R. *Employment and earnings inadequacy: A new social indicator.* Baltimore: Johns Hopkins University Press, 1974.

Ludwig, D. *Stochastic population theories.* New York: Springer-Verlag, 1974.

Mason, K. O., Mason, W. M., Winsborough, H. H., & Poole, W. K. Some methodological issues in cohort analysis of archival data. *American Sociological Review,* 1973, *38,* 242–258.

Matras, J. *Population and society.* Englewood Cliffs, N.J.: Prentice-Hall, 1973.

Montagna, P. D. *Occupations and society: Toward a sociology of the labor market.* New York: Wiley, 1977.

Moore, W. E. The exportability of the "labor force" concept. *American Sociological Review*, 1953, *18*, 68–72.

Nelson, C. R. *Applied time series analysis for managerial forecasting*. San Francisco: Holden-Day, 1973.

Morgan, J. N. *et al. Five thousand American families—patterns of economic progress*. Ann Arbor, Mich.: Survey Research Center, 1974.

Morton, J. E. *On the evolution of manpower statistics*. Kalamazoo, Mich.: The Upjohn Institute.

Myrdal, G. *Asian drama*. New York: Pantheon, 1968.

National Bureau of Economic Research. *The measurement and behavior of unemployment*. Princeton, N.J.: Princeton University Press, 1957.

Ott, L. *An introduction to statistical methods and data analysis*. North Scituate, Mass.: Duxbury Press, 1977.

Perry, G. M. Changing labor markets and inflation. *Brookings Papers on Economic Activity*, 1970, *3*, 441–448.

Pollard, J. H. *Mathematical models for the growth of human populations*. Cambridge: Cambridge University Press, 1973.

Preston, S. H. *Mortality patterns in national populations*. New York: Academic Press, 1976.

Preston, S. H., Keyfitz, N., & Schoen, R. *Causes of death: Life tables for national populations*. New York: Academic Press, 1972.

Proctor, C. H. A probabilistic formulation and statistical analysis of Guttman scaling. *Psychometrika*, 1970, *35*, 73–78.

Pullum, T. W. *Measuring occupational inheritance*. New York: Elsevier, 1975.

Pullum, T. W. Parametrizing age, period, and cohort effects: An application to U.S. delinquency rates, 1964–1973. In K. F. Schuessler (Ed.), *Sociological methodology 1978*. San Francisco: Jossey-Bass, 1977.

Rao, C. R. *Linear statistical inference and its applications* (2nd ed.). New York: Wiley, 1973.

Rawls, J. *A theory of justice*. Cambridge, Mass.: Harvard University Press, 1971.

Reynolds, H. T. *The analysis of cross-classifications*. New York: Free Press, 1977.

Robinson, J. Disguised unemployment. *Economic Journal*, 1936, *46*, 225–237.

Rogers, A. *Matrix methods in urban and regional analysis*. San Francisco: Holden-Day, 1971.

Rogers, A. *Introduction to multiregional mathematical demography*. New York: Wiley, 1975.

Ryder, N. B. The process of demographic translation. *Demography*, 1964, *1*, 74–82.

Ryder, N. B. The cohort as a concept in the study of social change. *American Sociological Review*, 1965, *30*, 843–3861.

Ryder, N. B. Fertility measurement through cross-sectional surveys. *Social Forces*, 1975, *54*, 7–35. (a)

Ryder, N. B. Notes on stationary populations. *Population Index*, 1975, *41*, 3–28. (b)

Shryock, H. S., & Siegel, J. S. *The methods and materials of demography* (2 vols.). Washington, D.C.: U.S. Government Printing Office, 1973.

Spiegelman, M. *Introduction to demography*. Cambridge, Mass.: Harvard University Press, 1968.

Stinchcombe, A. *Constructing social theories*. New York: Harcourt and Brace, 1968.

Stone, R. *Mathematics in the social sciences and other essays*. London: Chapman and Hall, 1966.

Stone, R. *Demographic accounting and model building*. Paris: Organization for Economic Co-Operation and Development, 1971.

Stone, R. Transition and admission models in social indicator analysis. In K. C. Land, & S. Spilerman (Eds.), *Social indicator models.* New York: Russell Sage Foundation, 1975.

Sullivan, T. A. *Marginal workers, marginal jobs: Underutilization in the U.S. work force.* Austin: University of Texas Press, 1978.

Sullivan, T. A., & Hauser, P. M. The labor utilization framework: Assumptions, data, and policy implications. A paper prepared for the National Commission on Employment and Unemployment Statistics, 1978.

Teachman, J. D. The relationship between Schoen's $\bigtriangledown$ and a log-linear measure. *Demography*, 1977, *14*, 239–241.

Theil, H. *Principles of econometrics.* New York: Wiley, 1971.

Torgerson, W. S. *Theory and methods of scaling.* New York: Wiley, 1962.

Turnham, D. *The employment problem in less developed countries.* Paris: Development Centre of the Organisation for Economic Co-Operation and Development, 1971.

United Nations. *Methods of analyzing census data on economic activities of the population.* New York: United Nations, 1968.

United Nations. *Determinants and consequences of population trends.* New York: United Nations, 1973.

U.S. Department of Commerce. *Census of population: 1960* (Vol. 1, Part 1), *United States Summary.* Washington, D.C.: U.S. Government Printing Office, 1961.

U.S. Department of Commerce, *The current population survey—a report on methodology.* Washington, D.C.: U.S. Government Printing Office, 1963.

U.S. Department of Commerce, *Characteristics of the low income population: 1973.* Washington, D.C.: U.S. Government Printing Office, 1975.

U.S. Department of Commerce. *Estimates of the population of the United States, by age, sex, and race: 1970 to 1975.* Washington, D.C.: U.S. Government Printing Office, 1975. (a)

U.S. Department of Commerce. *Social and economic characteristics of the metropolitan and nonmetropolitan population: 1974 and 1970.* Washington, D.C.: U.S. Government Printing Office, 1975. (b)

U.S. Department of Commerce. *The current population survey, design and methodology.* Washington, D.C.: U.S. Government Printing Office, 1978.

U.S. Department of Health, Education, and Welfare. *Vital statistics—special reports* (Vol. 47). Washington, D.C.: U.S. Government Printing Office, 1961.

U.S. Department of Health, Education, and Welfare. *Vital statistics of the United States, 1970.* (Vol. II, Section 5), *Life Tables.* Rockville, Md.: National Center for Health Statistics, 1974.

U.S. Department of Labor. *Concepts and methods used in manpower statistics from the Current Population Survey.* Washington, D.C.: U.S. Government Printing Office, 1967.

U.S. Department of Labor. Occupational outlook for college graduates, 1978–1979. *Bulletin 1956.* Washington, D.C.: U.S. Government Printing Office, 1978.

U.S. President's Committee to Appraise Employment and Unemployment Statistics. *Measuring employment and unemployment.* Washington, D.C.: U.S. Government Printing Office, 1962.

Vietorisz, T., Mier, R., & Giblin, J. E. Subemployment: Exclusion and inadequacy indexes. *Monthly Labor Review*, 1975, *98*, 3–12.

Vigderhous, G. Forecasting sociological phenomena: Application of Box-Jenkins methodology to suicide rates. In K. F. Schuessler (Ed.), *Sociological methodology 1978.* San Francisco: Jossey-Bass, 1977.

Viner, J. Full employment at whatever cost. *Quarterly Journal of Economics*, 1950, *64*, 394–405.

Weiss, Y., & Lillard, L. A. Experience, vintage, and time effects in the growth of earnings: American scientists, 1960–1970. *Journal of Political Economy,* 1978, *86,* 427–447.

Winsborough, H. H. Age, period, cohort, and education effects on earnings by race—an experiment with a sequence of cross-sectional surveys. In C. Land, & S. Spilerman (Eds.), *Social indicator models.* New York: Russell Sage Foundation, 1975.

Wiorkowski, J. J. Estimation of proportion of variance explained by regression, when the number of parameters in the model may depend on the sample size. *Technometrics,* 1970, *12,* 915–919.

Wunsch, G. J., & Termote, M. G. *Introduction to demographic analysis.* New York: Plenum Press, 1978.

Yule, G. U. On methods of measuring association between two attributes. *Journal of the Royal Statistical Society,* 1912, *75,* 579–642.

index